TERRY RUDD

W9-CKM-000

D. EDMOND HIEBERT is widely recognized as a leading scholar in the field of biblical exegesis. As an ordained minister of the Mennonite Brethren Church, he served as a pastor for some time. Since 1955 he has been professor of Greek and New Testament at the Mennonite Brethren Biblical Seminary in Fresno, California, joining the faculty at the time of the school's opening. Before that he served as professor of New Testament at Tabor College in Hillsboro, Kansas, for nearly fifteen years.

He gained his academic training at John Fletcher College, where he earned an A.B. in history, and at Southern Baptist Theological Seminary, where he earned a Th.M. and a Th.D. in religious education and Greek.

A prolific writer, Dr. Hiebert has authored three volumes of Moody Press' Everyman's Bible Commentary series: *First Timothy*, *Second Timothy*, and *Titus and Philemon*. He has also written a major commentary on First and Second Thessalonians entitled *The Thessalonian Epistles*. A two-volume introduction to the epistles is another of Dr. Hiebert's achievements: *An Introduction to the Pauline Epistles* and *An Introduction to the Non-Pauline Epistles*.

Personalities
Around
Paul

Personalities Around Paul

D. EDMOND HIEBERT

MOODY PRESS

CHICAGO

© 1973 by

THE MOODY BIBLE INSTITUTE
OF CHICAGO

All rights reserved. No part of this book may be
reproduced in any form without permission in writing
from the publisher except in the case of brief
quotations embodied in critical articles or reviews.

Library of Congress Catalog Card Number: 72-95028
ISBN: 0-8024-6473-4

Printed in the United States of America

CONTENTS

FOREWORD

CASUAL READERS of the New Testament might easily draw the conclusion from its narratives that Paul almost single-handedly evangelized the Roman world. Such a conclusion would be unwarranted, but very few are aware of the fact that Paul's ministry was supplemented by the work of a host of persons who might have been equally devoted and effective in their respective spheres. Dr. Hiebert has brought out of obscurity nearly a hundred such persons who were actively engaged in the gospel witness during the middle years of the first century.

The evidence concerning them is fragmentary at best, and in most instances a line or two of text is all that is available. Without straining the evidence or indulging in any airy flights of imagination, Dr. Hiebert marshals the existing facts, enabling the reader to see at least a glimpse of these personalities who were participants in the apostolic mission. He presents and evaluates the theories proposed to explain the more obscure references, and has shown both breadth of knowledge and restraint in his conclusions.

Although some other works deal with the minor characters of the New Testament, only one or two specialize in the associates of Paul or deal with them as completely as this volume does. For the Bible student who wishes to gain a fuller understanding of the constituency and mission of the early church, this book will be a valuable tool.

MERRILL C. TENNEY

WHEATON, ILLINOIS

7

PREFACE

THIS VOLUME does not aim to make a study of the life and work of the apostle Paul but rather to center attention on those around him. It offers scriptural studies of a number of the apostle's companions. While his prominent associates have been dealt with frequently in separate studies, the larger circle of people appearing around Paul has often not been observed sufficiently. In this book, all the individuals mentioned with him are brought into view.

Following the brief introduction, which centers on Paul as the natural point of orientation for the individuals studied, the material is divided into three major parts. Part 1 comprises scriptural studies of "Prominent Personalities" around Paul. Not all the biblical information concerning these distinguished companions relates directly to their association with the apostle, but is included to complete the biblical portrait.

Part 2 deals with "Lesser Lights" around Paul, people who were more or less closely related to Paul's work, yet about whom not a great deal of scriptural information is given.

Part 3, "All the Others, Named and Unnamed," consists of two lists of all the individuals mentioned in relation to Paul in one way or another but not previously covered. The first list contains in alphabetical order all those referred to in the New Testament by name. The second list records the various anonymous individuals who appear in Acts and the Pauline epistles.

Being intended as scriptural studies, the material covered here leaves almost wholly untouched the accumulated traditions concerning Paul's various companions. The studies are grounded in the Scriptures and proceed on the assumption that all the scriptural in-

9

formation concerning each individual may be accepted as reliable. I do not follow the view of certain modern, critical scholars who maintain that some of the Pauline epistles are really "Pseudo-Pauline Epistles,"* which carries with it the corollary that the information in them concerning these individuals is not truly Pauline and consequently unauthentic.

In seeking to relate information of these individuals to the life of Paul, free use has been made of the familiar designations — the first, second, or third missionary journey. I recognize that this traditional division of the missionary labors of Paul is somewhat inaccurate and leaves something to be desired, but I have retained it because it is well known and sufficiently accurate for the present purpose.

Unless otherwise indicated, the scripture texts quote the American Standard Version (1901).

My heavy indebtedness to many different sources is readily evident from the notes and the bibliography. Special thanks are due to the staff of Moody Press for their gracious encouragement and cooperation.

---

* See W. Marxsen, *Introduction to the New Testament,* pp. 176-222. Under the "Pseudo-Pauline Epistles," he includes Colossians, Ephesians, and the pastoral epistles, as well as Hebrews because of its traditional association with the name of Paul. For my view concerning these epistles see D. Hiebert, *An Introduction to the Pauline Epistles* and *An Introduction to the Non-Pauline Epistles.*

INTRODUCTION

In the Center — Paul

IN RECORDING the events of the first missionary journey, Luke concisely marks the passing of the leadership of the missionary party from Barnabas to Paul when he writes, "Now Paul and his company set sail from Paphos, and came to Perga in Pamphylia" (Ac 13:13). This rendering reveals the fact of the change in leadership, but it does not adequately convey Luke's precise picture in the original statement. The original may be literally translated, "Now having put to sea from Paphos, those around Paul (*hoi peri Paulon*) came unto Perga of Pamphylia." Luke's arresting expression assumes the fact that Paul was now the recognized leader and centers attention on the other members of the party as they array themselves around him.

HIS DYNAMIC LEADERSHIP

Paul, pictured as the natural leader of those around him, well portrays this dynamic personality in the rest of the New Testament. In the second half of Acts, Paul becomes the central figure of the story. The thirteen epistles which bear his name as their author give eloquent testimony to his aggressive leadership in the propagation and exposition of Christianity. Peter's complimentary remark in 2 Peter 3:15-16 further underlines the fact that Paul's importance as a leader in the Christian church was accepted and appreciated in non-Pauline circles as well. Paul has well been described as "the most outstanding and commanding personality the Christian faith has produced."[1]

This eminent figure among New Testament personalities is first introduced in Acts as "a young man named Saul" at whose feet the witnesses who stoned Stephen "laid down their garments" (7:58).

11

Their action before stoning Stephen, as also Luke's explanatory comment "Saul was consenting unto his death" (8:1), indicates that this forceful young man had already attained a position of recognized importance in the battle against the young church at Jerusalem. He promptly demonstrated his native leadership ability by personally pressing the persecution that arose against the church upon the death of Stephen (Ac 8:3; 9:1-2; 22:4; 26:10-11). His leadership of the persecution was officially accepted and sanctioned by the Jewish religious officials in Jerusalem (Ac 9:2; 22:5; 26:9-11).

Saul's prostrating encounter with the living, glorified Jesus on the Damascus road, abruptly terminated his zealous career as a persecutor. It left his views of Christianity and all that he had confidently espoused and vigorously fought for, lying in shambles at his feet. The Lord further humbled the blinded terrorist by revealing to him that he must receive the personal ministry of one of the very group of believers at Damascus against whom he had planned to act (Ac 9:12; 22:10-16). The Spirit-directed ministry of Ananias opened the door for the new convert to the company of the disciples of Christ at Damascus (Ac 9:19*b*). In their midst, Saul experienced the first rich blessings of fellowship with the saints.

After some years in obscurity, Saul of Tarsus was brought into the work of the church at Antioch of Syria through the thoughtful action of Barnabas (Ac 11:22-26), who some years earlier had befriended Saul as a suspected Christian when he had first returned to Jerusalem following his conversion (Ac 9:26-27). Saul's presence in Antioch added greatly to the effectiveness of the Lord's work in that pagan city (Ac 11:26). In assuming his position as a co-worker with older and more experienced Christian men in the church at Antioch, Saul received valuable training for his future ministry (Ac 13:1).

When the Holy Spirit inaugurated the enterprise of Gentile foreign missions at Antioch, with His call to set aside two of the leaders for that work, "Barnabas and Saul" were commissioned for the new assignment (Ac 13:2-4). During the first stage of the missionary tour, Barnabas was the obvious leader of the party. This is evident from Luke's use of the order "Barnabas and Saul" in describing the work (Ac 13:6-12).

Saul's Spirit-initiated demonstration of leadership in defeating

the opposition of Bar-Jesus at Paphos (Ac 13:6-11) made it clear to
the other members of the party that he was the logical leader for the
work that lay ahead. Until this clash with Bar-Jesus, Luke always
used his Hebrew name, Saul (Greek, Saulos). In introducing this
confrontation, Luke writes, "But Saul, who is also *called* Paul" (Ac
13:9), and thereafter in Acts always calls him Paul (Greek, Paulos).
In his epistles, the apostle always calls himself Paul. As the son of a
Pharisee who was also a Roman citizen (Ac 22:28; 23:6), he doubtless bore both names from birth. His double name is clearly implied
in Luke's statement which literally reads "But Saul, the one also Paul"
(*Saulos de ho kai Paulos*). The change to the Gentile name Paul was
appropriate at the time he assumed his position of leadership in bringing the gospel to the Gentile world.

As the apostle to the Gentiles, Paul held a position of leadership
throughout the rest of his story in the New Testament. He was the
acknowledged leader not only in his own circle of co-workers, but also
by other prominent leaders in the church (Ac 21:18-25; Gal 2:6-9).
His importance as a director in the Christian movement was also
readily recognized by non-Christians. In the varied attacks staged by
hostile Jews upon the heralds of the gospel, Paul commonly bore the
brunt of the attack as the acknowledged head (Ac 14:19-20, 17:13-15,
18:12-16). Gentiles, hostile to the spread of the gospel, likewise
aimed their attacks at Paul (Ac 19:23-31). Paul's dynamic personality could not be ignored.

His Polarizing Impact

The apostle Paul had one of those arresting, magnetic personalities that inevitably produces a polarizing effect upon those around
them. Men could not remain neutral toward him. When confronted
with his dynamic, disciplined, decisive character, they were compelled
to react.* They were either strongly repelled by him or strongly
drawn to him. Paul was both fiercely hated and devoutly loved. He
had strong antagonists, but he also had many staunch friends who
were bound to him by strong cords of love.

Paul's life centered in an unswerving committal to Jesus Christ,

---

* For an analysis of the character of Paul based on the "four temperaments"
theory, see Tim LaHaye, *Transformed Temperaments*, pp. 63-95.

whose cause and approval were of supreme importance to Paul. His committal to the truth that is in Christ Jesus allowed no temporizing for the sake of expediency. Having once seen the truth and understood his duty, he unflinchingly adhered to his convictions, undeterred by the possible consequences to himself. Those who categorically rejected the truth so uncompromisingly espoused by Paul, inevitably were his determined opponents. Paul had enemies not merely because of what he was but also because of the truth he disseminated. For Paul maintenance of the truth was more important than retention of the good will of men (cf. Gal 1:6-10).

Those who were nearest to Paul and knew him best were his staunchest friends. He was able to draw around himself a wide variety of loyal friends and co-workers and effectively lead them in the cause of worldwide Christianity to which his whole life was committed. White remarks,

> A man's power to attract and harness others to his own ideals, his positive contribution to others' lives, his appreciation of other types of people, are reliable indications not only of the breadth of his sympathies but of the genuineness of his self-assessment and the sincerity of his work. And they are indications of character, all the more significant because they are objective, and impossible to counterfeit. One cannot pretend to be a leader of men.[2]

Paul proved his powers of leadership by drawing around himself friends from diverse cultural backgrounds and with varied gifts and achievements, and molding them into a strong working team in the furtherance of the gospel.

His Treasured Friendships

The apostle Paul revealed "a genius and a hunger for friendship."[3] He had the ability to make and retain loyal friends. His powers of friendship sprang from his deep interest in people, his tender sensibility to their need, and his heartwarming love for them. He yearned for friendship and proved himself a loyal friend.

Paul had a keen personal interest in people wherever he met them. While working with the masses, he did not lose sight of the individual. This is reflected in his statement of his ministerial aim, "Admonishing every man and teaching every man in all wisdom, that we may present every man perfect in Christ" (Col 1:28). Having personally experienced the mighty transforming power of Christ, he was always eager to lead other lives into an experience of His power and love.

> Yes, without cheer of sister or of daughter,
>> Yes, without stay of father or of son,
> Lone on the land and homeless on the water
>> Pass I in patience till the work be done.

> Yet not in solitude if Christ anear me
>> Waketh Him workers for the great employ,
> Oh not in solitude, if souls that hear me
>> Catch from my joyaunce the surprise of joy.

> Hearts I have won of sister or of brother
>> Quick on the earth or hidden in the sod,
> Lo every heart awaiteth me, another
>> Friend in the blameless family of God.[4]

Paul was keenly sensitive to the needs of people and actively sympathetic toward men in their need. He was ready to "spend and be spent" (2 Co 12:15) in their service, whether they were menial servants or dignified masters, men in straitened material circumstances or possessing an abundance of this world's goods, unknown members of the common masses or men in high governmental position. Because they were all the objects of Christ's redeeming love, his own compassionate heart made him willing to give himself in unsparing toil for their spiritual welfare.

As a man of strong affections, Paul made fast friends. He "possessed that tender love which is the truest magnetism."[5] His warm, sincere love for others drew out a response of love from them. "He loved his way into the hearts of men. . . People were devoted to him because they were so sure of his devotion to them."[6] His letters mirror his deep love for his friends. His letter to the Philippians is essentially a friendship letter, written out of a heart overflowing with love for his dear Philippian friends. First Thessalonians has well been called "a classic of Christian friendship."[7] In it he revealed his yearning love for his converts and displayed his deep anxiety for them because he did not know what effect the experience of persecution was having on them. Second Corinthians shows how deeply Paul was grieved when his converts questioned the sincerity of his love and motives, and failed to return his unselfish love for them; it also reflects his heartfelt rejoicing when the sense of estrangement between them was removed (cf. 2 Co 7:2-11; 10:7-10; 12:11-18).

Paul treasured every friend he made and deeply appreciated every expression of love he received from them. His letters "show a heart that treasured each human contact, and held undimmed the memory of the person, the circumstances, and the character of each fellow Christian."[8] Again and again in his letters he unveiled "his store of felicitous memories and allows his heart to speak as friend speaks of friend."[9] Nowhere is this aspect of Paul's character more clearly seen than in the last chapter of Romans, where he revealed his tenacious memory and lasting appreciation of every kindness shown him. His brief characterizations of the various individuals are rich with personal memories and full of tenderness. Deissmann remarks, "The emotional strength especially which pulses in these names was one of the magic charms wielded by Paul, the leader of men."[10] They also reveal that Paul was a shrewd but honest judge of the qualities and activities of his friends.

The story of Acts suggests that Paul personally felt a deep need for the presence of fellow workers in his missionary activities. He knew the strength that comes from companionship and wisely made it a practice always to have some assistants with him in his missionary labors. Lees remarks that Paul could "toil at the loom, deal and take hard knocks in the fight, and emerge smiling at the close, if only some one is with him."[11] He worked most efficiently when he had some co-workers with him and was uneasy without any attendants. Farrar asserts, "His nature imperiously demanded the solace of companionship; without this he found his work intolerable, and himself the victim of paralysing depression"[12] (cf. 2 Co 2:13; Phil 2:19-20; 1 Th 3:1; 2 Ti 4:11). Only once, in Athens, was Paul left without any of his co-workers (Ac 17:14-16). So keenly did Paul feel the need of their presence that he sent back word at once to Silas and Timothy to join him as soon as possible.

Paul deeply appreciated the contribution that his friends made to his own life and placed a high value on their friendship. But most of all Paul appreciated the value of Christian friends because of his deep conviction that fellowship with other believers was the true outcome of the experience of salvation in Christ. Paul preached the gospel of reconciliation, not only of sinful men with God but also of men with their fellowmen, regardless of racial, social, or former religious backgrounds (Eph 2:13-19). He believed and knew from personal experience that the saving work of Christ found its richest and fullest expression not in isolation but in the Christian community held together by a mutual love, grounded in a common love for Christ Jesus as Saviour and Lord.

The apostle Paul truly towers among the figures of the New Testament. The concentrated attention that he has rightly received has often unintentionally resulted in throwing a shadow over the proper appreciation of the greatness of some of the men around him. But "it does not detract from his greatness to bring into greater prominence those with whom he served, those whom he was glad to praise and pleased to call his co-workers."[13] A closer acquaintance with his numerous friends and fellow workers can only enhance our appreciation of the true stature of Paul the apostle of Christ.

Part 1

PROMINENT PERSONALITIES

1

APOLLOS

Acts 18:24-28; 19:1
1 Corinthians 1:12; 3:4-6, 22; 4:6; 16:12
Titus 3:13*

APOLLOS was a man with a touch of native genius. With his rare gifts and thorough training, he left his mark wherever he went. Although some zealous Corinthians wished to set him up as a rival to the apostle Paul, Apollos deliberately avoided all such rivalry and self-exaltation. He subordinated his remarkable gifts and attainments to the larger interests of the kingdom of God.

NAME AND NATIONALITY

The name Apollos is apparently a contraction of the common name Apollonius,† or possibly Apollodorus. But the Vulgate gives his name as Apollo, the name of a deity familiar to the Greeks and Romans. Some scholars,[1] accepting this connection of his name, have wondered how a Jew could bear the name of a heathen deity, in view of the Jewish aversion to idolatry. Carter seems to agree with Clarke's suggestion that "his parents were Gentiles who were converted to Judaism as proselytes after his birth and christening, and thus Apollos was a Jew by religion but not by nationality."[2] But Luke's designation of Apollos as "a certain Jew" (Ac 18:24) seems to point clearly to his national extraction; he was a native Jew rather than the son of a proselyte.

---

* All the scripture references are placed at the beginning in order to enable the reader to turn readily to all the scriptural data at once.
† Codex Bezae (D) gives his name as Apollonius at Ac 18:24.

21

He is further identified as "an Alexandrian by race"; that is, born in Alexandria, the noted Egyptian city founded by Alexander the Great in 332 B.C. Presumably, Apollos grew up in Alexandria, which from the first was the home of numerous Jews. Jews were very influential, for it was the literary center of the Hellenistic world, where Gentile and Jewish learning met and interacted. Alexandria boasted the greatest library of antiquity and earned notice for its school of philosophy, literature, and rhetoric. Here was translated the Septuagint (Old Testament rendered in Greek), which spread the knowledge of the Jewish Scriptures throughout the Greek-speaking world and proved to be a mighty, preparatory agent for the coming of Christianity. Apollos read the sacred books in the Septuagint version.

TRAINING AND LIMITATION

Apollos had keen intellectual ability and thorough educational training. He was also an accomplished scholar. "Books always abounded in Alexandria, and were within the reach of this man who had both the taste and talent to use them."[3]

Luke characterized Apollos as "an eloquent man." The margin of the American Standard Version (ASV) suggests the alternative rendering "a learned man." The Greek adjective *logios,* occurring only here in the New Testament, carries both meanings, indicating not only knowledge but also the ability to set it forth with ease and attractiveness. Apollos had not only a trained and well-stored mind but also a natural facility of speech. Moulton and Milligan suggest that a general phrase, such as "a man of culture" gives the best meaning here.[4] But perhaps "eloquent" is best retained; by contrast with his other notable characteristics, a natural rather than an acquired ability seems in view. (The ancient versions also preferred "eloquent.") It was clearly because of his eloquence that some Corinthians preferred Apollos to Paul (1 Co 1:12).

Apollos was also "mighty in the scriptures." His teaching in the Ephesian synagogue at once evidenced this fact. He possessed a thorough knowledge of the Old Testament. "In a day when a knowledge of the Scriptures had to be acquired from manuscripts, and in which even the art of reading was acquired by only a few, it was no ordinary accomplishment to be thus familiar with the Scriptures."[5] But he also knew how to handle them effectively in teaching and debate. "As a loyal Jew he devoted his learning and eloquence to the exposition of scripture."[6] His native abilities and educational advantages had been sanctified in their subjection to the task of communicating revealed truth in a vivid and arresting manner. This occupation with the Old Testament Scriptures laid the foundation for his future usefulness in the Christian church. No substitute yet exists for an experiential mastery of the Word of God.

Apollos diligently studied and accurately taught the Word. "He spake and taught accurately the things concerning Jesus" (Ac 18:25); that is, accurately as far as his knowledge went. Exactness is an important trait of an effective teacher. Howson remarks,

> He had that habit of mind which we call accuracy; and it is a most important habit — far more important than is commonly supposed. The difference between one man and another in regard to real influence in the world relates not so much to amount of knowledge as accuracy of knowledge.[7]

In his teaching, Apollos kept his enthusiasm under the restraint of his knowledge. Here again he offers a ringing challenge to the modern preacher. "Incorrectness in teaching is detrimental to all concerned."[8]

Luke noted that Apollos "had been instructed in the way of the Lord" (Ac 18:25). The word rendered "instructed" generally meant "to be instructed by word of mouth" (our English word *catechize*) and "implies a course of instruction distinct from his own study of the O.T. Scriptures."[9] Where and from whom he received the instruction is not stated.‡

Luke pointed out that there existed a definite limitation in the knowledge and message of Apollos. He "spake and taught accurately the things concerning Jesus, knowing only the baptism of John" (18:25). It is not quite clear how much defect is indicated in Luke's statement.

Some, like Barnes and Hackett, think that Apollos had correct views concerning the coming Messiah, which he had derived from a study of the Old Testament and that he had accepted John's testimony

---

‡ Codex D adds "in his country," i.e., Alexandria.

concerning the Messiah's imminent coming, but that he had not yet heard that Jesus was He.[10] But then more naturally Luke would have written, "the things concerning the Christ," the coming Messiah, instead of "the things concerning Jesus." Also, such a limited knowledge would offer an inadequate basis for controversial discussion and teaching of the things concerning Jesus in the synagogue. That he taught accurately "the things concerning Jesus" implies that he did have a general acquaintance with the facts of the ministry of Jesus and that he was convinced He was the promised Messiah. Moe remarks, "Inasmuch as it is emphasized that he was *mighty in the Scriptures,* this cannot mean only that he told about Jesus but that he elaborated on the relationship between Jesus and the Old Testament; in other words, that he showed that Jesus is the promised Messiah."[11] But Apollos' knowledge was limited in that he knew "only the baptism of John." He knew what John's baptism meant, as pledging its recipients to follow the Messiah when He came; but concerning the outcome and results of Christ's mission, he had incomplete information. He also did not know about His crucifixion, resurrection, ascension, Pentecost, and the divine provisions of grace in the establishment of the Christian church. "He was on the threshold of the first principles, and knew nothing of any greater things. He was in the dimness of the dawn, and he mistook it for noonday."[12] Clearly Apollos had received his knowledge concerning the things of Jesus apart from the mainstream of apostolic witness.

ZEAL AND ENLIGHTENMENT

Apollos providentially came to Ephesus some time after Paul had left Aquila and Priscilla in that city (Ac 18:18-21). Whether he came directly from Alexandria is not indicated. Neither did Luke explain why Apollos left Alexandria, beyond the fact of his zeal to proclaim his faith. Some, like Blaiklock, have suggested that Apollos left Alexandria because he had come under the unfavorable notice of the Alexandrian authorities due to his Christian testimony.[13]

This view is based on the discovery in 1920 of a letter written to the Alexandrian Jews by the emperor Claudius in A.D. 41, expressly forbidding them "to bring or invite other Jews to come by sea from Syria. If they do not abstain from this conduct," the emperor wrote,

"I shall proceed against them for fomenting a malady common to the world." Some interpret this to reflect a situation in Alexandria similar to that in Rome which caused Claudius to expel the Jews from the capital (Ac 18:2). Thus Apollos felt it expedient to leave because of the possibility of official action against him. But such an inference from the letter is quite uncertain. That Apollos felt compelled to leave Alexandria because of political pressure cannot be established. More probable is the natural implication that Apollos came to Ephesus under the inspiration of his spiritual zeal.

"Being fervent in spirit, he spake and taught accurately the things concerning Jesus" (Ac 18:25). The word for "fervent," meaning "boiling over, bubbling," is a picturesque expression of Apollos' zeal and spiritual enthusiasm. His message stirred him deeply. "What he had discovered appealed to him not only intellectually, it captivated his very spirit; he glowed with holy enthusiasm and zeal."[14] It burned like fire in his bones; he could not rest until he had taught others what he knew.

That Apollos "spake and taught" the things he knew may mean that he first spoke in private conversation and then taught publicly in the synagogue, but the distinction cannot be pressed. The imperfect tense of the verbs indicates that it was his practice to speak and teach these things. Thus upon his arrival in Ephesus, Apollos "began to speak boldly in the synagogue" (18:26). Availing himself of the opportunity offered him as a visiting rabbi, Apollos faithfully presented his message to his Jewish audience. The verb rendered "to speak boldly" means "to speak freely, openly, fearlessly." Apollos did not lack the courage of his convictions but "boldly" spoke forth. Doubtless, experience had already taught him that his Jewish audience would not receive his message without strong questioning.

Apollos boldly "began" to speak forth his limited message in the synagogue, but providentially there were two humble Christians in his audience who soon detected his need and personally knew the corrective for his limited knowledge. Being sensitive to the leading of the Spirit, they became the human channels to give Apollos the knowledge that he still lacked. "God has His own strange ways of giving more light to those who love light."[15]

"When Priscilla and Aquila heard him, they took him unto them, and expounded unto him the way of God more accurately" (Ac 18:26). As they listened to Apollos, this Christian couple was keenly impressed with the speaker's fervor and ability but soon became sharply conscious of his imperfect message. Instead of publicly criticizing his inadequate message, they courteously invited him to share the hospitality of their home. Probably after partaking of an enjoyable meal, Priscilla and her husband tactfully began to unfold to Apollos the truths of the gospel, of which he obviously was uninformed. They "expounded," stated, set forth, and explained to him "the way of God more accurately," the gospel in its fullness, as they had learned to know it from Paul. What they taught him did not contradict his faith but rather completed and confirmed it. The comparative adverb "more accurately" indicates that Priscilla and Aquila also had a deep concern about dealing accurately with revealed truth. It required courage and tact on the part of these humble lay workers thus to instruct this eloquent university graduate and noted rabbi. It is equally to the credit of Apollos that he willingly and eagerly received their instruction. He did not allow any false sense of pride to keep him from profiting by what they had to offer. Certainly his evident love for truth made it easy for them to lead him into the full light.

While not expressly stated, it seems obvious that Apollos had been baptized with the baptism of John. But in view of the fact that Paul baptized the twelve Johannine disciples (Ac 19:1-7), the question naturally arises whether Apollos was also rebaptized. Those who hold that the position of Apollos was the same as that of these Johannine disciples, or even hold that they were his converts, generally conclude that he was baptized a second time. Carter says, "He seems to have received Christian baptism at the hands of Priscilla and Aquila."[16] But Luke gives no hint of it. If he knew no more than the twelve whom Paul baptized, it is difficult to see how Luke could have spoken of the teaching of Apollos as being "accurate" as to the things concerning Jesus. There is also no evidence that these twelve were the converts of Apollos.

It may well be that while attending one of the Jewish feasts at Jerusalem, Apollos went out to hear John the Baptist preach and received baptism from him.§ This was the only baptism that the disciples of Jesus received. If Apollos received his baptism before the institution of Christian baptism after the resurrection of Christ, it would be valid baptism like that of the twelve apostles; only he was much longer in being brought into a full understanding of the full truth. But the twelve Johannine disciples at Ephesus apparently became followers of the John the Baptist movement after the resurrection and exaltation of Jesus. Paul accordingly regarded them as not having been baptized at all, since they gave no evidence of the presence of the Spirit in their lives.

HELPFULNESS AND POPULARITY

Apollos showed himself an apt and responsive pupil who warmed the hearts of his teachers. Their mutual fellowship forged an enduring bond of friendship among the three. From the lips of Priscilla and Aquila, Apollos heard the story of the flourishing church that had been founded by Paul at Corinth. Soon there arose in his heart a yearning to bring to others the blessings that gripped his own soul. His conversations with the godly couple turned his thoughts to the province of Achaia, prompting him to express his wish to go and minister there. This wish met with their warm approval. Knowing the needs of the Corinthian church, they probably felt that Apollos would be better qualified to build on the foundation that Paul had already laid there than to attempt to anticipate Paul's work at Ephesus.

When Apollos announced his decision to minister in Achaia, "the brethren encouraged him, and wrote to the disciples to receive him" (Ac 18:27). The term rendered "encouraged" means "to urge forward" (like a runner), to persuade, while the middle voice indicates the particular interest of "the brethren" in giving him their support for this move. Luke's expression "the brethren" can scarcely mean Aquila and Priscilla alone. Apparently the testimony of Aquila and Priscilla had already drawn together a nucleus of Christian believers in Ephesus. This group gladly provided Apollos with a letter of commendation to the Corinthian church. It is the first known instance of

---

§ Of course, the possibility exists that he had been baptized by a disciple of John who had traveled to Alexandria. Codex D assumes this. It is another gloss by the reviser of this Codex.

the use of such letters in the Christian church (cf. 2 Co 3:1), a practice which afterward became usual throughout the churches.

Codex D, in a effort to connect the movement of Apollos directly with the Corinthian church, makes this lengthy insertion at Acts 18:27, "Now there were certain Corinthians sojourning in Ephesus, and having heard him they besought him to cross over with them to their own country. And when he had consented the Ephesians wrote to the disciples in Corinth that they should welcome the man." This addition is not authentic, although such a request could have stimulated the desire of Apollos. However, "If Apollos arrived at Corinth with a group of Corinthian Christians, all of whom came from Ephesus, the commendatory letter prepared for him to present at Corinth seems entirely superfluous."[17]

Apollos left Ephesus for Achaia and began his ministeries at Corinth before Paul returned to Ephesus (Ac 19:1). The report of Priscilla and Aquila concerning Apollos must have interested Paul very deeply. He would have a heartfelt interest in any worker carrying on the work at Corinth.

Luke indicated that the ministry of Apollos in Achaia was twofold. His ministry had positive value for the church members, for he "helped them much that had believed through grace" (18:27). His ministry in their midst contributed much to them. "Through grace" may be connected with "believed," as above, or it may be connected with the more remote verb "helped." The former is more natural from the word order, but the latter seems preferable, since Luke is not describing the characteristics of Paul's converts but the ministry of Apollos.‖ Thus Rotherham renders, "who arriving was very useful unto them who had believed with his gift." This connection makes clear that "his success was not due to his eloquence and his learning, but to divine grace, the grace with which he had made contact in the home of Aquila and Priscilla."[18] Thus Apollos effectively "watered" the work at Corinth that Paul had planted (1 Co 3:6).

Apollos also helped the believers by his powerful ministry in defense of the faith. "He powerfully confuted the Jews, *and that* publicly" (Ac 18:28). The original is very strong; he continued to

---

‖ The marginal rendering of NASB is, "helped greatly through grace those who had believed."

thoroughly and completely refute them. "He argued them down; but to confute is not of necessity to convince."[19] He was able to do this because of his thorough mastery of the Old Testament Scriptures. With irrefutable logic he proved from those Scriptures that "Jesus was the Christ," the promised Messiah. This was a ministry beyond the confines of the Christian assembly. Clearly Apollos extended his efforts to the Jewish synagogue in Corinth, and in synagogues beyond Corinth. Luke referred to the ministry of Apollos as being in "Achaia," although certainly much of his work was done in the Corinthian assembly.

The learned and eloquent Apollos apparently carried on his work at Corinth for over a year. Although, as a fellow worker with God, Paul had planted the seed of the Word, Apollos, as a diligent worker, continued to water the young, growing church (1 Co 3:6). He proved to be a powerful and popular worker in the Corinthian assembly.

However, the very popularity of Apollos proved to be a snare. His brilliant presentation charmed those who were thrilled under the dazzling oratory of the Greek sophists. Carried away by the eloquence of this powerful preacher, these philosophy-loving Corinthians began to discuss the different servants, compare their merits, and openly praise the merits of Apollos to the disparagement of the others. In comparing the servants, they forgot the Master. They failed to recognize that all the laborers were under the authority of Christ as "God's fellow-workers" (1 Co 3:9). In thus forming parties and crying either "I am of Paul" or "I am of Apollos" (1 Co 3:4), they were only spiritually impoverishing themselves, failing to realize that "whether Paul, or Apollos, or Cephas . . . all are yours" (1 Co 3:22). Paul devoted the first four chapters of 1 Corinthians to a rebuke of the Corinthian factions, seeking to show them the folly of thus splitting the church over their favorite preacher.

LOYALTY AND FRIENDSHIP

Whether these factions at Corinth began while Apollos was still there or after he left, is not certain. But certainly Apollos did not further or condone them. Nor did Paul feel any jealousy toward the popular Apollos who had unwittingly drawn to himself the allegiance of some of Paul's converts. Paul's rebuke was not aimed at Apollos but at the Corinthians themselves. He mentioned himself and Apollos "in order that no one of you might become arrogant in behalf of one against the other" (1 Co 4:6, NASB).

From 1 Corinthians 16:12 it is clear that Apollos returned to Ephesus and there associated with Paul. It is the first indication of a personal encounter between these two men. Because of the close maritime connections between Ephesus and Corinth, Paul doubtless had received and followed with keen interest the reports of the work of Apollos at Corinth. Paul warmly welcomed the opportunity to enter into personal association with this noted Christian worker. To the Corinthians, Paul appreciatively spoke of him as "Apollos the brother" (16:12).

Judging from his use of the introductory formula in 1 Corinthians (7:1; 8:1; 12:1; 16:1, 12), Paul's words "Now concerning Apollos" (*peri de Apollō*) imply that the Corinthians in their letter to him had expressed a request that Apollos might return to Corinth. Paul warded off any suspicion of rivalry between himself and Apollos by informing the Corinthians that he had strongly urged Apollos to make the requested visit. "But," he informed them, "it was not at all *his* will to come now." Clearly, Apollos was working independently and not under the direction of Paul, like Timothy and Titus. Ellis sees confirmation of the independent ministry of Apollos in the fact that "Paul can 'urge' Apollos to go (but not 'send' him) to Corinth with a party of 'the brothers' (I Cor. xvi. 11f.; cf. Tit. iii. 13)."[20] Apollos already had made plans and did not feel that he could go to Corinth as Paul requested. Paul's use of the past tense *was* implies that at the time of writing, Apollos was not at Ephesus. The absence of any greeting from Apollos points to the same conclusion. It seems clear that Paul and Apollos had discussed the situation at Corinth and that Apollos himself was adamantly opposed to going back. He did so because he had no desire to give encouragement to his admiring partisans who had elevated him to a position of rivalry with Paul. Paul clearly appreciated this "high-minded delicacy which made him refuse to revisit Corinth."[21]

Nothing further is heard of Apollos for some seven or eight years. Since Apollos worked independently of Paul, Luke's limited narrative

did not leave room for any further account of the work of this remarkable man.

The last biblical glimpse of Apollos is found in Titus 3:13. Those
who reject the Pauline authorship of this epistle hold that the reference has little historical value, or, as a compromise, accept it as giving
valid information "to the extent that we may assume that Titus pre-
serves fragments of a genuine letter to Titus."[22] But conservatives,
who accept the authenticity of the letter, find this brief reference to
Apollos to be significant as giving a final touch to the New Testament
account of the friendship between Paul and Apollos.

In closing his letter to Titus, who was working on the island of
Crete, Paul added, "Set forward Zenas the lawyer and Apollos on their
journey diligently, that nothing be wanting unto them" (3:13). His
words, though brief and apparently unimportant, indicate that the
warm friendship between Paul and Apollos had continued unabated.
Clearly Zenas and Apollos were with Paul when he wrote the letter
to Titus, and since their journey was taking them through Crete, Paul
entrusted to them the delivery of his letter to Titus. He urged Titus
to supply their needs for their continued journey. With that journey
toward its unnamed destination, we lose our last glimpse of Apollos.
Lees remarks, "When we first meet him he is a Bible student; when
we last see him he is in company with another Bible student."[23]

Paul's location when he wrote the letter to Titus is unknown.
The subscription in the King James Version (KJV), "from Nicopolis
of Macedonia" is a later, unauthoritative, scribal addition, based
on the mistaken assumption that Paul was already at Nicopolis
when he wrote. But Paul's remark "for there I have determined to
winter" rather indicates that he had not yet arrived there when he
wrote. More probably, Paul was at Corinth when he wrote the letter
to Titus. If so, we have the happy suggestion that now the two men
could be personally present in the Corinthian assembly without stimulating anew the unhappy party spirit in that church.

The suggestion, first made by Luther, that Apollos was the author
of the epistle to the Hebrews has found favor with many scholars.
While Apollos seems eminently qualified to be the scholarly author of
this important New Testament book, no known historical facts sub-
stantiate the suggestion.

Both intellectually and morally, Apollos was one of the great men of the New Testament. He enhanced his great natural gifts by years of patient toil. Although acquainted with the literature and philosophy of his day, his chief love was the Word of God. "Wholly free from the pride of intellect, he was alert to welcome fresh truth, however unexpected its form and source."[24] Having been brought into the full light of the Christian revelation, he zealously continued to devote himself to the cause of Christ and His church. He refused to allow his success and acclaim to foster a spirit of self-aggrandizement; loyally he continued to put first the welfare of the church. Apollos remains the shining example of a gifted scholar who brought all of his remarkable talents and attainments into full obedience to the Lordship of Jesus Christ. In him Paul found a highly appreciated kindred spirit. Who follows in their train?

2

AQUILA and PRISCILLA

Acts 18:1-3, 18-19, 26
Romans 16:3-5a
1 Corinthians 16:19
2 Timothy 4:19

AQUILA AND PRISCILLA provide a beautiful scriptural example of an ideal Christian couple, together in work and faith alike. Their names are mentioned six times in the New Testament and always together. If in Ananias and Sapphira (Ac 5:1-10) we have the tragic example of a couple united in the commission of sin, here we have the challenging example of a Christian couple wholeheartedly united in spirit, aim, and deed. As McGiffert says, "They furnish the most beautiful example known to us in the apostolic age of the power for good that could be exerted by a husband and wife working in unison for the advancement of the Gospel."[1] Lees compares them to "a double star" among "the group of bright lights which cluster round Paul the Apostle."[2]

BACKGROUND

Aquila and Priscilla are first mentioned in Acts in connection with Paul's arrival at Corinth on his second missionary journey, and the working partnership he established with them. Luke's introductory remarks give us a glimpse into the background of this remarkable couple. Upon arriving from Athens, Paul "found a certain Jew named Aquila, a man of Pontus by race, lately come from Italy, with his wife Priscilla" (Ac 18:2).

33

Although Aquila was a Jew, he bore a Latin name meaning "eagle." It was a common occurrence for Jews of the dispersion to have non-Jewish names. Aquila was a native of Pontus, apparently the Roman province located on the southern shores of the Black Sea and forming an administrative unit with Bithynia, rather than the more easterly non-Roman kingdom of Pontus. Numerous Jews inhabited the district. Jews from Pontus were present in Jerusalem at Pentecost (Ac 2:9). Another Jew named Aquila, known for his Greek translation of the Old Testament around A.D. 130, also came from Pontus.

At what age and under what circumstances Aquila moved to Rome, we do not know. Perhaps he went there as a young man to seek his fortune, attracted by the inviting commercial opportunities in the imperial city. But he may have been taken there as a slave. Most people agree that Aquila was a freedman, since the name appears among Roman slaves as well as freedmen. Knowling points out that "the greater part of the Jews in Rome were freedmen."[3] LaSor regards it as "possible that Aquila had been a slave in a Roman household and had married one of the daughters of that family."[4]

His wife, Priscilla, likewise has a Roman name. While some have held that Priscilla was a freedwoman, it is more commonly held that she belonged by birth to an aristocratic Roman family. LaSor points out that her name "is purely a Roman name" and asserts that "Aquila's wife was not a Jewess."[5] This seems harmonious with Luke's method of introducing Priscilla. While informing us that Aquila was a Jew, by saying "with his wife Priscilla," Luke seems to have carefully avoided asserting that she was Jewish. Ramsay thinks that "it is characteristic of Luke to suggest by subtle arrangement of words a distinction which would need space to explain formally."[6] If Priscilla was not a Jew, we may well assume that she had become a proselyte to Judaism, a common occurrence in Rome,[7] before she married Aquila. This means that she had early revealed herself as a woman of deep religious interests.

Although Aquila and Priscilla are always named together, the order varies. In four of the six occurrences of their names, her name stands before his name (Ac 18:18, 26; Ro 16:3; 2 Ti 4:19). The King James Version reverses the order in Acts 18:26. Ramsay suggests that perhaps the order of the Textus Receptus was due to the influence of the reviser of Codex D, whose revisions of the text show "his dislike to the prominence assigned to women in Acts."[8]

The fact that the name of Priscilla stands before that of her husband four out of six times gives prominence to Priscilla, presumably indicating the superior abilities of this remarkable woman. Certainly Priscilla was very gifted and capable. Lenski asserts, "In character, ability, devotion she excelled her husband so evidently that her name had to precede his."[9] The fact that she took a prominent part in the instruction of Apollos (Ac 18:26) indicates that "she was a woman of more than ordinary culture, a student and interpreter of the Old Testament Scriptures."[10] Harnack suggests that Priscilla, aided by her husband, might have authored the epistle to the Hebrews. But Harnack's arguments from the supposed feminine touches in the epistle are not convincing. The contents of Hebrews imply a more intimate acquaintance with Judaism than Priscilla apparently possessed, especially if she were not Jewish. Hunter records a "sneaking sympathy with Hausrath's sarcastic remark that there is no evidence that Aquila was plagued with a learned wife."[11]

Ramsay, however, thinks that the prior position of Priscilla's name in four of the six instances was due to the fact that she "was of higher rank than her husband, for her name is that of a good old Roman family."[12] But Adeney well questions whether both Paul and Luke would name her first on such grounds. He adds,

> In the free democracy of a Christian Church she was but a sister among brothers and sisters. It is much more likely that her name stands before her husband's because she was the more prominent in the service of the gospel.[13]

Sanday and Headlam object to the view of Ramsay, with the comment that "for a noble Roman lady to travel about with a Jewish husband engaged in mercantile or even artisan work is hardly probable."[14] Robertson counters with the reply, "If she had accepted Judaism, like many educated Roman women, she would do so, especially when both had become Christians."[15] Her patrician connections need not be rejected; nor need we conclude with Ramsay that her name came first because of her aristocratic background. But her Roman background may indicate that she had some personal wealth which enabled them to travel and permitted them to further the cause of Christ by acting as hosts to the saints where they lived.

Luke always uses the name "Priscilla," the diminutive of "Prisca." According to the Greek text of Nestle, Paul always uses the diminutive form. (KJV uses "Prisca" only in 2 Ti 4:19.) Ramsay points out that "Luke regularly used the language of conversation, in which the diminutive forms were usual."[16] In his letters, Paul avoids the diminutive of familiar conversation. Lees asserts, "Paul, mindful of her social standing, and careful as a Roman of her dignity, always speaks of her as Prisca."[17]

CORINTH

Aquila and Priscilla, having but "lately come from Italy," were just getting established at Corinth when Paul arrived there. Luke explains that they moved to Corinth "because Claudius had commanded all the Jews to depart from Rome" (Ac 18:2). Note, the imperial decree had expelled them only "from Rome," not from Italy; but for some unstated reason, they had felt it best to go as far as Corinth. Perhaps they felt that the thriving, commercial city of Corinth offered better business opportunities than other cities, especially in Italy.

This decree of expulsion is apparently that mentioned by the Roman historian Suetonius, who says, "Since the Jews constantly made disturbances at the instigation of Chrestus, he expelled them from Rome"[18]* The precise meaning of the historian's reference to "Chrestus" and the "disturbances" caused by him has been much debated. Some, like Lenski, hold that he was an agitator who was living in Rome at the time.[19] Most others feel that "Chrestus" refers to Christ, the form "Chrestus" deriving from a popular mispronunciation of the name "Christus." Then the disturbances mentioned by Suetonius were due to the disputes of the nonchristian Jews in Rome with Jewish Christians concerning the preaching of Christ as Messiah. According to this interpretation, we have evidence here for the early penetra-

---

* For a discussion of the actions of several emperors against the Jews at Rome, see George Ogg, *The Chronology of the Life of Paul,* chap. 13.

tion of Christianity into the Roman synagogues. Blaiklock says that "Claudius was faced with problems arising from the first impact of the preaching of Christianity on the Jews of Rome."[20] He holds that the amazing "Nazareth Decree," apparently by Claudius, is confirmatory archeological evidence.[21] To rid himself of this religious controversy, Claudius simply expelled all the Jews from Rome, making no distinction between Jews and Jewish Christians. In any case, the decree of Claudius was divinely employed to bring a great blessing into the life of Aquila and Priscilla, by throwing them into intimate fellowship with the apostle Paul.

It is an open question whether Aquila and Priscilla were Christians when Paul met them at Corinth. Luke's language gives no positive aid on the question. The interpreters either disagree or are noncommital in their conclusions. Meyer supports his view that they were not Christians when they met Paul by pointing out that Luke simply called Aquila "a Jew" without adding the usual designation that he was a disciple; that "all the Jews" naturally included Aquila as such; and that Paul associated himself with Aquila and Priscilla because of their common trade, not their common faith.[22] In reply, one may say that calling Aquila a Jew accounts for the fact that the decree affected him. Since the imperial policy as yet made no distinction between Jews and Jewish Christians, as a Jewish Christian, Aquila would be included in the emperor's edict. While clearly their common trade brought Paul into association with Aquila, a common spiritual interest is not thereby ruled out.

The fact that Luke gives no hint of conversion through Paul favors the view that they already were Christians. Considering the important place they held in the later ministry of Paul, it does not seem logical that he should omit such an important fact. Nor does Paul ever suggest that they were his converts. Plumptre holds that they already were converts to Christianity since Paul "joins himself to them, as able to share his thoughts and hopes, even before he begins preaching in the synagogue, as in verse 4."[23] If Aquila was not already a Christian, why would he so readily accept as a business partner this man whom the bulk of his fellow Jews regarded with such strong disfavor? Clearly Aquila and Priscilla did not harbor any definite antagonisms to Christianity when they met Paul. The assumption that they had already accepted at least the basic principle of Christianity that Jesus was the Messiah accounts for the ready welcome they accorded Paul when he came to reside with them. Lees thinks that "they knew *about* Christ perhaps more than they knew Himself."[24] Their associations with Paul soon led them into an experiential understanding of the deeper truths of the Christian faith.

Paul established a working partnership with Aquila because they engaged in "the same trade" (Ac 18:3). After a long period of preaching daily in Athens (Ac 17:17), Paul's funds were exhausted when he reached Corinth, and he found it necessary to resort to the trade that he had been taught as a youth. The Jews wisely insisted that every boy should learn a manual trade. They knew from the vicissitudes of life that every Jewish boy needed a means whereby he could earn his own living in foreign cities, where the chances of war or persecution might transport him. The Jews dignified manual labor and believed that even a rabbi must have a skill. Having no mission board to finance him, Paul regularly resorted to tentmaking to support himself.

As a youth in Tarsus, Paul had learned the trade of tentmaking (Ac 18:3), a flourishing occupation in that city. Of Cilicia, Olshausen says, "The hair of a species of very shaggy goat was there wrought into a thick stuff like felt, which was very much employed in covering tents."[25] This often used material, called *cilicium*, made tents that were in great demand all over the East. Some, like LaSor, hold that Paul and Aquila actually wove the tent cloth.[26] Others point out that the word etymologically means "tentmaker, tent tailor" and see no need to depart from the original import of the term.[27] Since Paul could find employment wherever he went, he probably worked at actually making tents.

During the first century, however, the term's connotation included the idea of a leather worker, and Origen and Chrysostom held that Paul worked in leather. Following a review of the usage of the term, Lake and Cadbury remark, "The early and widespread nature of this evidence seems to prove that though *skenopoios* etymologically means 'tentmaker' it does actually mean 'leather-worker'."[28] They accordingly rendered, "for they were leather-workers by trade." Some scholars, like Bruce, accept this interpretation, but there is no widespread agreement on the view.† Since Paul's father was a strict Pharisee (Ac 23:6) and thus regarded contact with the skins of dead animals as defiling, it seems improbable that he would have permitted his son to learn such a trade. It is however entirely possible that later – when as a Christian, Paul was freed from all such ceremonial scruples – he may at times have used leather to manufacture tents.

Upon arrival at Corinth, Paul would have no trouble finding others of his occupation, since they would all be concentrated in one place in the city. Shortly before, Aquila and Priscilla had found their way to the street of the tentmakers and had established their business. Luke's statement, "They were tentmakers," clearly indicates that the wife also used her skills in cutting and sewing the tent cloth. Paul found employment with them and "wrought," the imperfect tense denoting his steady work with them at the task. He also boarded with them during his stay at Corinth. Acts 18:7 indicates a change in the place of *preaching* at Corinth, rather than a change of Paul's *residence*. Moe says that the home of Titus Justus "also furnished him lodging facilities," and thinks that Paul thus "emphasized the significance of his move away from the Jew Aquila to the Gentile Titius Justus" as evidence that he "was to become a Greek to the Greeks."[29] But his willingness to preach openly in the home of a Gentile next to the Jewish synagogue gives sufficient evidence that an open break with Judaism had been made by Paul as the messenger of Christ.

A lifelong association with Aquila and Priscilla resulted, a fellowship in Christian service as well as daily labor. The arrival of Silas and Timothy from Macedonia with a monetary gift (Ac 18:5; 2 Co 11:9), enabled Paul to launch out in aggressive evangelistic efforts at Corinth, but he never broke off his business connections with Aquila. Tentmaking allowed Paul, during the year and a half that he remained at Corinth (Ac 18:11), to keep himself financially independent of the Corinthian church (2 Co 11:9). Through their partnership with Paul, Aquila and Priscilla received a priceless spiritual boon and rendered the church a great service.

---

† F. F. Bruce, *The Dawn of Christianity*, calls Paul "a leather-worker" (p. 12) but notes that this is an extended meaning of the Greek term (p. 13, note). Cf. "Commentary on the Book of the Acts," in *New International Commentary*, p. 367.

EPHESUS

So profitable and mutually satisfactory did their association with Paul prove, that Aquila and Priscilla agreed to shift their business to Ephesus when Paul determined to begin his ministry there. When Paul sailed from Cenchreae, the eastern seaport of Corinth, he had "with him Priscilla and Aquila" (Ac 18:18). Luke's added words, "for he had a vow," have occasioned much discussion as to whether Paul or Aquila had taken the vow. Although grammatically the reference points to Aquila, the natural emphasis of the narrative makes it more probable that Paul had taken the vow.

Arriving at Ephesus with Aquila and Priscilla, Paul "left them there" (Ac 18:19) while he went on to Jerusalem. Their presence in Ephesus would not only lay the groundwork for his intended work there but would also provide a means of livelihood for him while preaching in that city.

Since no Christian assembly existed then in Ephesus, Aquila and Priscilla attended worship services in the Jewish synagogue (Ac 18:19, 24-26). This illustrates "how close and intimate at first were the bonds between the synagogue and the church."[30] They sat in the audience when a noted preacher from Alexandria, Apollos, began to preach in the Ephesian synagogue. His eloquence and thorough knowledge of the Scriptures deeply impressed them, but they soon noticed the serious limitations in his message. Realizing that Apollos was a man with great potential for the kingdom of God, "Priscilla and Aquila . . . took him unto them, and expounded unto him the way of God more accurately" (Ac 18:26). The order of their names here implies that Priscilla led in their ministry to Apollos, not merely joining her husband in his conferences with Apollos, which in itself would have been a commendable indication of her interests. Lenski comments, "She was by nature more gifted and able than her husband, also spiritually fully developed, due to her having had Paul in her home for 18 months in Corinth. Aquila seems to have been a gentle, quiet soul, genuine in this unobtrusive way."[31] It is eloquent testimony to Priscilla and Aquila's tact and graciousness that this university graduate and noted rabbi readily received their instruction. The ministry that they rendered in the privacy of their home proved

to be a great boon for the cause of Christ; for Apollos, having been
fully illuminated concerning the gospel, became an effective worker.
With the other believers in Christ who resided in Ephesus, Priscilla
and Aquila encouraged Apollos in his desire to carry his ministry to
Achaia (Ac 18:27).

Aquila and Priscilla lived in Ephesus for nearly three years (Ac
20:31) while Paul worked there on his third missionary journey. Apparently, here, as at Corinth, he lived and worked with them (cf. Ac
20:34). First Corinthians 16:19 asserts this, according to the reading
of some manuscripts, "Aquila and Prisca with whom I lodge."‡ Although this reading is not authentic, it makes a correct inference.

When Paul wrote 1 Corinthians from Ephesus, Aquila and Priscilla, as former members of the Corinthian church, sent warm greetings. "Aquila and Prisca salute you much in the Lord" (1 Co 16:19).
Their hearty greeting reflects their real affection for the Corinthian
believers, the overflow of their common fellowship in the Lord.

To the personal greeting to the Corinthian church sent by Aquila
and Prisca, Paul added, "with the church that is in their house" (1 Co
16:19). It gives us an added glimpse into the ministry of this hos-
pitable couple. Not only did they furnish Paul a home and a means
whereby he could maintain his financial independence, but they also
threw open their home as a regular assembly place for believers in
Ephesus. Since they had no special building specifically reserved for
worship, the early believers gathered for worship wherever they
could. Priscilla, no doubt, eagerly sanctioned Aquila's willingness to
use their home for this purpose. It was evidence of their earnest desire to use their means for the furtherance of the cause of their Lord.
"Their occupation as tent-makers probably required spacious apart-
ments, suited for the purpose of such assemblies."[32] Thus their home
became a center for mutual help, Christian instruction, and united
worship. In this use of their home as a means for Christian witness,
Aquila and Priscilla offer a timely challenge to our own day.

Aquila and Priscilla's spiritual ministries at Ephesus are not
further delineated. That they added great strength to the Ephesian
church is obvious. Isabella Buchanan's remark that "in all probability

---

‡ The reading in the uncials D and G, the majority of the Old Latin manuscripts,
and the Clementine Vulgate.

Priscilla and Aquila were assistant teachers"[33] with Paul in the school of Tyrannus (Ac 19:9-10) lacks convincing support.

Scripture gives one other glimpse of Aquila and Priscilla that seems to belong chronologically to this time of their sojourn in Ephesus. In Romans 16:4, speaking of Prisca and Aquila, Paul says, "who for my life laid down their own necks." The picturesque expression, "laid down their own necks," is apparently figurative, as evidenced by the singular *neck* in the original. It expresses some extreme peril to which they voluntarily exposed their lives in order to save Paul. Luke does not say what that peril entailed. Some would connect it with the riot of the silversmiths (Ac 19:29-30). Thus Lees conjectures that "the rioters appear to have come in search of Paul, and Prisca and her husband covered his retreat at the risk of being torn to pieces by the angry mob."[34] But the Acts account does not speak of such a danger in relating the events of that riot. More probably the reference is to some other unrecorded danger which befell Paul in Asia; it may have been connected with the unidentified "affliction" mentioned in 2 Corinthians 1:8. Paul's list in 2 Corinthians 11:23-27 shows that he was no stranger to perils of various kinds, many of which went unrecorded. His reference to the "trials which befell me by the plots of the Jews" in his farewell to the Ephesian elders (Ac 20:19) reveals that dangers often menaced his ministry at Ephesus.

Paul deeply appreciated the brave action of Aquila and Priscilla. He gratefully added his comment, "Unto whom not only I give thanks, but also all the churches of the Gentiles" (Ro 16:4). Whatever had happened, the event remained vivid in Paul's mind and left him with a lively sense of gratitude for his devoted friends. Their willingness to hazard their own lives to save Paul's, bears eloquent testimony to their high esteem and strong affection for him. It touched Paul deeply. Lard says, "The heroism which the act displays is simply sublime. Could Paul possibly have had it in mind at Rom. 5:7?"[35] Their brave deed "was loyalty to the limit and Paul cherished the memory of their courage."[36]

ROME

Paul keenly realized the importance of Rome in his plans for the evangelization of the Roman empire. His discussions with Aquila and Priscilla deepened this conviction in him. While still at Ephesus, Paul laid plans to go to Rome (Ac 19:21). Some months later when Paul wrote the epistle to the Romans from Corinth, he sent greetings to "Prisca and Aquila my fellow-workers in Christ Jesus" (Ro 16:3). When Paul terminated his work at Ephesus after the Ephesian riot (Ac 20:1), Aquila and Priscilla also decided to leave the city. Undoubtedly by agreement with Paul, they decided to return to Rome. Their presence there would assure him a ready acceptance by the church in Rome when he arrived, and would do much toward furthering the cooperation of the church in Paul's plans for missionary work in Spain (Ro 15:22-24).

The view that Aquila and Priscilla had already returned to Rome when Paul wrote Romans assumes that Romans 16 is a genuine part of the epistle to the Romans. But this assumption has been strongly questioned. Some writers claim that Romans 16 was originally a letter to the church at Ephesus and has mistakenly become attached to the epistle to the Romans. Some plausible arguments, drawn from its contents and advanced in support of the view, have met with considerable favor.§ But no manuscript evidence supports the theory, and the internal features of the chapter have a fully satisfactory explanation on the common view that the chapter always belonged to the epistle to the Romans. After reviewing the evidence for the Ephesian hypothesis, Guthrie comments that "Harnack's conclusion that this Ephesian destination theory is a 'badly supported hypothesis' is fully justified."[37] Knox has recently advanced a third possibility. Unwilling to accept the traditional view and aware of the difficulties to the Ephesian hypothesis, he postulates that chapter 16 of Romans is most probably "a pseudonymous addition to the Letter to the Romans designed to bind the apostle more closely to Rome and to strengthen the hands of that church in its battle with the Gnostics in the second century."[38] The conservative rejects this view because it denies the authenticity of the chapter as from the hand of Paul. The

---

§ *For* the Ephesian hypothesis, see Farrar, *The Life and Work of St. Paul,* p. 450, footnote; McGiffert, pp. 275-279; James Moffatt, *An Introduction to the Literature of the New Testament,* pp. 134-139. *Against,* see James Denney, "St. Paul's Epistle to the Romans," in *The Expositor's Greek Testament,* 2:580-582; C. H. Dodd, "The Epistle of Paul to the Romans," in *Moffatt New Testament Commentary,* pp. xvii-xxiv; Donald Guthrie, *New Testament Introduction,* pp. 400-404.

Ephesian hypothesis sees no reason to believe that Aquila and Priscilla returned to Rome and maintains that they remained at Ephesus; those of this opinion claim support from the fact that in 2 Timothy Paul includes them in those he greets in Ephesus. The suggestion of Knox denies any historical validity to this reference to Aquila and Priscilla. I accept neither view as justified.

Paul's close ties with "Prisca and Aquila my fellow-workers in Christ Jesus" led him to give them first place in the long list of Christian residents in Rome to whom he sent his greetings (Ro 16:3-4). He had good reason for his high esteem of them. In affectionately calling them "my fellow-workers in Christ Jesus" Paul set them side by side with himself in the service of Christ. He worked with them at their trade of tentmaking, and they shared with him aggressive efforts to spread the gospel. They made a vital contribution through their zealous activities as lay workers. Paul further felt personally indebted to them for their brave intervention on his own behalf, and remarked that in saving his life, all the Gentile churches were likewise indebted to them (Ro 16:4).

In conveying his greetings to Prisca and Aquila at Rome, Paul added "and *salute* the church that is in their house" (Ro 16:5). At Rome they had again shown their spirit of hospitality by opening their home as a place for the saints in Rome to assemble. When he concluded the epistle, Paul had already received a report of their characteristic action.

Aquila and Priscilla must have experienced deep disappointment when they learned of Paul's arrest in Jerusalem, an event which delayed his arrival in Rome for over two years. We have no evidence that they were still in Rome when Paul did arrive there as a prisoner. If they were, they doubtless joined the Christians who went out to meet Paul before his arrival in the imperial city (Ac 28:15). Since, however, Paul never mentions their names in any of the epistles written during his two years as a prisoner in Rome (Ac 28:30-31), they apparently had left the city.

EPHESUS

The last scriptural reference to this remarkable Christian couple is found in 2 Timothy 4:19, which reads, "Salute Prisca and Aquila."

Those who deny the Pauline authorship of this epistle naturally conclude that this greeting "throws no further light on the later residence
of the two."[39] But conservatives, accepting the Pauline authorship,
find here a welcome final glimpse of these staunch friends of Paul.
Since it is generally accepted that Timothy was stationed in Ephesus
when Paul wrote the letter, it seems obvious that Prisca and Aquila
again resided in Ephesus. That at a later period they should again
make their home in that city is quite comprehensible. They would be
drawn back not only because of the trade connections they had established there previously but also because of their strong ties with the
Ephesian church, with whose founding they had been intimately
connected. This return to Ephesus may well have been their last
move.

Among the friends to whom Paul sent his greetings, Prisca and
Aquila again received first mention. As a devoted Christian couple,
they still lived and worked together, the recipients of the dying
apostle's heartfelt love.

3

BARNABAS

Acts 4:36-37; 9:27; 11:22-30; 12:25; 13:1 — 14:28; 15:1-40
1 Corinthians 9:6
Galatians 2:1, 9, 13
Colossians 4:10

A WARM HEART and a helping hand for those in need well characterize Barnabas. The character and service of this man of God left an
abiding mark upon the early church. While he does not rank in importance in the Bible with the twelve or with Paul, it would do an
injustice to Barnabas simply to call him one of the "lesser lights"
around Paul. He was a worthy peer of Paul, and the apostle set
Barnabas side by side with himself in Christian service (1 Co 9:6;
Gal 2:9). Because he was overshadowed by his more gifted and
capable companion, the true greatness of Barnabas has not always
been sufficiently recognized.

"SON OF CONSOLATION"

His original name was "Joses" (KJV); or more probably "Joseph"
(Ac 4:36, ASV). *Joseph* is the form found in the earliest manuscripts and versions. They are apparently simply variant forms of the
same name since "Rabbinic writers often give *Jose* for Joseph."[1] From
the apostles he received the familiar name "Barnabas," which, because
of its felicity, completely superseded his original name. His friends
bestowed it upon him in recognition of his character. The name says
something about the man. It individualizes and characterizes him as
"The son of consolation" (KJV) or "Son of exhortation" (ASV). Both

46

renderings are legitimate and either gives an attractive portrait of the man.

Although the scholars debate the true derivation of the name, Luke at once gave the interpretation or translation by adding "Barnabas (which is, being interpreted, Son of exhortation)." The original reads, "Son of *paraklesis.*" Coming from a verbal form meaning "to summon to one's side to help," the designation denotes that spiritual help which one Christian extends to another in coming to his aid and assistance. At one time, the help given may take the form of comfort or consolation; while at other times, it may take the form of exhortation or appeal. To cover both meanings, the rendering "Son of encouragement" has been suggested, and the story of Barnabas shows it eminently fitted the man. Barnabas' disposition led him to help those who needed encouragement.

Opinions differ as to which of Barnabas' qualities earned him his new name. Those who favor the rendering "son of exhortation" say that he received it because of his ability to give inspiring exhortation, to arouse and stimulate fellow believers. Thus Hervey holds that "his exhortations under the influence of the Holy Spirit in the Church assemblies were particularly stirring and edifying."[2] Acts 11:23 and 13:43 show that he did have a gift of kindly exhortation. But this view would be more convincing if the name had originated later, in connection with his ministry in the Word. Luke's word choice, using an aorist tense, supports the view that a definite occasion in the early church called forth the name in relation to the events. Bartlet favors the rendering "son of consolation" and points out that, since Luke mentions it in connection with Barnabas' generous deed, "such a rendering makes the reference to the surname all of a piece with the matter in hand, if we suppose the apostles signalized Joseph's exemplary love by hailing him a veritable 'son of comfort' for the needy."[3] Lenski would connect the bestowal of the name with his conversion. Noting that Barnabas is introduced as a Levite, Lenski remarks,

> His conversion was the first breach in the hierarchial walls, and, coming at just this critical time, brought great consolation and encouragement to the apostles. That is why they gave him the new name.[4]

Whatever the immediate occasion for the name, it was probably intended to designate him as a "son of consolation" rather than "exhortation." The picture of him in Acts stresses the excellence of his heart rather than his eloquence. Barnabas doubtless was an able speaker, but Paul clearly was his superior in speech (Ac 14:12).

One wonders how Barnabas reacted when the apostles first applied this name to him. Was he reluctant to accept it for fear that he might not be able to live up to it, or did he rejoice at this honor and regard it as a stimulating challenge to prove worthy of it? Acts reveals that he did prove worthy of his new name, manifesting the grace of consolation as well as exhortation.

NATIVE OF CYPRESS Sp!

In introducing Barnabas, Luke further described him as "a Levite, a man of Cyprus by race" (Ac 4:36). This does not mean that his ancestors were natives of Cyprus, but rather that Barnabas himself was born there of Jewish parents then residing on the island (cf. Ac 18:2, 24). Numerous Jews lived there at the time. Some have conjectured that, because of its proximity to Tarsus, Barnabas as a young man was sent to the famous university at Tarsus for his education and there became acquainted with Saul before either of them became Christians.[5] Plumptre even speculates that there Barnabas "practiced with Saul in early life the craft of tent-making, for which Tarsus was famous and in which they were afterwards fellow-labourers (I Cor. 9:6)."[6] While such hypotheses in themselves are not improbable, they are entirely devoid of any scriptural foundation.

Being a Levite, as distinguished from a priest, Barnabas apparently performed Levitical duties in the temple at Jerusalem. Filson thinks it "highly probable that he had heard Jesus teach, at least in Jerusalem, and had been a follower of the Master before the crucifixion."[7] The tradition that he was one of the seventy is very improbable.

He had relatives living in Jerusalem. Mary, the mother of John Mark, was his aunt (Ac 12:12; Col 4:10), apparently a widow. After her conversion she threw open her home as a place of assembly for the Christians. Barnabas may have made his home with her. From

1 Corinthians 9:5-6, some have inferred that Barnabas remained a bachelor. In verse 5, Paul discussed his right to be married and in verse 6 his right to support from his ministry. Since he named Barnabas in verse 6 it seems that he would also be included in the "we" of verse 5.

CONTRIBUTOR TO THE POOR

Barnabas first appears in Acts in connection with his liberal contribution to the poor members of the Jerusalem church (4:37). This first reference to him reveals him as a generous, sympathetic individual, characterized by his practical helpfulness. Rees comments that Barnabas "had a *stewardship* rather than an *ownership* view of property."[8] He had a love-prompted willingness to sacrifice for the welfare of others. In this voluntary act of sharing his material means, he gave an illustration of the "great grace" that characterized the early church in Jerusalem (Ac 4:33).

He possessed a certain "field," a plot of ground used mainly for farming. Whether this field was in Cyprus or in Palestine the Bible does not say. Some have thought that the Mosaic regulations which excluded the Levites from a share in the land of Palestine (Num 18:20-24; Jos 18:7) necessitate the view that the land was in Cyprus, outside the Holy Land. But this need not follow. The case of Jeremiah (Jer 32:7-12) shows that it was not considered illegal for a Levite to own a field in Palestine.

When material needs became evident among the members of the church, Barnabas, like some others who had possessions, sold his land "and brought the money and laid it at the apostles' feet" (Ac 4:37). The use of the singular "the money" (*to chrēma*), instead of the plural, points to a definite sum and implies that Barnabas gave the total amount received for the field, quite in contrast to the duplicity of Ananias and Sapphira (Ac 5:1-2). Robertson remarks that Barnabas thus showed himself "the true Levite with the Lord as his portion. He had spiritual wealth that far outweighed the value of his land."[9]

First Corinthians 9:6 makes it clear that Barnabas, like Paul, was dominated by a noble spirit of independence as a missionary and toiled at a trade to earn his living while preaching the gospel free of charge. The nature of his trade is not known, but perhaps he also was a tentmaker.

SPONSOR OF SAUL

The next reference to Barnabas in Acts shows him proving himself "a son of encouragement" in courageously befriending the suspected Saul (Ac 9:26-27). When Saul suddenly reappeared in Jerusalem three years after his conversion (Gal 1:18), where the memories of the persecutor were still vivid, and sought to enter into intimate communion with the disciples as a recognized member of their group, "They were all afraid of him, not believing that he was a disciple." They doubtless had heard reports about his conversion but regarded as incredible any claim that the notorious Pharisee had become a Christian. Their fear of him is understandable, if not wholly pardonable. The welfare of the church demanded the exercise of great vigilance concerning those welcomed into the intimacy of their fellowship. The Christians feared that Saul might actually be a wolf in sheep's clothing, seeking to gain their confidence for their more effective undoing. Such methods of infiltration were well known. Perhaps also, garbled and insinuating reports concerning his conversion had been circulated by the attendants who had accompanied him on the trip to Damascus. Matthew Henry justly observes,

> There is need of the wisdom of the serpent, to keep the mean between the extremes of suspicion on the one hand and credulity on the other; yet methinks it is safer to err on the charitable side.[10]

Providentially, one man in the Jerusalem church had this charitable spirit and the faith to believe in Saul's spiritual transformation.

This coolness and suspicion must have been a trying and humbling experience to Saul, but Barnabas proved himself the needed friend in that crucial hour. "But Barnabas took him, and brought him to the apostles" (Ac 9:27). Barnabas was ready to hear the story of Saul. He received Saul warmly but made an investigation. He may have had other confirmatory sources available to him. Convinced of the genuineness of Saul's conversion, he took him to Peter and James (Gal 1:18-19), the representatives of "the apostles" then in Jerusalem. He made a twofold appeal on behalf of Saul. He recounted to them what Christ had done for Saul, "how he had seen the Lord in the way, and that he had spoken to him," and what Saul had since done for Christ, "how at Damascus he had preached boldly in the name of Jesus" (Ac 9:27). When Barnabas, one of the esteemed members of the church, thus willingly stepped forward to sponsor and vouch for Saul, the fears and suspicions of the brethren were relieved and they gladly received Paul into their fellowship.

It is the lasting honor of Barnabas that he proved himself a genuine friend to Saul in his hour of need. The question naturally arises why Barnabas rather than someone else first befriended Saul. It might have been due to his previous acquaintance with Saul of Tarsus. Some feel that Barnabas was convinced that the suspected applicant was incapable of such duplicity. Plumptre asserts, "He knew enough of his friend to believe every syllable of what he told him as to the incidents of his conversion."[11] But this explanatory assumption of a previous acquaintance has no shred of evidence in Acts to support it. Rather, this action of Barnabas adds another proof of the kindly nature of the one whom the apostles called "a son of consolation." Seekings perceives here another instance of that quick discernment which characterized Barnabas. "He possessed that rare gift of insight which enables men to get beneath the surface and discover the deeps of another's soul; and often in the face of popular prejudice he was courageous enough to act as he saw."[12] This is in harmony with the key which Luke himself furnished in a subsequent manifestation of this same trait in Barnabas' discernment (Acts 11:23-24).

When after the short period of fifteen days (Gal 1:18) Saul's bold witness to the Hellenistic Jews in Jerusalem evoked a death plot against him, "the brethren" averted possible tragedy by sending him to Tarsus. Doubtless, Barnabas, concerned for the safety of this aggressive young worker, had a hand in it.

LEADER IN ANTIOCH

When news of the development of a predominantly Gentile church in Syrian Antioch reached the Jerusalem church (Ac 11:19-22), they recognized the novelty of the movement and felt bound to take cognizance of the situation. The narrative does not indicate any hostile reaction to the report, as in the case of Peter's work with Cornelius (Ac 11:1-3). "And they sent forth Barnabas as far as Antioch" (11:22). He held the confidence of the Jerusalem church, and they considered him the best choice for this important mission. As a Hellenist, Barnabas could sympathetically evaluate this new step taken by his Hellenistic brethren (11:20-21).

The record does not state Barnabas' specific assignment. We only know that he went to investigate and report back. Doubtless, the church commissioned him to determine if this new Gentile movement was genuine and to take such steps as he found necessary to correct and direct it.

Upon his arrival in Antioch, Barnabas "wisely played the part of an unbiased auditor and observer of the Gentile revival."[13] Having spiritually opened eyes, he readily saw "the grace of God" (Ac 11:23), the unmistakable evidence of God's grace operative in the lives of both Jews and uncircumcised Gentiles. He was convinced that it was a genuine work of God. He found nothing to censure or correct. "Like Julius Caesar, *He came, he saw, he triumphed;* but triumphed in the conquests not of war, but of grace."[14] That he could thus enthusiastically commend a work that he had neither originated nor directed, reveals the true greatness of the man.

Barnabas wisely decided not to return to Jerusalem but to stay and associate himself with the work in Antioch. Giving his full support to the work, "He exhorted them all, that with purpose of heart they would cleave unto the Lord" (Ac 11:23). With his exhortations, he encouraged the Christians to persevere and progress in their new found faith. He rose above his Jewish conceptions and accepted these uncircumcised believers as true brethren in the Lord. He recognized that God had started a new work in them, and he refused to lay the burden of Jewish ceremonialism on them. He sanctioned and furthered the practice, already begun in the Antioch church, of Jewish and Gentile converts joining in Christian fellowship without ceremonial restrictions.

Luke's rare eulogy underlines that Barnabas' Christian character prompted his kind actions. "For he was a good man, and full of the Holy Spirit and of faith" (Ac 11:24). As a "good man" he embodied kindness, generosity, and a winning and persuasive form of holiness.

But his naturally generous disposition was refined and transformed by the indwelling grace of the Spirit, while his faith gave him insight into spiritual realities and enabled his heart thus to encourage these new brethren.

Barnabas entered actively into the work at Antioch, and his efforts further stirred the revival fires. "And much people was added unto the Lord" (Ac 11:24). Barnabas soon became the church's acknowledged leader, and this spirit-filled ministry no doubt extended over a considerable period. "It is a tribute to his worth and ability that although he had not helped to found the church, all accepted his leadership."[15]

The rapid growth of the work soon made the need evident for an assistant in the work. Wisely, Barnabas did not turn to Jerusalem for the needed helper, for "he wished to bring no disturbing element into the life of the Greek Church in Antioch."[16] His thoughts turned rather to Saul of Tarsus as the best-qualified man. He had a vivid recollection of the miraculous conversion of the capable man whom he had introduced to the church at Jerusalem and remembered the zeal Saul had shown in preaching to the Hellenists at Jerusalem (Ac 9:27-29). He must also have had some acquaintance with Saul's subsequent activities (Gal 1:23) and of his commission from the Lord as an apostle to the Gentiles (Ac 9:15; 22:21; 26:16-18). He felt assured that the work at Antioch needed Saul.

"And he went forth to Tarsus to seek for Saul" (Ac 11:25). The verb *seek*, which in the papyruses "is specially used of searching for human beings, with an implication of difficulty,"[17] indicates that Barnabas was aware that Saul was not idle and that he might have trouble finding him. That this proved to be the case is shown by the added words "and when he had found him" (11:26).

Glad to hear of the developments in Antioch, Saul accepted the urgings of Barnabas to join in the work in that important center. So, Barnabas "brought him unto Antioch." Thus for the second time, Barnabas sponsored Saul, giving him his great opportunity. In bringing this capable and aggressive worker to Antioch, Barnabas must have already realized the possible threats to his acknowledged leadership there. He had none of the littleness which cannot endure the presence of a possible rival in a church.

The results proved the wisdom of Barnabas; a very fruitful year in the work at Antioch followed. The united teaching ministry of these workers reached "much people." Large numbers of converts came from various classes and circumstances. To the members of this aggressive church, which could rightly be classified as neither a Jewish nor a Gentile movement, the epithet "Christian" was first applied (Ac 11:26).

BEARER OF RELIEF

When the prophet Agabus predicted the coming of a severe famine, the Antiochene church demonstrated its spiritual oneness with the Judean church by immediately commencing a relief fund for the Judean saints (Ac 11:27-29). They sent the collected sum "to the elders by the hand of Barnabas and Saul" (11:30). The order of the names indicates that they selected Barnabas to head the delegation. Filson remarks, "It is worth noting that he was trusted in this financial ministry. Those who sent the gift knew that it was being put into the hands of a capable representative."[18]

Quite probably, Barnabas and Saul, while in Jerusalem, lodged in the home of Mary, the mother of Mark. How long they remained in Jerusalem, Luke does not say, but the stay probably was short. Since the two men delivered the collection "to the elders," the apostles apparently were not present in Jerusalem at the time.* Ramsay indeed conceived of Barnabas and Saul as bringing in loads of provisions instead of money, and pictured them personally distributing these provisions; hence he concluded that "their ministration" (Ac 12:25) lasted a considerable time.[19] But the term *ministration* does not require that they personally distributed the relief. In Romans 15:31, Paul used the same term for the offering which he took to Jerusalem on the third missionary journey, an offering which he did not distribute. Thayer notes that the word is used "of those who

---

* Scholars have difficulties in seeking to correlate this "famine visit" with the visits to Jerusalem mentioned by Paul in Gal. A number of recent scholars would equate this visit with that in Gal 2:1-10. But Ac gives no hint that the circumcision controversy seen in Gal had as yet arisen. I follow the view of those who equate Gal 2:1-10 with the visit in Ac 15. This means that the "famine visit" was not mentioned in Galatians, since Paul did not personally meet any of the apostles on this visit. For a full discussion see Ogg, *The Chronology of the Life of Paul*, chaps. 9 and 11.

succor need by either collecting or bestowing benefactions."²⁰ The collection was bestowed upon the needy through the hands of the elders. When they had completed their assignment, Barnabas and Saul returned to Antioch, "taking with them John whose surname was Mark" (Ac 12:25).

MISSIONARY TO GENTILES

Barnabas appears first among the five "prophets and teachers" who ministered in the church at Antioch (Ac 13:1). Luke does not specify when the other three men began their ministry there. Whether one must regard all five men as both prophets and teachers, Barnabas, who had already exercised an effective teaching ministry in Antioch (Ac 11:23-26), is here designated a prophet, one through whom the Holy Spirit made known His will and message to the people.

The command of the spirit, "Separate me Barnabas and Saul for the work whereunto I have called them" (Ac 13:2), inaugurated the new missionary endeavor and designated the workers. Barnabas' name came first as the accepted leader, while Saul became his capable lieutenant. The church promptly obeyed the command of the Spirit; they "laid their hands on them" and dismissed them to take up their new work (13:3). This laying on of hands was not an ordination of these two men to the apostolic office. Paul strongly insisted that human agency had no part in making him an apostle (Gal 1:1; 2:6). Nor can Barnabas be considered an "apostle" in the narrower technical sense of the term, like Paul and the twelve. Although the term *apostles* (plural) refers to Paul and Barnabas on this missionary tour (14:4, 14), in its primary and wider sense, it means messengers sent on a special mission. The term *apostle* is never used of Barnabas alone. In the words of Ramsay, "The Apostle was always appointed by God and not by the church."²¹ Nor does the modern sense of the term *ordination* apply to this ministry, for both men had long served in the ministry full time. It should rather be recognized as a commissioning service, whereby "the church of Antioch, through its leaders, expressed its fellowship with Barnabas and Saul and recognized them as its delegates or 'apostles'."²² Acts 14:26 indicates that it was a commissioning for a definite type of service, foreign missionary work.

Accompanied by John Mark, Barnabas and Saul began their

work in Cyprus, with Barnabas as the acknowledged leader (Ac 13:7). But with the departure of the missionaries from Paphos, following the encounter with Bar-Jesus (13:6-12), a clearly marked change in the leadership of the mission took place. Luke indicated this by his expression "Paul and his company" (13:13). The original reads literally "those around Paul," and marks him out as the center of the group, with the other members of the party clustering around him. The expression may imply that the party comprised more than two others, although no others are named. Luke made plain the recession of Barnabas to second place by using the order "Paul and Barnabas" (13:43, 46, 50) for the remainder of the journey, with one notable exception. That Barnabas faithfully continued the work with Paul as leader, shows that he did not yield to the common temptation to desire to be first. A familiar couplet says,

> It takes more grace than I can tell
> To play the second fiddle well.

But Barnabas had that grace, and he did not play any discordant notes in that position, even though Mark left the party (13:13). Another evidence of the greatness of Barnabas is that he doubtless recognized the fact that in personality, education, and eloquence, Paul outranked him; so he graciously deferred to Paul's leadership.

In describing the work of the missionaries in the cities of South Galatia, Luke reverted to the order "Barnabas and Paul" on one memorable occasion and thus introduced an event where Barnabas appeared in a superior position to Paul (Ac 14:9-14). When a congenital cripple at Lystra was miraculously healed, the excited Lycaonians, on the basis of their local traditions, concluded that they were witnessing another theophany of their gods. Their tradition asserted that years before, the gods Zeus and Hermes (counterparts to the Latin gods Jupiter and Mercury) had visited their region in human form. With this demonstration of supernatural power before their eyes, they promptly identified the visitors as gods and "called Barnabas, Jupiter [Greek, Zeus]; and Paul, Mercury [Greek, Hermes]" (14:12).† Luke indicated that they identified Paul as

---

† Bruce reprehensively remarks, "The Latin equivalents Jupiter and Mercury (Mercurius, AV) given in AV, ERV, ARV, are due to an old and foolish fashion of replacing Greek proper names by their Latin equivalents in English translations from the Greek" ("Commentary on the Book of the Acts," p. 291, note 21).

Hermes "because he was the chief speaker" (v. 12); but Luke gave no reason for identifying Barnabas as Zeus. Zeus, the chief god of the Greek pantheon, fathered Hermes, the one considered the traditional spokesman for the gods. Paul, quick and active, the chief speaker during the mission at Lystra, was thus readily identified with Hermes; hence Barnabas, older and more venerable in appearance, was naturally, without further question, identified as the superior Zeus. Ramsay points out that this is in perfect harmony with the workings of the Oriental mind which "considers the leader to be the person who sits still and does nothing, while his subordinates speak and work for him. . . . The more statuesque figure of Barnabas was therefore taken by the Orientals as the chief god, and the active orator, Paul, as his messenger, communicating his wishes to men."[23]

When "Barnabas and Paul" (14:14) learned of the intentions to pay them divine honors they vigorously protested and with difficulty restrained the intention to offer sacrifies to them. While Luke's order of the names aptly brings out the fact that the people were according chief honor to Barnabas, his account yet makes it clear that Paul was the master spirit amid the excitement. He continued to play the spokesman, the part assigned to him by the people; for the speech made to the idolaters (Ac 14:15-17) is distinctly his in thought and diction.

Luke did not explain how Barnabas escaped the stoning inflicted upon Paul when the fanatical Jews from Antioch and Iconium came to Lystra (Ac 14:19). Both had been in danger of this at Iconium (14:6). But obviously, from their previous encounters with the missionaries, the Jews clearly recognized Paul as the leader, and held him chiefly responsible for the mischief being done by all the missionaries, and so vented their hatred on him.

When the missionary party departed from Syrian Antioch, Barnabas had been the acknowledged leader. But when the missionaries returned to Antioch, the natural leadership of Paul was recognized and accepted. Luke indicates this by his use of the order "Paul and Barnabas" as he narrates subsequent events at Antioch (Ac 15:2, 35).

CHAMPION OF GENTILE LIBERTY

When certain Judaizers from Judea appeared at Antioch with

their insistent teaching that circumcision was necessary for salvation, Barnabas wholeheartedly joined Paul in opposing this legalism (Ac 15:1-2). "When Paul and Barnabas had no small dissension and questioning with them, *the brethren* appointed that Paul and Barnabas, and certain other of them, should go up to Jerusalem unto the apostles and elders about this question" (15:2). The church at Antioch, having followed the position of Paul and Barnabas, recognized the crucial importance of this question and sent their trusted leaders to Jerusalem for a conference on this grave matter. At a report meeting, the missionaries recounted "all things that God had done with them" on their tour (15:4), but this report of Gentile conversions only intensified the demand of the Pharisee element in the Jerusalem church (15:5).

The view that the conference in Acts 15 is to be equated with the visit to Jerusalem recorded in Galatians 2:1-10 goes back to Tertullian and Irenaeus. I agree with Ogg in accepting the identification; he remarks that the correctness of this identification "is still recognized by a very large number of New Testament scholars."[24] These scholars have repeatedly shown that the two accounts essentially agree. Thus, one can also understand that Paul and Barnabas held a private meeting with the Jerusalem leaders, James, Peter, and John, who found themselves in perfect agreement with the position of Paul and Barnabas on the question. In recognition of their agreement, they gave Paul "and Barnabas the right hands of fellowship" (Gal 2:9).

At the formal meeting called to discuss the problem (Ac 15:6), after free discussion, Peter spoke the key word in his rehearsal of what God had done in the house of Cornelius. "Barnabas and Saul" (15:12) then told what God had continued to do through them among the Gentiles. Paul wisely let Barnabas take the lead in Jerusalem; for in Jerusalem it was the word of Barnabas, rather than of Paul, which carried weight. The superior esteem accorded Barnabas in Jerusalem is reflected in the commendation embodied in the letter drawn up by the conference, regarding "our beloved Barnabas and Paul, men that have hazarded their lives for the name of our Lord Jesus Christ" (Ac 15:25-26). They received commendation as men who had heroically made themselves potential martyrs for the spread of the gospel among the Gentiles.

Upon returning with the favorable decision reached at the conference, "Paul and Barnabas tarried in Antioch, teaching and preaching the word of the Lord" (Ac 15:35). Apparently during this time, the incident recorded in Galatians 2:11-14 occurred. Most scholars generally accept this view, but some propose to correlate the time with Acts 15:1. The issues in Acts 15:1 and Galatians 2:12-13 are not the same, however. When Peter withdrew from social fellowship with the Gentile believers at Antioch, the impact of his dissimulation (Greek, hypocrisy) was so strong that the rest of the Jewish believers also withdrew from table fellowship with Gentile believers, and "even Barnabas was carried away with their dissimulation" (Gal 2:13). Paul's very statement of the unexpected, momentary wavering of Barnabas carries a clear note of his deep appreciation for him. That "even Barnabas" was thus carried away indicated the tremendous pressure exerted by Peter's example. "It reveals an esteem for Barnabas, on the part of Paul, surpassing that which he had for Peter."[25] He could think of the wavering of Barnabas only with sorrowful surprise. Paul recorded no censure of Barnabas for his momentary equivocation; Paul addressed his rebuke to Peter. But the fact that Barnabas did yield "shows that he lacked something of that deep insight into fundamental truth which marked the career of Paul and made him the outstanding apostle to the Gentiles."[26]

CO-WORKER IN OTHER FIELDS

The missionary heart of Paul soon prompted him to propose to Barnabas that they return to visit the churches that they had founded. Barnabas readily agreed and expressed his wish‡ "to take with them John also, who was called Mark" (Ac 15:37). ("Also" may imply that Barnabas suggested that they take along other helpers beside Mark.) But Paul reacted strongly against taking John Mark. As indicated by Luke's use of the imperfect tense, Paul refused "to have with them day by day one who had shown himself unreliable."[27] He could not overlook the fact that Mark "withdrew from them from

---

‡ The rendering "determined" in the KJV is too strong, especially if we read the imperfect *ebouleto* of the critical text.

Pamphylia, and went not with them to the work" (15:38). Their diverse positions resulted in "a sharp contention" between these two co-workers. The word rendered "contention" (our word *paroxysm*) "intimates a temporary rather than a prolonged dispute, although it may for the time be severe."[28] When neither man would willingly modify his position, "they parted asunder one from the other" (15:39). They parted not as enemies but as co-workers, each working henceforth in his own field. "And Barnabas took Mark with him, and sailed away unto Cyprus" (v. 39), and thus sailed out of the story that Luke recorded.

In this regrettable event, neither man shines. It is neither easy nor pleasant to seek to apportion blame in this story. Bruce considers it a token of Luke's honesty that "he does not relate it in such a way as to put Paul in the right and Barnabas in the wrong."[29] Obviously both men stand guilty of ruffled feelings and sharpness in their reactions. Robertson suggests that the disagreement caused Barnabas to let loose the hitherto suppressed resentment in his heart that Paul had superseded him, while Paul allowed his resentment at the wavering of Barnabas to put heat into his rejection of the suggestion of Barnabas.[30] The suggestion compliments neither man, even though it well reflects human nature. Neither man seemed to behave in accordance with his highest spiritual attainments. The Scripture gives no indication that they turned to prayer for divine guidance to settle the disagreement. Carver remarks that the incident shows that "true devotion to a great cause does not guarantee infallibility of judgment nor imperturbability of temper."[31] Jacobson generously remarks, "Excess of sharpness was perhaps the only thing really wrong."[32]

Both men had strong personalities, and each had a phase of truth on his side that he felt he must not compromise. Barnabas, true to his gracious and gentle nature, with an easy forgetfulness of danger, felt that they should not throw Mark aside without first giving him another chance. The fact that Barnabas and Mark were cousins (Col 4:10) adds another motivating factor. Barnabas apparently had strong loyalties to kindred and country. But Paul regarded the matter as an ethical problem. "Paul thought not good [worthy] to take with them" the one who had previously deserted the work. He felt it was unjustified in the coming campaign to assume the risk of again taking

along one who had not shown himself dependable. As Meyer remarks,

> *Fickleness* in the service of Christ was to Paul's bold and decided
> strength of character and firmness in his vocation the foreign ele-
> ment, with which he could not enter into any union either abstractly
> or for the sake of public example.[33]

Paul's unswerving nature did not enable him to appreciate the lenient
reaction of Barnabas, who, looking beyond Mark's present failure, dis-
cerned the promise of recovery if only he were given another opportunity. If Barnabas erred on the side of leniency, Paul erred on the
side of sternness.

The tragic disagreement ended the beautiful and profitable working partnership of Paul and Barnabas, but it did not end their friendship. Paul's continued high esteem for Barnabas is evident from his
references to him in his epistles (1 Co 9:6; Gal 2:13). In the stormy
days that followed, Paul often must have missed the generous and
stimulating presence of Barnabas, the son of encouragement. But the
event was providentially overruled for good. As a result, two missionary parties went forth, and more workers were called into service. But
Adeney thinks that even if the contention had not taken place, it
would have been difficult for the two men to continue to work closely
together.

> Paul was bound to be the leader; more and more, as time went on,
> his powerful personality dominated the Churches he had founded.
> And yet deference was always felt to be due to Barnabas, as the
> senior. It was easier for both to work apart.[34]

One can only wish that Luke had given us further glimpses of the
work of Barnabas. We have no positive scriptural evidence that Paul
and Barnabas ever worked together again. Calvin's theory that "the
brother" of 2 Corinthians 8:18-19 means Barnabas, cannot be proved.[35]
That Barnabas went to Cyprus does not mean that he lost his interest
in the wider fields of heathen evangelism. The fact that Barnabas
went to Cyprus while Paul went through Syria and Cilicia (Ac
15:39-41) rather implies a purposeful division of fields of labor. One
need not assume that Barnabas confined his labors to Cyprus; rather,
the allusion to Barnabas in 1 Corinthians 9:6 implies that he extended

his labors more widely. From Paul's remark, we may conclude that Barnabas continued to labor upon the same principles as before.

Uncertain traditions concerning Barnabas abound. The view of Tertullian that Barnabas wrote the epistle to the Hebrews has had support from some modern scholars.[36] In favor of this, stands the fact that Barnabas was a Levite and closely linked with Paul. But Barnabas apparently had a closer relation to the original apostles than that implied in Hebrews 2:3. Nor is it easy to understand, if Barnabas wrote Hebrews, why tradition has associated it with Paul. That the spurious Epistle of Barnabas, apparently written by an unknown Christian of Alexandria late in the first or early second century, was attributed to him, indicates the high esteem in which people continued to regard Barnabas.

Barnabas stands out as one of the choicest saints of the early Christian church. He had a gracious personality, characterized by a generous disposition, and possessed a gift of insight concerning the spiritual potential of others. He excelled in building bridges of sympathy and understanding across the chasms of difference which divided individuals, classes, and races. He lived apart from petty narrowness and suspicion, and had a largeness of heart that enabled him to encourage those who failed and to succor the friendless and needy. He did have his faults and shortcomings, but those faults arose out of the very traits that made him such a kind and generous man — his ready sympathy for others' failings and his eagerness to think the best of everyone.

4

LUKE

Luke 1:1-4
Acts 1:1; 16:10-18; 20:5 — 21:18; 27:1 — 28:16
Colossians 4:14
Philemon 24
2 Timothy 4:11

OF ALL THE PEOPLE around Paul, Luke's name probably comes to one's mind first. Yet his name appears only three times in the entire New Testament (Col 4:14; Phile 24; 2 Ti 4:11). But our wide familiarity with Luke does not depend upon these few references, important as they are. It was his authoring the third gospel and the book of Acts that has established Luke's importance in Christian circles. In the prologue of both these books, the author refers to himself with the first person singular pronoun, yet does not include his name. The unanimous teaching of early Christian tradition made Luke the author of the Luke-Acts narrative.* The two books were clearly intended to form one continuous work. The book of Acts establishes Luke's position as one of Paul's close companions in travel by means of its so-called "we" sections (16:10-18; 20:5 — 21:18; 27:1 — 28:16). By his unobtrusive change from the third to the first person, the author indicated his participation in certain events which he narrated. The

---

* On the Lucan authorship see Bruce, *The Acts of the Apostles,* pp. 1-8; John Martin Creed, *The Gospel According to St. Luke,* pp. xi-xxi; Norval Geldenhuys, *Commentary on the Gospel of Luke,* pp. 15-22; Guthrie, *New Testament Introduction,* pp. 98-109; Alfred Plummer, "A Critical and Exegetical Commentary on the Gospel According to S. Luke," in *International Critical Commentary,* pp. xi-xvii; C. S. C. Williams, "The Acts of the Apostles," in *Harper's New Testament Commentaries,* pp. 1-13.

Lucan authorship of Acts has been vigorously assailed since the nineteenth century, but today many scholars accept the traditional view.† This is in keeping with the current emphasis upon the unity of the Luke-Acts narrative.

NAME

In form, the name Luke (Loukas), which the KJV gives as Lucas in Philemon 24, is doubtless a contraction of Loukanos; and several Old Latin manuscripts of the fifth century give his name as Lucanus.

Others think that the derivation comes from Loukios (Latin, Lucius). Scholars in the past asserted that the names Loukas and Loukios were quite distinct and separate names. But recent inscriptional evidence has shown that writers might have used the two names as variant forms for the same man.[1]

Calder argued that the formal name of the evangelist was Lucius rather than Lucanus from "the frequency of the former and the rarity of the latter name in the Greek East."[2] Paul in each case used the name Loukas. Such contracted names ending in -as were quite common for slaves. It is a pet name for Loukios.

NATIONALITY

Luke's nationality has caused great dispute. Some scholars, like Reicke and Ellis, say that he was a Hellenistic Jew.[3] This view identifies Luke with the Lucius of Acts 13:1 and Romans 16:21. Although the name offers no objection, this proposed identification is questionable. Blair points out that the author of Acts, "who seems studiously to avoid direct reference to himself, would hardly have flatly named himself in Acts 13:1."[4] The fact that Luke did show an interest in New Testament prophets and prophecy does not warrant Ellis' conjecture that "Luke was a Christian prophet with contacts among others exercising the same gift" in the Antioch church.[5] That the "Lucius of Cyrene" named in Acts 13:1 as one of the five "prophets and teachers" in that church was actually Luke, the companion of Paul in his later missionary work, one has reason to doubt. No scriptural evidence or tradition connects Luke with Cyrene.

---

† On the arguments for and against the Lucan authorship of Acts, see F. J. Foakes Jackson and Lake, eds., *The Beginnings of Christianity*, 2:207-359.

Most authorities generally agree that Luke was a Gentile. This seems a necessary conclusion from Paul's reference to him in Colossians 4:14 when taken in its context. In naming his companions who were sending their greetings to the Colossian church, Paul clearly divided them into two groups. In verses 10-11 he named Aristarchus, Mark, and Jesus Justus; designated them as "of the circumcision"; and appreciatively added, "These only are my fellow-workers unto the kingdom of God." He next named three others, Epaphras, Luke, and Demas, who therefore by clear implication were Gentiles. Epaphras, a native of Colosse (v. 12), certainly was a Gentile. If Luke was a Jew, Paul would not have failed to name him in the former group. Such a failure would have been a direct slap at Luke, as a Jewish Christian who had not brought cheer to Paul's heart. But such an implied rebuke to Luke is inconsistent with Paul's warm commendation of him as "the beloved physician" (v. 14). One must infer that Luke did not belong among those "of the circumcision." Bruce says, "It is from this reference that we may most surely conclude that Luke was a Gentile by birth — as the author of Luke-Acts appears to have been, to judge by some internal evidence."[6]

Grosheide further argues that Luke's designation of the inhabitants of Malta as "barbarians" (Ac 28:2, 4) indicates that he was a Gentile. He asserts, "At the time no Jew would employ this word for these people, who were Phoenicians, and thus related to the Jews."[7] And Farrar thinks that Luke's non-Jewish background shines through in Acts 1:19 where he slipped in the words "in their language" in recording Peter's speech.[8]

Most likely, Luke was a Gentile. He thus has the honor of being the only non-Jewish writer of the Bible. As God broke down the wall of separation between Jew and Gentile in the church, He appropriately used a Gentile believer to record that story in the book of Acts.

The conclusion that Luke was not a Hebrew Christian, rules out the suggested identification with the Lucius of Romans 16:21. This man who joined Paul in sending greetings to the Roman saints from Corinth was a Jew by nationality, for Paul included him among "my kinsmen."

Luke's Gentile background further eliminates such conjectures as that he was one of the "seventy" (Lk 10:1-7), or the companion of

Cleopas in the walk to Emmaus (Lk 24:13-33). That he joined the Greek proselytes who asked Philip to introduce them to Jesus during Passion Week (Jn 12:20-21) is not impossible but highly improbable. All such suggestions that Luke had any personal contacts with the events in the life of Christ contradict his statement that he was not an eyewitness of the events he recorded in his gospel (Lk 1:2).

Whether Luke was a Greek or a Roman we do not know, but we may safely suppose that he was a native Greek. He revealed the traits of the Greek. Rackham comments that Luke's Greek stamp is shown "by his ready pen, his versatility, and not least by his interest in the sea."[9]

Neither do we know for certain whether Luke was a free Hellene or a Greek slave set free by his master. Probably the latter is true. If he was a freedman, he was probably set free with Roman citizenship.

Birthplace

Scripture does not tell Luke's native city, and different conclusions have been formed on the basis of inferences from Scripture. Scholars seem impressed differently by Luke's evident personal interest and accurate information about various places.

Syrian Antioch has a strong claim. Codex Bezae (D) inserts an interesting "we" passage in Acts 11:28: "And there was much rejoicing; and when we were gathered together one of them stood up and said." It is doubtless an unauthentic Western addition, but it obviously embodies an early tradition connecting Luke with the church of Antioch. A similar assertion connecting Luke with Syrian Antioch is also found in the so-called Anti-Marcionite prologue to Luke. Eusebius and Jerome likewise regard Antioch in Syria as Luke's residence.

Luke certainly showed a deep interest in Syrian Antioch (cf. Ac 11:19-30; 13:1; 14:26-28; 15:22, 30-35; 18:22). The only deacon whose place of origin Luke mentioned was Nicolas (KJV) of Antioch (Ac 6:5). Obviously Antioch played an important part in the development of Christianity beyond Jerusalem, but Luke's record reveals trifling touches which seem to betray his personal familiarity with the scenes. The evidence does not squelch all doubt, but does make it very probable that Luke was born and reared in Antioch of Syria.

Philippi has also received support for the honor of being Luke's birthplace. Ramsay argues for Philippi on the basis of the strong interest that Luke showed in that city.[10] But Luke's love for and interest in Philippi is naturally explained by his long residence there.

Rackham, much impressed by the accuracy and intimacy of Luke's knowledge concerning the South Galatian cities of Lystra, Iconium, and Pisidian Antioch, suggested Antioch of Pisidia rather than Antioch of Syria as the birthplace of Luke.[11] But Luke's accurate information concerning widely different localities simply proves that he was a much traveled and accurate observer. His keen Greek mind made him an exact observer and faithful recorder.

EDUCATION

That Luke had received an excellent education we can discover from his writings. They reveal a man possessed of remarkable literary skill, with a fine sense of form and a beautiful style. By casually referring to Luke as a physician (Col 4:14), Paul adds much to our understanding of this thoroughly trained man. Where Luke received his medical training, we do not know, but Tarsus, Athens, and Alexandria merit consideration. If he came from Syrian Antioch, Tarsus would be very probable. "Nowhere else in Asia Minor," says Plummer, "could he obtain so good an education."[12] Luke's writings reveal his vast knowledge of the classics. He could have obtained that training also at the university at Tarsus.

Luke was a man of genuine culture. As a doctor, he stood in the middle or higher planes of contemporary society. Among the Greeks, the profession of medicine enjoyed high esteem, being ranked next to philosophy. The Romans did not regard the physician as highly; and in wealthy Roman houses, the part of the family doctor was often played by a slave or freedman. Luke may have studied medicine as the slave of some rich householder and later been given his freedom.

The practice of medicine, an old and venerable profession, had reached a high level of achievement in the days of Luke. By the second century A.D., medical science had more knowledge than at any time in history before the nineteenth century. The Greeks had developed medicine into an organized science. LaSor remarks, "Luke was heir to a science of medicine that could compare favorably with any medical practice up to the early part of the last century."[13]

Luke apparently first came into contact with Paul in connection with his services as a doctor. Where their acquaintance began is conjectural. In later years, as Paul's traveling companion, Luke continued to minister to the apostle's physical needs. Lockyer claims that "Luke must have been a man of some wealth, otherwise he could not have traveled with Paul as his friend and useful companion."[14] But doubtless Luke's medical skills financed his travels with Paul.

CONVERSION

Where and how Luke became a Christian has aroused much speculation. If he was a native of Syrian Antioch, perhaps someone had reached him for Christ during the missionary work among the Greeks there, described in Acts 11:20-21.

Nowhere does Scripture hint that he was Paul's convert. He apparently had already become a Christian before he first met Paul. If the "we" section at Acts 11:28 in Codex D is authentic or embodies a reliable tradition, Luke belonged to the early church at Antioch.

Luke probably converted to Christianity directly from heathenism. Since Paul did not group him with those "of the circumcision" (Col 4:10-14), Luke clearly had not previously converted to Judaism. He may, however, have belonged to that class of God-fearing Gentiles who frequented the synagogue as "proselytes of the gate," a group frequently mentioned by Luke in Acts.

TRAVELS WITH PAUL

Luke modestly revealed his presence as Paul's traveling companion by means of his three "we" sections in Acts (16:10-18; 20:5 − 21:18; 27:1 − 28:16). But the dropping of the "we" does not prove that Luke was no longer with Paul. We note with interest that Luke used "we" while recounting the progress of the journey but dropped it soon after the arrival at their destination. Thus in chapter 28 the "we" is dropped as soon as the party reached Rome, but we know from Paul's letters that Luke remained with Paul in Rome.

Luke first clearly revealed his presence with Paul at Troas on the second missionary journey. "And when he had seen the vision, straightway we sought to go forth into Macedonia, concluding that God had called us to preach the gospel unto them" (Ac 16:10).

Either Luke first joined the missionary party at Troas, or up to this time he had felt himself a minor participant in the mission. Moe thinks that at first Luke had "accompanied Paul and Silas only as an attendant in practical matters, possibly not least as Paul's physician. . . . But more and more the missionary call penetrated into his consciousness," and that at Troas he fully committed himself to active participation in the mission.[15] But whatever the nature of his initial relations with Paul, the events at Troas marked the beginning of a close and lasting companionship in spiritual ministry between the apostle and the doctor. Luke's interests extended beyond the medical profession. He specifically felt himself included in the call to preach the gospel to the Macedonians. When Luke revealed his presence with Paul at Troas, he was already a Christian worker personally committed to the spread of the gospel. This is evident from his participation in the service out by the riverside (Ac 16:13).

Obviously, Luke witnessed the stirring events recorded of the mission at Philippi. Why Luke and Timothy escaped arrest and imprisonment, he does not inform us. Probably, since Paul and Silas were the recognized leaders of the group, they caught the fury of the enemy attack.

In recounting the departure of the missionaries from Philippi, Luke dropped the "we." The obvious implication is that he remained there to superintend the young church. Along with his missionary activities, he most likely continued his medical practice. We need not suppose that Luke remained stationary at Philippi in the years that followed, but apparently he considered it his headquarters.

Some propose to find evidence for Luke's gospel activities during these years by equating him with "the brother" mentioned in 2 Corinthians 8:18, whom Paul sent with Titus from Macedonia to Corinth in the interest of the collection. This unnamed companion of Titus was a Christian worker whose activities in behalf of the gospel had made him well known in all the churches. This suggestion, which goes back to Origen, has many supporters.‡ The Luke theory harmonizes

‡ For a full survey of the various individuals who have been suggested, see Philip E. Hughes, "Commentary on the Second Epistle to the Corinthians," in *New International Commentary*, pp. 312-316.

well with known circumstances, and it even corresponds to the scribal subscription to 2 Corinthians which states that the epistle "was written from Philippi, a city of Macedonia, by Titus and Lucas." But it must remain an unverified conjecture. No doubt it originated in the mistaken notion that "the gospel" here meant the written gospel (the gospel of Luke).

In adopting the suggestion that "the brother" of 2 Corinthians 8:18 was Luke, Ramsay and others conclude that the verse means that he was the physical brother of Titus.[16] Some hold that this kinship explains why the name of Titus never appears in Acts, a strange phenomenon indeed, in view of the importance of Titus in the Pauline epistles. The suggestion in itself has merit, but one cannot draw support for it from Paul's expression "the brother." While the original may denote such a physical relation, more probably it simply designates him as a fellow Christian. Kelly points out that if the expression meant his brother after the flesh, "The object and character of the association would have been frustrated by selecting one so near to Titus."[17] The purpose in sending this brother was to shield Titus against insinuations of unworthy dealings in connection with the collection money.

Luke again joined Paul at Philippi when Paul left there for Jerusalem on the third missionary journey. This is indicated by the second "we" section (20:5 — 21:18), which gives a diary-type account of the trip to Jerusalem. Although Luke dropped the "we" with Paul's visit to James in Jerusalem, Luke obviously remained in Jerusalem during the stirring days that followed. He must have witnessed much of what he recorded of those eventful days (Ac 21:17 — 23:31).

Luke did not indicate his presence with Paul at Caesarea during the two years of his imprisonment there, but doubtless he was among the friends who were allowed to minister to the apostle (Ac 24:23). During this time, Luke would have ample opportunity to travel in Palestine to become acquainted with the surviving leaders of the church there and to interview the various "eyewitnesses and ministers of the word" (Lk 1:2), from whom he gathered much of the material for his gospel and the early story of the Christian church.

When the governor transferred Paul from Caesarea to Rome, Luke and one other friend accompanied Paul on the long and haz-

ardous journey. The "we" section recording that journey (Ac 27:1 –
28:16) demonstrates Luke's remarkable powers of accurate observation and graphic description. The account is generally acknowledged
as one of the most instructive documents for a study of ancient sea-
manship available today.

Ramsay believes that the presence of these two friends with Paul
on the journey could only be accounted for on the assumption that
they passed as Paul's slaves. He felt that this would greatly enhance
Paul's importance in the eyes of the Roman officer, Julius.[18] But one
wonders whether Paul would stoop to such a pretense. While admit-
ting Ramsay's great knowledge of social history in the Roman empire,
Carter aptly suspects that "Ramsay unconsciously read into the narrative more of the aristocratic cultural influence of the British society of
his day than the known facts of the case would warrant."[19] The
lenient treatment accorded Paul by Felix (Ac 24:23-24) and Festus
(Ac 25:22-26, 26:32), as well as the kindly attitude of Julius toward
Paul in 27:3, gives ample grounds to believe that these officials
would have permitted Paul the privilege of having these two friends
with him on the journey.[20] Since they left Caesarea on an independent, commercial vessel, they may have traveled with Paul as
independent passengers.

Did Luke cure the sick on the island of Malta? The opinion of
scholars like Ramsay, Rackham, and Robertson is that Luke's terminology implies this (Ac 28:8-10).[21] He recorded how Paul "healed"
(*iasato*) the father of Publius through prayer, adding that when this
healing became known, "the rest also that had diseases in the island
came and were cured" (*etherapeuonto*). This latter verb is a medical
term properly denoting to receive medical treatment. Robertson asserts that it indicates that "the medical missionary and the preacher
were at work side by side."[22]

Luke continued the account of the journey with "we" until the
party entered Rome. He left no hint of his known presence with Paul
in Rome during much of the next two years (Ac 28:30-31).

FRIENDSHIP WITH PAUL

How precious Luke's friendship was to Paul we gather from his
few references to Luke in his letters written from Rome. Of the

different companions of Paul, Timothy alone seems to have gotten a
stronger hold on the heartstrings of Paul than Luke. The hearts of
these two co-workers were knit together in tender and enduring
affection.

In Colossians 4:14, Paul's deep love for Luke burst through the
conventionalities of the greetings being sent to the Colossian saints.
Affectionately he called him "Luke, the beloved physician." Of the
six companions named as sending greetings, only Luke is described in
terms of Paul's own affection for him. "The term of endearment
stands out like a lighthouse in the dark."[23] It confers upon Luke a
distinctive title of affectionate nobility. Luke's tenderness and solicitude drew out Paul's warm and deep affection in return.

Unquestionably, Luke endeared himself to Paul through his
thoughtful and gentle ministrations to the apostle's physical needs.
But a higher basis for the love and esteem of Paul for Luke was their
fellowship in the service of the Lord.

In the note to Philemon, written as a companion letter to the
Colossian epistle, Paul included the name of Luke among four companions sending their greetings, whom he designated as "my fellow-
workers" (Phile 24). At Rome, Luke actively continued in the furtherance of the gospel, probably in connection with his medical services. He laid his medical skills at the feet of his Lord and combined
his practice with the preaching of the gospel.

When Paul wrote the letter to the Philippians, near the end of
his first Roman imprisonment, he did not mention Luke's name. Since
Luke had close connections with the Philippian church, absence of
reference to him in the letter can only be explained on the assumption that Luke was not in Rome when Paul wrote. Lees suggests
that Luke had returned to his old flock at Philippi, and even thinks
that "the gifts of money carried by Epaphroditus to Paul at Rome
look like the renewal of the old habit of Luke's pastorate in the earlier
years."[24] But his further suggestion that Luke was the "true yokefellow," whom Paul bade to settle the feminine bickerings in the
Philippian church (Phil 4:3), is mere conjecture.[25]

We catch our last scriptural glimpse of Luke in 2 Timothy, written during the rigorous bondage of Paul's second Roman imprisonment. Paul writes simply, "Only Luke is with me" (4:11). The brief

words are freighted with significance. When others did not wish to identify with Paul or deserted him for other reasons, Luke remained constantly at his side. He was the only one of the old group of companions left with Paul. He was Paul's one link of communication with the outside world. Luke may have penned the letter to Timothy for Paul, who, according to tradition, was confined in the dark, Mamertime prison. Surely Luke witnessed the execution of his dear friend and arranged for the burial of his body.

Radical critics doubt the validity of the picture conveyed in this last reference to Luke. Lake, who put a question mark behind the authenticity of Colossians, remarked, "In somewhat greater measure the reference in 2 Timothy must be discounted, on the ground of doubts as to the authenticity of the Epistle. So long as these doubts exist, the possibility cannot be entirely excluded that the references to Luke ought to be regarded as the result of the tradition, rather than as proof of its accuracy."[26] I do not share Lake's doubts concerning the accuracy of this final glimpse of Luke.

CONTRIBUTION

Luke's priceless legacy to the Christian church is his two-part history which constitutes invaluable portion of our New Testament. In his gospel, which Renan called the most beautiful book in the world, he portrayed the incarnate Son of God as the perfect man, while the book of Acts recorded the world impact of God's revelation in His Son. In the gospel, Luke recounted the matchless story of God incarnate in a human body, while in the Acts he set forth the story of the formation of the church, the mystical body of Christ, under the direction of the Holy Spirit.

We are indebted to Luke for some of our most beautiful and treasured passages concerning the life and teaching of our Lord. To him we also owe our only systematic scriptural account of the begin ning and development of the Christian church. The value of his work for our knowledge and understanding of the life and labors of Paul is incalculable.

Luke's two books also have immense value for what they reveal of the writer himself. He revealed himself as a highly cultured man with remarkable literary ability. The prologue of his gospel (Lk

1:1-4) is fully worthy to stand with the prefaces of such noted Greek masters as Herodotus, Thucydides, and Polybius. Luke's writings demonstrate a keen power of accurate observation, a vividness of expression, and the ability to delineate a character or a scene in a few vigorous lines or words. Tradition, traceable to the sixth century, declares that Luke was a painter; obviously he was a master at painting word pictures.

He was a competent scholar and first-rate literary historian.[27] His preface to the gospel (Lk 1:1-4), which answers also for the book of Acts, reveals his method of research and his qualifications for the task. His work was characterized by comprehensiveness, thoroughness, accuracy, and orderliness. While he revealed the methods of the literary historian, his stated purpose (v. 4) was evangelistic.[28]

For years the storm of hostile criticism has raged around Luke. His abundant historical data has undergone the most searching critical investigation. On those points that can be tested by the results of historical and archeological investigation, Luke has been gloriously vindicated.[29] Currently, New Testament study has renewed a strong interest in the Lucan writings with special emphasis upon the theological contribution of Luke and its relationship to history.[30]

CHARACTER

Many points in the life of Luke must remain in obscurity, but the outlines of his character emerge with considerable clarity. He was a man of high and noble character, whom Paul trusted implicitly and loved wholeheartedly.

Cultural achievements, professional skills, a rare gift of observation and vivid expression, and accurate scholarship, Luke brought into captivity to the obedience of Christ to further His cause. Throughout the gospel and the Acts, we feel that the presence and power of the risen Lord were a living reality to Luke.

He had an affectionate and gentle disposition. The sweetness of his character earned for him the apostle's grateful designation, "the beloved physician." His writings reveal that he was "broad in his sympathies, compassionate toward the poor and the outcasts of society."[31] A prominent feature in his gospel and in Acts is his unflagging interest in the part women played in the story which he recorded.

Luke's character included self-effacing modesty. He had a marked faculty of being serviceable, but he studiously kept himself in the background. He never intruded upon the scenes that he described, even when he had a share in them. In his gospel, he has given us a matchless picture of our Lord Jesus as the perfect, universal man; in writing the story of the advancement of the gospel he drew a graphic picture of Paul, his hero; but he quite contentedly left both works without his name attached to them.

He was a man of steadfast loyalty. Having actively associated himself in the work and cause with Paul, he steadfastly remained with him through weal and woe. While others, consulting their own safety, deliberately avoided close association with Paul or fearfully forsook him, Luke never left his side. His faithful loyalty earned for him the grateful testimony of Paul, "Only Luke is with me." Not only was he physically with Paul but he was also wholeheartedly "with" Paul in everything that pertained to the spread of the knowledge of his blessed Saviour and Lord.

5

MARK

Acts 12:12, 25; 13:5, 13; 15:36-39
Colossians 4:10
2 Timothy 4:11
Philemon 24
1 Peter 5:13

MARK'S NAME rings a familiar bell to Bible readers as the author of the second gospel, but comparatively few realize that Mark had the unique distinction of having three of the great men of the apostolic church lean upon his arm for assistance and friendship. Barnabas claimed him as his cousin and protégé; Peter acknowledged him as his son and affectionate disciple; and Paul relied on him as his helpful servant and valued friend. Mark lacked the personal greatness of these men, but he had the gift to make himself useful as their valued supporter.

NAME

Mark, a Jewish young man, is first formally introduced in Acts as "John whose surname was Mark" (Ac 12:12). John was his Jewish name, while Mark is Latin.* In Acts, Luke refers to him three times by both names (12:12, 25; 15:37), twice as John (13:5, 13), and once as Mark (15:39). The writers of the epistles simply call him Mark. That the Mark of the epistles is the same as the John Mark of Acts we know from the fact that the epistolary references always link him with the same people (Paul, Barnabas, and Peter) as in Acts.

---

* The KJV uses the form "Marcus" in Col 4:10; Phile 24, and 1 Pe 5:13.

The earliest tradition assumes the identification without question.

In those days, Palestinian Jews commonly adopted or accepted a second name. The use of such Latin second names was quite frequent among Greek-speaking Jews, although the name "Mark" was rare. Why he assumed or had imposed upon him the Latin name, no one mentions. Luke's use of the aorist participle in Acts 12:25 may imply that Mark started this surname when he went to Antioch with Barnabas and Paul. It may however be an indication of Roman citizenship. Farmer thinks that such a supposition is quite in harmony with the standing of the family of Mark.[1]

Plummer reminds us that the two names were not separate, like our English "John Smith," but were alternatives.[2] He used either name, according to the circumstances or the occasion. In Jewish circles, they appropriately would call him John, a common Jewish name; but in a Gentile environment, he would appropriately use his Latin name. That Mark's Jewish name disappears entirely in the epistles indicates that Mark had moved out into the Gentile world as the sphere of his activities.

EARLY HOMELIFE

Mark first appears in Acts as an inhabitant of the city of Jerusalem (12:12). Mark's parents, like his kinsman Barnabas, may have been Jews of the dispersion, perhaps natives of Cyprus. If so, they must have moved to Jerusalem some years before, for they had become well established in the holy city.

Since Barnabas was a Levite (Ac 4:36), some have conjectured that Mark too was a Levite. But most do not concur. His relationship with Barnabas (Col 4:10) apparently was through his mother's side.

In A.D. 44 when we first hear of her, Mary, the mother of Mark, was evidently a widow. We believe this because no mention is made of her husband and Luke calls her residence "the house of Mary" (Ac 12:12). She was one of that group of Marys "whose praise was in the early church."[3] To distinguish her from the others named Mary, Luke designates her as "the mother of John whose surname was Mark." By this means, Luke, who wrote in the light of later developments, let the mother bask in the glory of her noble son. To be known as the mother of a son who has risen to usefulness and recognition, is one of the highest honors a Christian mother can receive.

Some, like Edersheim, think that Jesus and His disciples observed the last Passover in Mary's home.⁴ Then "the goodman of the house" (Mk 14:14) must have been the father of John Mark. Certainly the owner who provided the room was a follower of Jesus. If he were Mark's father, he must have died shortly after those eventful days. While this identification sounds probable, it must remain a mere guess.

The Scriptures imply many things about Mark's remarkable home. First, the family lived in comfortable financial circumstances. We infer this from the fact that the house was pretentious enough to have a "gate," with a "door" in it, opening upon a passageway leading to an inner court; the family had at least one servant; and the home had sufficient space to permit a large group to gather at one time (Ac 12:12-13). It may have been Mary's "upper room" where the disciples gathered after Jesus' ascension to pray and wait for the promise of the Spirit (Ac 1:13).

Second, Mark's home was a busy center of social and religious activities. His mother, a conspicuous and devoted member in the early Christian community, threw open her spacious home as a place of assembly for the believers in Jerusalem. It became a well-known rendezvous for the early Christians. When Peter suddenly found himself miraculously delivered from prison, he naturally made his way to Mary's home. There he found a large group of believers assembled. Rhoda, a "servant-girl" (Williams), immediately recognized his voice (Ac 12:14), which shows that Peter frequently visited at the home.

Third, in Mark's home, the Christian spirit prevailed, and Christian activities were welcomed and encouraged. The young lad came to know and be deeply impressed by the spiritual leaders of the early church who frequented it. Even during the dark days when governmental persecution struck the church and James was beheaded and Peter was imprisoned, the home remained a center of Christian activity. Mary bravely opened her home to the disciples to gather in earnest prayer for Peter. In that home, spiritual values were placed uppermost.

As a lad, Mark must have felt the excitement of the sensation caused in Jerusalem and throughout Judea when, after centuries of silence, the voice of John the Baptist began proclaiming that the kingdom of heaven was at hand (Mk 1:5), for at that point, Mark began the story of his gospel.

That the "young man" in Gethsemane mentioned in Mark 14:51-52 refers to Mark himself seems a natural assumption. It explains most reasonably the insertion of this trifling incident, otherwise so irrelevant to the circumstances. Surely it is Mark's covert reference to his own connections with the stirring story he was recording. We know that he did not learn of this unimportant incident from Peter or the other apostles from the fact that in the preceding verse he recorded that "they all left him, and fled" (14:50). Obviously Mark's knowledge of the young man's presence came from his own experience. This supposition fits all the details. Bickersteth remarks, "The action corresponds with what we know of his character, which appears to have been warm-hearted and earnest, but timid and impulsive."[5] The incident seems to offer an accurate picture of the early life and character of Mark — impulsively eager to help but fleeing in sudden and complete recoil when unexpected danger loomed.

Objection to this suggested identification has been made on the ground that Eusebius quoted Papias as saying that Mark "neither heard nor followed our Lord."[6] Mark obviously was not one of the recognized followers and regular attendants of our Lord, perhaps because he was too young or had not yet made a personal commitment to Him. But his brief contacts with the horrible events of the closing hours in the life of Jesus would naturally make a deep impression on his young soul. Morison thinks that the incident marked "the vital turning point of his spiritual career."[7]

When and how Mark came to personal faith in Jesus as his Saviour is not known. The influence of his pious mother and his contacts with the early Christians in his home were doubtless instrumental in heading him to such a decision. That Mark became saved under Peter's influence many scholars assume from 1 Peter 5:13 where the apostle calls Mark "my son." No doubt Peter did make a deep and lasting spiritual impression upon the young man.

Another prominent leader in the early church at Jerusalem who exerted a deep influence on young Mark was his relative, Barnabas.

Barnabas was Mark's cousin (Col 4:10),† and his contacts with Mary's home seem to have been frequent. Barnabas' gracious and sympathetic nature as well as the high esteem in which he was held in the church, must have made Mark proud of his outstanding relative.

Mark must have been at the prayer meeting in his mother's home on the night that the angel miraculously delivered Peter from the hand of Agrippa. As he listened to Peter's account, this unmistakable instance of the intervening hand of God must have made a deep impression on him. It stimulated and deepened the faith of the timorous young man.

EARLY ACTIVITIES

Mark lived in famine-stricken Jerusalem when Barnabas and Paul arrived with the relief funds from the church in Antioch (Ac 11:30). That they stayed in the home of Mary, the aunt of Barnabas (Col 4:10), seems obvious. It afforded Mark an invaluable opportunity to form a personal acquaintance with "Saul of Tarsus," the capable associate of his well-known cousin.

How long the bearers of the relief fund remained in Jerusalem is not known, but it was long enough to have their attention drawn to the young John Mark. Swete suggests that this was due to his "services rendered during the distribution of the relief fund which revealed in him a capacity for systematic work."[8] Perhaps at this time Barnabas detected possibilities of greater usefulness for the young man. When they were ready to return to Antioch, he probably took the initiative in suggesting that "John, whose surname was Mark" be taken along (Ac 12:25). Paul consented to the suggestion.

Mark readily agreed to go forth in the company of his honored cousin. That Mark took seriously the opportunity thus being presented to him is questionable. It offered the prospects of a pleasant journey, new and exciting adventures, and the important chance of being of service, even though in quite a secondary position, to these Christian leaders. It marked the close of the first stage in the life of Mark and the beginning of his real career.

Nothing is stated concerning Mark's work in the flourishing

---

† The Greek word *anepsios* means "cousin" rather than "nephew," as suggested by the KJV rendering.

Gentile church at Syrian Antioch. Mark's presence there gave him an excellent opportunity to observe the Holy Spirit working with and for Gentiles who had accepted Jesus Christ as their Saviour and Lord. The growing work there kept the leaders busy, and Mark's association with the missionaries comprised personal assistance to them in their work. That his services were acceptable and appreciated is obvious from the sequel.

EARLY FAILURE

When the Holy Spirit inaugurated the program of foreign missions in the Antioch church by calling Barnabas and Saul, the missionaries took with them "John as their attendant" (Ac 13:5). He either volunteered or accepted the invitation to join in the work. That he went along in a secondary position Luke indicated by designating him as "their attendant." Ramsay characterizes Mark as "an extra hand, taken by Barnabas and Saul on their own responsibility."[9]

The term *attendant* (*hupēretēs*) originally meant an "under-rower" on a Roman trireme with three banks of oars. Then it evolved into one who serves under a superior, an underling. Mark served under the direction of the missionaries, performing the varied tasks appointed him by them.

Precisely what work Mark did, attracts speculation. Some, like Hackett, think that Luke's "also" suggests that his work included assisting the missionaries in preaching the Word.[10] This would make him "a sort of apprentice missionary."[11] That Mark would speak at opportune times and give his testimony, we assume. But Mark had not been included in the Spirit's commission, and apparently his duties were not directly evangelistic. Swete thinks that "his work would include all those minor details which could safely be delegated to a younger man, such as arrangements for travel, the provision of food and lodging, conveying messages, negotiating interviews, and the like."[12] Rackham objects to the thought that the missionaries required personal service and asserts that Mark baptized the converts, since the missionaries generally did not baptize with their own hands (1 Co 1:14-17).[13] With this would go the further duty of instructing the converts. While Paul and Barnabas may well have used him occasionally for baptizing and teaching, as their "attendant," Mark would

also perform any other service which would free them for their primary work.

When the missionary party, with Paul as its recognized leader,
left Cyprus and came to Perga in Pamphylia, "John departed from
them and returned to Jerusalem" (Ac 13:13). Luke assigned no reason for Mark's departure, but Paul's later reaction (Ac 15:36-39)
proves that he regarded it as wholly unjustified.

Speculation abounds as to why Mark failed to continue with the
work. The charge that Mark deserted the work due to homesickness
for his mother seems rather unfair to him.

A change in leadership of the party had taken place, and apparently also a change in plans of work took place at Perga. Some scholars suggest that it offended Mark that Paul had taken the leadership
from his cousin, so he decided not to go on with the new arrangement. If his elders could change their plans, so could he. But Mark
had joined them as the attendant of both men, and as long as Barnabas
did not object to the change in leadership, which came about very
naturally, Mark would have no reason to take offense.

More probable is the suggestion that Mark had a theological
reason. Thus, Farmer holds that Mark was dissatisfied with and ob-
jected to Paul's offer of salvation to the Gentiles directly on the basis
of faith alone.[14] Seekings thinks that Mark was still too much under
the influence of the narrow religious conceptions concerning the gospel, which he had imbibed under the influence of Peter, and so could
not sympathetically enter into Paul's aggressive spirit to press on to
the Gentiles.[15] LaSor, who thinks that Paul's strong rejection of Mark
later can only be understood as "arising from the Judaizer problem,"
construes the situation thus, "Mark had found Paul's work with Gentiles contrary to his own view of the Law. When it became obvious
that they were going to move into territory where Gentiles would
predominate, Mark drew the line. He went home."[16]

But if Mark harbored narrow and legalistic views of the gospel,
as LaSor implies, it is difficult to see how he could feel at home in the
predominantly Gentile church at Antioch. Certainly, Paul and Barnabas had both escaped from such legalistic attitudes, and it seems
strange that they should invite one with such prejudice to participate
in a mission directed to the Gentiles.

Lenski contends that the simplest and best explanation for Mark's defection was his lack of courage.[17] The proposed journey into the highland interior of Asia Minor threatened danger. The road from Perga on the coast to Antioch of Pisidia in the interior was mountainous and difficult, and notoriously robber-infested. "The roads all over the Roman Empire were apt to be unsafe, for the arrangements for insuring public safety were exceedingly defective; but probably the part of his life which St. Paul had most in mind when he wrote about the perils of rivers and of robbers, which he had faced in his journeys, was the journey from Perga across Taurus to Antioch and back again."[18] The prospects of such a journey unmanned Mark and filled his heart with dark apprehensions and prostrating fears. "He may have felt," says Swete, "that duty to his mother and his home required him to break off at this point from so perilous a development of the mission."[19] And so in the hour of crisis, when suddenly confronted with unexpected danger, the promising young assistant flickered, turned his back, and fled to his home. "He did not possess staying qualities. He wanted the grace of perseverance. Having put his hand to the plow, he looked back."[20]

Since the causes for our actions generally are not simple, several motives may have entered into Mark's departure. Whatever the true cause or causes, Mark tragically failed by deserting his post of duty in the hour of crisis.

SECOND CHANCE

At the conclusion of the Jerusalem Conference, Paul and Barnabas returned to Antioch. They tarried there and preached the word for "some days" (Ac 15:36). That Mark was also at Antioch before the beginning of the second missionary journey is clear, but when and why he returned to Antioch is unknown. He may have come up with Peter whose visit to Antioch led to the unfortunate episode recorded in Galatians 2:11-21. Certainly Paul willingly associated with Mark in the work at Antioch.

When Paul proposed to Barnabas that they revisit the churches they had founded, Barnabas readily agreed and expressed his wish‡ "to take with them John also, who was called Mark" (Ac 15:37). But

---

‡ The rendering "determined" in KJV is too strong.

Paul stoutly refused to have Mark on his hands again for the proposed journey. Their diverse stands resulted in "a sharp contention," and when neither man was willing to modify his position, "They parted asunder one from the other" (15:39). "Mark, the shaken reed, had become also an apple of discord."[21] He had become the unwitting cause for the breaking up of a fruitful partnership. The possible repercussions of our unworthy actions is a sobering thought.

Paul and Barnabas each had a phase of truth which he felt he could not compromise. Paul felt it would endanger the success of this campaign to take along one who had shown himself unreliable in a crisis. A general cannot afford to plan his campaign around undependable men. But Barnabas, true to his gracious and helpful nature, felt that Mark should not be thrown aside without giving him another chance. Characteristically, Barnabas looked beyond the present failure to discern the promise of recovery and future usefulness. Mark was fortunate indeed to have a friend like Barnabas, who, with love and patience, helped him to overcome his failure.

Paul's sharp rebuff undoubtedly shook Mark's complacency concerning the gravity of his defection. It made him realize the seriousness of responsibility and the far-reaching possible consequences of faithfulness. He came to see that Christian service requires that a man be found faithful.

"Barnabas took Mark with him, and sailed away unto Cyprus" (15:39), and with that they sailed out of the story that Luke told in Acts. The Scriptures are entirely silent concerning the activities of Mark for the next eleven or twelve years.§

LATER SUCCESS

Further scriptural information concerning Mark is confined to four references in the New Testament epistles, all apparently written from Rome. These references reveal the encouraging truth of Mark's complete restoration and faithful service.

We find Mark again in Paul's company during the apostle's first Roman imprisonment. This we learn from Paul's letters to the Colos-

---

§ Tradition fills in this gap by asserting that Mark founded the church of Alexandria. But that does not prove that it is true. The great Alexandrian Fathers, Clement and Origen, make no reference to any sojourn or work of Mark in Alexandria.

sians and to Philemon, apparently written during the middle of that
two-year imprisonment.

In sending greetings to the Colossian church, Paul named three
Jewish Christians who had been a comfort to him, including "Mark,
the cousin of Barnabas" (Col 4:10-11). This interesting reference reveals not only that Mark and Paul were together again but that the
breach had been completely healed and Mark had become an honored
and trusted assistant worker, a comfort or encouragement to Paul in
his confinement.

By what process Mark earned his way back into Paul's confidence
and approval, we are not informed. Paul had held no permanent
grudge against Mark, and when Mark proved himself, Paul gladly
welcomed him back. Mark had come to see also that Paul's rejection
of him had worked for his good. The discipline had stimulated him to
overcome his defects and had brought out the best in him.

Paul named Mark as one of his "fellow-workers unto the kingdom
of God" (Col 4:11; Phile 24), men who assisted Paul in spreading the
gospel. In conveying Mark's greetings to the Colossians, Paul by
means of a parenthesis — "(touching whom ye received command-
ments; if he come unto you, receive him)" — added his commendation of Mark. This studious recommending of Mark would efface
any unfavorable impression of the past concerning him.

Mark was contemplating a mission that would take him into the
province of Asia, and the Colossians were directed to receive him as
Paul's friend and co-worker. The mission was apparently being carried out for Paul. The Colossians had already received some instructions concerning Mark, apparently from Paul himself. If however, as
Lenski affirms, Paul is using an epistolary aorist, he was now informing the Colossians that he was sending Mark.[22] Then Mark would be
scheduled to arrive some time after the arrival of Tychicus with the
letter. Of the actual trip, we have no information.

Chronologically the next reference seems to come at 1 Peter
5:13,|| where we read, "She that is in Babylon, elect together with
you, saluteth you; and so doth Mark my son." Here we again find

---

|| Assuming a date of A.D. 64, before the outbreak of the Neronian persecution.
See Hiebert, *An Introduction to the Non-Pauline Epistles*, pp. 126-127.

Mark in the company of Peter, joining him in sending greeting to the Christians in the five provinces of Asia Minor (1:1).

Peter's reference to him as "Mark my son" is generally taken to mean that Mark owed his conversion to Peter. But others, like Swete,[23] consider it merely an expression of Peter's personal affection. It is true that Peter used the term *huios* (son) rather than *teknon* (child), which Paul commonly employs to indicate his relationship between himself and his converts. But according to Robertson, it is "quite possible that Peter employed this word in the sense of spiritual sonship."[24] Mark may well have been Peter's convert, but his use of the term here clearly conveyed his affection for his former pupil and present associate. Mark was again an intimate member of Peter's circle.

When and where Mark again became closely associated with Peter is not certain. Peter wrote the epistle while "in Babylon" (1 Pe 5:12-13), but the precise significance of that expression raises debate. Those who interpret it as the literal city of Babylon, think that Mark went on to the city on the Euphrates after making his visit to Colosse. More probably the expression is a cryptic designation of Rome.[25] Early tradition places Peter and Mark together in Rome.[26]

Since there is no mention of Peter in Paul's prison epistles, we may assume that Peter did not arrive at Rome during Paul's first imprisonment there. Probably, Peter arrived shortly after Paul's release, and Mark remained in Rome to resume labors with Peter.

Early tradition firmly asserts that in writing his gospel, Mark was largely dependent upon Peter's teaching.[27] While there is some divergence concerning the precise relation of Peter to Mark's composition of his gospel, Peter's close connection with the second gospel is uniformly stressed. The content of Mark's gospel in itself does not prove this close connection. But as Robertson shows, when once the suggestion is accepted, there is much in it to confirm and illustrate that assertion.[28]

The gospel of Mark gives us the beautiful picture of Jesus Christ as the perfect Servant. It was the manifest grace of God that chose Mark, the servant who had failed, to record the story of the Son of God in unwearied and unbroken service for man. As an older and wiser man, Mark could more fully appreciate that example of perfect service. He had discovered his own weakness and had found the answer to his own need in the strength and greatness of Christ. The drawing of his pen picture of the incarnate Son of God as the perfect Servant was the greatest service that Mark rendered to the Christian church.

The last scriptural mention of Mark is in 2 Timothy 4:11, written by Paul under the shadow of his own impending martyrdom. In summoning Timothy to his side at Rome, Paul adds, "Take Mark, and bring him with thee; for he is useful to me for ministering." Paul's desire to have Mark with him testifies remarkably to the value he had learned to place upon Mark's services. Lees aptly remarks, "No man could pray for a better testimonial from a dying friend than this."[29]

"Useful for ministering" offers an accurate, final evaluation of the status and services of Mark. The word *ministry* (*diakonia*) stresses not the office but the service rendered. Mark had demonstrated his power of organization and practical usefulness; so Paul felt that he was just the man he now needed in Rome.

While not gifted with outstanding abilities, Mark had proved himself "a practical industrious subordinate."[30] Mark always appears in the position of a subordinate. He contentedly devoted his energies to the service of others. His own greatness lay in his extraordinary gift of being the prop of truly great men. In the words of Swete, "He knew how to be invaluable to those who filled the first rank in the service of the Church, and proved himself a true servant of the servants of God."[31]

Mark's biography offers hope for those who have failed. There is hope for the coward, the deserter, if only he will turn back to Christ. The possibility of recovery, of renewed and enlarged usefulness, is open to all. Mark challenges us to learn the secret of success by taking advantage of our blunders and failures in turning them into stepping-stones in the struggle for respect and usefulness. One who has failed need not remain a failure.

6

SILAS

Acts 15:22, 27, 32-34, 40-41; 16:1–17:15; 18:5
2 Corinthians 1:19
1 Thessalonians 1:1
2 Thessalonians 1:1
1 Peter 5:12

SILAS CAME INTO PROMINENCE in the scriptural account as the intimate companion of Paul during his second missionary journey. As a prophet and a leading member of the early Jerusalem church, he had eminent qualifications to be Paul's co-worker in the furtherance of the gospel. He gladly worked in cooperation with others as their willing and effective assistant.

NAME

Silas' name appears under two forms in the New Testament. The shorter form, "Silas," always appears in Acts, while "Silvanus" is uniformly employed in the epistles. Silas is apparently the Greek form of the Aramaic name for Saul, a Jewish name, while Silvanus was his Latin name. Silas may have chosen that Latin name because of its similarity in sound to his Jewish name. His double name is in harmony with the fact of his Roman citizenship (Ac 16:37). Luke in Acts retained the name Silas went by in the Jerusalem community; while the epistles referred to him by the Latin name he would employ in Greek and Roman circles. Although some question the identification of Silas of Acts and Silvanus of the epistles as the same person, that fact is established by Paul's statement in 2 Corinthians 1:19, where Paul reminded the Corinthians that Christ was first preached to them "by me and Silvanus and Timothy." Since Acts recorded that Silas and Paul worked together to establish the Corinthian church, the identification is certain.

PLACE IN JERUSALEM CHURCH

Silas is first mentioned in Acts in connection with the close of the Jerusalem Conference (Ac 15:22). Upon reaching their decision, the apostles and elders of the Jerusalem church thought it well "to choose men out of their company" to bear the findings of the conference to Antioch. They chose "Judas called Barsabbas, and Silas, chief men among the brethren." The designation of these two as "chief men," literally, "leading men," has been differently understood, as the word is employed in connection with various forms of authority and leadership. Since the term designates the religious leaders of a local church (Heb 13:7, 17, 24), some have thought that it denotes they were eminent among the elders in the Jerusalem church. Selwyn feels that it indicates a recognized standing in that church "such as would hardly have been conceded to any but members of the original circle of Christians there."[1] Plumptre even thought it implied that they held "a position of greater authority than the other elders" because "they had been disciples of Christ, who as the number of witnesses diminished came more and more into prominence."[2] Later tradition made Silas one of the "seventy" (Lk 10:1). Selwyn thinks that this tradition "receives some support from the fact that St. Paul in I Thess. ii. 6 speaks of Silas and himself as 'apostles of Christ' — a phrase which suggests an actual commission from the Lord."[3] But more probably, Paul used the term *apostles* in the wider sense as denoting "missionaries."[4] Alexander insists that the restriction of the term "leading men" to ministers or elders "is without foundation in the text or context."[5] The term as applied to them need only indicate the high personal esteem in which Judas and Silas were held in the Jerusalem church. To achieve such recognition in the large Jerusalem church was no small tribute. One possible source of that esteem comes from Luke's statement that they were "prophets" (Ac 15:32). Both men belonged to that select group of men in the early church through whom the Lord gave fresh communications of His will for His people.

Although occasionally the prophets predicted future events, they primarily served to interpret and apply the will of God to the present circumstances. Judas and Silas were Christian teachers thoroughly able to set forth the will of God authoritatively on the basis of His Word.

Luke mentions nothing concerning the parents or background of Silas. He was certainly a Jew by birth; otherwise one has difficulty accounting for the esteem the Jerusalem church had for him. Carter's suggestion that "Silas was likely a Gentile proselyte" is less likely.[6] But he definitely belonged to the Hellenistic section of the Jerusalem church; this we know from his hearty agreement with the decision of the conference upholding the liberty of Gentile believers, as well as the fact that he was a Roman citizen.

ROLE IN JERUSALEM CONFERENCE

The Jerusalem Conference leaders embodied their decision in an epistle addressed to the Gentile believers in Antioch and the surrounding regions of Syria and Cilicia (Ac 15:23). When the Antioch delegation left for home, Judas and Silas accompanied them with the letter. Williams thinks that the two men chosen "represented the Jewish-Christian and the Hellenist points of view."[7] They were commissioned not only to deliver the letter but also to confirm orally the conference decision (v. 27). The selection of these two men and the commission given them was a wise move. McGarvey points out,

> The wisdom of sending Judas and Silas is seen in the fact that they had not been connected at all with the work among the Gentiles, and that their personal influence would tend to silence any objections which might be raised by refractory Jews. They could explain, without suspicion of bias, anything in the written document which might appear to any as obscure.[8]

It was an important assignment, and the Jerusalem church considered the two men fully qualified to carry it out.

The church at Antioch felt greatly encouraged upon hearing the letter read by Judas and Silas (Ac 15:31). The two also strengthened and encouraged other believers by their personal ministry (v. 32); they served to ground and settle these Gentile converts in their faith. They demonstrated that they came not only as the formal representatives of the Jerusalem church but had a personal interest in the work at Antioch. After having spent some time there, the messengers "were dismissed in peace" and returned to Jerusalem (v. 33).

At this point the personal movements of Silas become somewhat obscure because of uncertainty in the text. Did Silas remain at Antioch or did he return to Jerusalem with Judas? Acts 15:33 implies that he did return, while verse 34, as given in the King James Version ("Notwithstanding it pleased Silas to abide there still"), declares that he did not return. But verse 34 has very slight manuscript support; all critical editions of the Greek text omit it. Bruce points to it as "a Western addition which was taken over by the Byzantine text."[9] Ramsay supported the verse with the argument that it did not declare that Judas and Silas actually *departed* but only that they were free to do so, adding that Silas did not avail himself of the permission.[10] But in view of the lack of manuscript support for verse 34 and the apparent contradiction to verse 33 which it produces, this seems improbable. Meyer asserts that "the return of Silas to Jerusalem was a necessary exigency of the commission which he had received."[11] While quite possibly Paul summoned Silas from Jerusalem, more probably Silas found the atmosphere in the Antioch church so exhilarating that he returned of his own accord before Paul chose him.

CAREER WITH PAUL

Following the unfortunate contention between Paul and Barnabas (Ac 15:37-39), Paul "chose Silas" as his co-worker (v. 40). The verb implies that there were others whom Paul might have selected and who would have been willing to go with him. "Indeed there was no lack of competent and devoted men in the Church of Antioch; but the fitness of Silas was pre-eminent."[12] Having observed his zeal at Antioch and appreciating his clear views as to the liberty of the gospel, Paul was convinced that Silas was the needed colaborer. The church of Antioch approved the choice; for when the missionaries started out, they were "commended by the brethren to the grace of the Lord" (Ac 15:40). Plumptre thinks that the statement "obviously implied a full gathering of the Church and a special service of prayer on the departure of the two Apostles."[13] Thus, sent forth by the Antioch church, according to Plumptre's view, Silas also was an apostle, in the sense of being the commissioned representative of the church. But Nixon points out that "nowhere is he referred to in a general way as an 'apostle' (contrast Barnabas in Acts xiv. 14)."[14]

Having the commendation and confidence of the Jerusalem church qualified Silas to work with Paul; choosing him confirmed that Paul did not wish to stir up any antagonism. It proved that there was perfect agreement between Paul and the leaders of the mother church. Another attractive factor was that Silas, like Paul, was also a Roman citizen and, if necessary, could claim with him the protection that such citizenship offered in facing "perils from the Gentiles" (2 Co 11:26). The possession of Roman citizenship would "give him a standing among the aristocracy of any provincial town."[15] Silas further had the rare qualification of being a good follower and steady companion to a man who, because of his apostolic commission and aggressive personality, was accustomed to lead. The call required deliberate self-effacement on the part of Silas, but he was willing to take second place.

Paul chose Silas to replace Barnabas, not Mark. Had Silas initially aspired to take the place of Barnabas, Paul might well have hesitated. Few men indeed would have been fully able to replace Barnabas. Lenski remarks, "It does not seem, from all accounts, that Silas fully filled the place of Barnabas with Paul; Barnabas was the greater man."[16]

In sketching the opening movements of the second missionary journey, Luke used the singular pronoun *he*, referring to Paul as the obvious leader, although we know that he had Silas along. The trip through Asia Minor, although a formidable undertaking, Luke sketched in a few verses, not stopping to name the different members involved unless he wanted to make a definite identification for a true understanding of the events. But Silas shared with Paul the joy of instructing and strengthening the young churches in that area (Ac 16:4-5). He stayed at Paul's side as his friend and ministering comrade during the dangers and toils as well as the triumphs.

When Paul expelled the demon from the soothsaying slave girl at Philippi, the owners took revenge by having "Paul and Silas" arrested and rushed before the magistrates. Although Paul cast out the demon, the arrest of Silas with him confirms that he was a prominent member in the missionary party. Clearly Paul and Silas were the recognized leaders. Silas shared with Paul the ill-treatment heaped upon the accused men — a merciless public beating without a trial, rude imprisonment though uncondemned, and the indignity of having their feet placed in the stocks as though they were dangerous criminals. Seekings well remarks, "It is under conditions such as these that the strength of a man's courage and the reality of his trust in God are tested."[17] How gloriously Paul and Silas passed the test! Instead of filling the jail with their groans and just complaints, "Paul and Silas were praying and singing hymns unto God" (Ac 16:25). We do not know whose idea it was to sing in their pain, but the amazing spiritual victory had shattering consequences. The divine applause to this first known Christian concert in a jail on the continent of Europe, shook the prison, opened all its doors, and loosed all the fetters of the prisoners (v. 26). The startled jailer, kept from impulsive suicide, "fell down before Paul and Silas, and brought them out and said, Sirs, what must I do to be saved?" (vv. 29-30). Not only was Silas the corecipient of his question but also the happy participant in the transforming events in the jailer's house that night. The next morning, the fact that both men were Roman citizens procured for them an honorable release. Paul's insistence upon the recognition of that fact served to establish the dignity of the young church at Philippi.

With their backs still sore from the shameful treatment at Philippi, Paul and Silas began their ministry in the Thessalonian synagogue. Paul apparently did most of the preaching at Thessalonica, for Luke emphasized his ministry to the extent of giving an actual quotation of his words (Ac 17:2-3). But both Silas and Paul actively gathered in the converts who "consorted" with them (v. 4). The jealous Jews at Thessalonica aimed their attack at the missionaries, and consequently both were hurried away from the city by the believers who were deeply concerned for their safety.

At Berea, Paul and Silas found a receptive and fruitful ministry in the Jewish synagogue, until it was disrupted by the fanatical Jews from Thessalonica (Ac 17:10-13). Because of the ensuing riot, the brethren at Berea immediately hurried Paul out of the city. The vicious Jewish opponents directed their efforts against Paul because they recognized him as the most influential member of the missionary party. They regarded Silas and Timothy as of minor importance, in their determination to crush the movement by destroying its leader. When the solicitous Berean brethren spirited Paul away from the danger, "Silas and Timothy abode there still" (17:14). For the first time on the trip, Silas left Paul's side. As the older member of the two who remained, Silas took the leadership in directing the young church at Berea through the crisis. Since they began traveling together, Silas had never worked independently of Paul.

The brethren who conducted Paul to Athens returned to Berea with instructions from him to "Silas and Timothy that they should come to him with all speed" (Ac 17:15). Luke did not add whether Silas and Timothy came to Paul at Athens as requested. He only mentioned that they rejoined Paul after he had taken up residence in Corinth (Ac 18:5). But obviously Luke did not record all the movements of Paul's assistants. From 1 Thessalonians 3:1-2, it appears that Timothy at least did arrive at Athens as directed, perhaps Silas also. But due to his deep concern for the Thessalonian believers, Paul sent Timothy back there to comfort and strengthen them. In saying "We thought it good to be left behind at Athens alone" (1 Th 3:1), Paul apparently implied that Silas also was sent on a mission to Macedonia. Apparently he went back to the Philippian church with which Paul was in frequent communication at this time (Phil 4:15).

"Silas and Timothy came down from Macedonia" (Ac 18:5) some time after Paul had gone to Corinth and found work with Aquila and Priscilla and had started weekly preaching in the Corinthian synagogue (18:1-4). Timothy's return from Thessalonica with his good report prompted the writing of 1 Thessalonians (1 Th 3:6). A few months later, 2 Thessalonians was dispatched to the church. In both epistles, "Paul, and Silvanus, and Timothy" are named as the writers. No further words of identification of the writers were added; none were needed. Any communication coming to them from these three men would at once evoke an eager interest in the members of the Thessalonian church. The order of their names correctly indicates their relative importance in relationship to the Thessalonian church.

In the first epistle, Paul reminded the church that while the missionaries ministered at Thessalonica, they had made it a practice of "working night and day, that we might not burden any of you" (1 Th

2:9). From this, we assume that Silas, like Paul, had a trade whereby he supported himself. While Paul was a "tentmaker" (Ac 18:3), we have no information concerning Silas' occupation. As a Jewish lad he too had wisely been taught a gainful trade.

When Silas and Timothy rejoined Paul at Corinth, they brought along a monetary gift from the Macedonian brethren, apparently from the Philippian church which Silas had revisited (2 Co 11:9; Phil 4:15-16). It relieved Paul of the necessity of working long hours at his trade, and enabled him to begin an intensive evangelistic ministry in Corinth (Ac 18:5-8). Paul's remark to the Corinthians that the gospel was brought to them "by me and Silvanus and Timothy" (2 Co 1:19) indicates that these two co-workers had an aggressive share in the campaign. Silas played an important part in the founding of the Corinthian church, but not so much that his name became a rallying point in their unhappy church factions (1 Co 1:12).

With the close of Paul's missionary work at Corinth, a curtain falls over the story of Silas. He apparently did not leave Corinth with Paul, since he is never mentioned again in the story that follows. Nor is there any mention of him in the Pauline epistles in connection with any subsequent events. That he did not permanently settle at Corinth we take from the fact that the Corinthian epistles contain no greetings to him. He probably returned to Jerusalem. The reason for the termination of the joint labors of Paul and Silas is unknown.

ASSOCIATION WITH PETER

Only once more does the name of Silvanus occur in the Scriptures, and then in connection with the work of the apostle Peter some thirteen years later. In 1 Peter 5:12 we read, "By Silvanus, our faithful brother, as I account *him*, I have written unto you briefly." Is he the former co-worker of Paul, or another otherwise entirely unknown individual? Jacobson asserts, "We have no materials for determining whether he was the same."[18] Savile felt that the identification was "doubtful,"[19] but Hart declares, "There does not seem to be any good reason for refusing to identify this Silvanus with the companion of St. Paul."[20] Most scholars accept the identification.

Once more we find Silvanus modestly serving in second place. "By Silvanus" may mean that he was Peter's envoy, the bearer of the letter to the Christians scattered in the five provinces of Asia Minor (1 Pe 1:1). Polkinghorne calls attention to the fact that in the original, "to you" stands immediately after the name of Silvanus, and thinks that it "suggests a close link between him and the recipients."[21] If so, Silvanus must have labored in those regions since the time of his ministry at Corinth. According to this interpretation, the commendation given Silvanus was intended to reveal Peter's esteem personally for the bearer of the letter. In support of this view, Lenski points out that the epistle contains "no salutation from Silvanus, while it does convey one from Mark."[22]

Peter's expression "by Silvanus" (*dia Silouanou*) could mean "through the agency of Silvanus," indicating that Silvanus served as Peter's amanuensis, taking down his dictation up to this point. Thus Selwyn points out that if he simply carried the letter, *sent* rather than *written* would have been the more natural word to use.[23] While some scholars, like Huther and Lenski reject this view,[24] it is finding increasing acceptance today. But Kelly believes that Silvanus, Paul's noted companion, was too important a figure to allow us to think of him here simply serving as a dictation clerk; he concludes that "Silvanus had been responsible for drafting the letter on the author's behalf and on his instructions."[25] Many assume that Silvanus had some freedom in writing out Peter's message. Ancient scribes occasionally had considerable freedom in writing out the message entrusted to them. Zahn surmises that Peter probably would not have referred to him as "our faithful brother, as I account him," if Silvanus' only part was taking Peter's dictation. Zahn thinks that this commendation of Silvanus can only be explained on the assumption "that Silvanus' part in the composition was so important and so large that its performance required a considerable degree of trustworthiness."[26] This view has great appeal to scholars today as helping to explain how Peter's thought found expression in the good Greek of this epistle. Many conservative scholars today feel that this "Silvanus hypothesis" need not be ruled out, and that it "forms a reasonable alternative for those whose main objection to Petrine authorship is linguistic."[27] This viewpoint adds yet another touch to our picture of Silvanus as a capable yet self-effacing servant of the Lord.

FINAL TRIBUTE

Peter's commendation of Silvanus as "the faithful brother as I account him" (1 Pe 5:12, Rotherham) well summarizes Silas' character. This evaluation was no mere conjecture on Peter's part, as the rendering "as I suppose" in the King James Version might suggest, but rather his considered estimate resting on rational and sure grounds.

Silas throughout appears as a faithful worker who worthily performed any assignment given him. He had already gained the recognition of this characteristic when the Jerusalem church selected him to convey and explain to the Gentile believers the letter formulated at the close of the Jerusalem Conference. The account of his work with Paul also strongly confirms that aspect of his character. It was likewise Peter's testimony concerning him in our last glimpse of Silas.

As a capable and dependable worker, Silas had the difficult task of assisting men whose dominating personalities always overshadowed him. In order to be their true collaborator, he had to possess qualities approaching those of his more gifted friends; yet he had to be willing to take second place while working with them. Silas did have the willingness thus to efface himself in the service of the Lord. Interestingly, except for the probable scribal gloss found in Acts 15:34 (KJV), Silas is never mentioned in Scripture as acting alone, but always in association with another. Clearly he did not prefer to work independently. Furthermore, except for three instances where his name is coupled with that of young Timothy (Ac 17:14, 15; 18:5), his name always stands second. Silas had that commendable Christian attitude which "gives men a readiness for unobtrusive service, and makes them content to offer for positions of secondary importance."[28]

But Silas was not a mediocre and colorless individual. Although he was overshadowed by the more brilliant men with whom he worked, we must not lose sight of his true greatness. He was indeed one of the "leading men among the brethren" (Ac 15:22, Greek).

7

TIMOTHY

Acts 16:1-3; 17:14-15; 18:5; 19:22; 20:4
Romans 16:21
1 Corinthians 4:17; 16:10-11
2 Corinthians 1:1, 19
Philippians 1:1; 2:19-23
Colossians 1:1
1 Thessalonians 1:1; 3:2, 6
2 Thessalonians 1:1
1 Timothy 1:2, 18; 6:20
2 Timothy 1:2; 4:9, 21
Philemon 1
Hebrews 13:23

APOSTOLIC HISTORY and Christian thought have lastingly enshrined
Timothy because of his long and intimate association with the apostle
Paul. Their association was longer and more continuous than that of
any other of Paul's companions, with the possible exception of Luke.
Of all his associates, none seems to have been so dear to Paul as
Timothy. Paul associated the name of Timothy with his own in the
salutation of no less than six of his epistles.* Only in 1 Corinthians is
another single individual thus named by Paul in the salutation of his
epistles. Timothy is the only *individual* to whom two canonical
epistles were addressed, epistles marked with such tenderness and
intimacy as to single him out as a close and beloved companion. Paul
always spoke of him in terms of unqualified affection and praise. In at

---

* Paul names only Timothy with himself in 2 Co, Phil, Col, and Phile; in 1 and
2 Th, Paul mentions Silvanus also.

least three passages (1 Co 4:17; 16:10-11; Phil 2:19-23), Paul strongly insisted upon the identity of thought and aim between himself and Timothy. Paul lavished upon Timothy the affection that he would have given his own son. Bourdillon remarks, "Timothy was most a son to him while he lived, and most his legatee when he died."[1]

BACKGROUND AND CONVERSION

With the first mention of Timothy in Acts, Luke gives us a sketch of Timothy's background and early life. "And he came also to Derbe and to Lystra: and behold, a certain disciple was there, named Timothy, the son of a Jewess that believed; but his father was a Greek. The same was well reported of by the brethren that were at Lystra and Iconium" (Ac 16:1-2). His interjection, "Behold," marks the importance which Luke attached to this introduction of Timothy as a member of the Pauline circle.

On beginning the second missionary journey, Paul returned to "Derbe and to Lystra" (16:1). The latter place was the home of Timothy. I conclude this from several considerations. In the best manuscripts, "to" (eis) also comes before Lystra, marking it as the scene of the events to follow. That Timothy was commended by the brethren "at Lystra and Iconium" also implies this. While Lystra and Derbe, both Lycaonian cities, lay in one administrative district, Lystra and Iconium appear together as the two places where Timothy was well known, implying that they did not know him in Derbe. Ramsay points out that this is in harmony with "the facts of commerce and intercourse. Lystra is much nearer Iconium than it is to Derbe; and geographically Lystra goes along with Iconium."[2] Lystra is also favored by Paul's remarks in 2 Timothy 3:11. (The view, as old as Origen, that Timothy came from Derbe is based upon a misunderstanding of Ac 20:4, where the expression "of Derbe" rightly applies only to Gaius, not to Timothy.)

Timothy was the son of a racially and apparently also a religiously mixed marriage. His mother was "a Jewess that believed" while his father was "a Greek." Such marriages were quite unthinkable by the exclusive standards of Palestine, but in the dispersion they occurred more or less frequently, especially if the husband became a proselyte. If Timothy's father did accept the Jewish God, he must have remained "a proselyte of the gate," refusing to accept circumcision for himself as well as his son. Otherwise Timothy would certainly have been circumcised. The fact that Luke twice called the father "a Greek" (16:1, 3) without any qualifying adjective, as in the case of the mother, strongly implies that he was a pagan. Timothy received instruction in the Jewish Scriptures, but that does not prove that he was a proselyte since he studied the Old Testament under his mother and grandmother (2 Ti 3:15). That the father had already died may be implied from Luke's "was" (Ac 16:1), although the language is not conclusive on the point. Plumptre indeed thinks that he was still alive.[3]

From 2 Timothy, we catch a glimpse of the home in which Timothy grew up. His mother, Eunice, and his grandmother, Lois (1:5), were both godly Jewish women characterized by "unfeigned faith," a faith devoid of sham or pretense. They grounded their faith and loyalty to the hope of Israel in the Old Testament Scriptures. This unhypocritical faith they successfully transmitted to young Timothy. Their sincerity made them receptive to the message of Christ when they heard it. Thus, on his mother's side, Timothy had the inestimable blessing of at least two generations of godly ancestors.

When her son was born, Eunice hopefully called him "Timothy," meaning, "honoring God." Determined to retrieve her disappointment with her marriage, she set herself to the sacred task of his godly training. Ably assisted by the grandmother, Timothy's mother poured into the lad a knowledge of the Old Testament (2 Ti 3:14-15). Lenski concludes from Paul's use of the expression "sacred letters" (2 Ti 3:15, Greek) that little Timothy was taught the letters of the alphabet from the Scriptures and first learned to read from the Bible.[4] Timothy's firm grounding in the Scriptures and his personal loyalty to them provided the basis for his later usefulness in the service of Christ.

The time came when Timothy's acceptance of the Scriptures as taught to him by his beloved mother and grandmother became vitalized by a personal acceptance of the Christ predicted in those Scriptures, thus making him "wise unto salvation" (2 Ti 3:15). That Timothy was converted through Paul seems assured from the fact that the apostle repeatedly spoke of him as his own "son" or "child" (1 Co 4:17; 1 Ti 1:2, 18; 2 Ti 1:2). Paul's characterization of Timothy as "my beloved and faithful child" (1 Co 4:17) cannot be reduced to mean simply that Timothy was in full accord with him, because Paul did not so designate others who were also in wholehearted accord with him.

Timothy's conversion, as perhaps also that of his mother, occurred during Paul's labors at Lystra on the first missionary journey (Ac 14:8-21). His training in the Old Testament Scriptures had instilled in Timothy the hope of a coming Messiah. When Timothy heard Paul proclaim Jesus as the Messiah, his heart was moved to accept Him in faith.

Timothy must have witnessed with deep interest the stirring events at Lystra: the healing of the congenital cripple, the followers of Zeus attempting to worship the missionaries, and the hateful Jews from Antioch and Iconium fomenting trouble that culminated in the stoning of Paul. Timothy may well have joined the group as "the disciples stood round about" Paul as he lay, apparently dead, outside the city gate. When Paul suddenly arose, they may have taken him to the home of Eunice, who would tenderly care for him until his departure for Derbe the next day. The spectacle of such innocent suffering and undaunted courage made a lasting impression upon the mind of young Timothy. In connection with these noble virtues, Timothy first came to know Paul as a messenger of the cross. In 2 Timothy 3:11 Paul reminded him of those sufferings, when seeking to arouse Timothy's courage to face impending danger.

Apparently at his baptism, young Timothy "professed a good profession before many witnesses" (1 Ti 6:12, KJV). Some connect this "good confession" (ASV) to the time of Timothy's ordination, but the combination of the confession with the call unto eternal life links it with his conversion and public confession of "the faith" at his baptism.

When Paul returned to Lystra after an interval of little more than a year, he found his young convert "well reported of by the brethren that were at Lystra and Iconium" (Ac 16:2). His activities in these two churches demonstrated his piety and talents, winning for him the respect and approval of "the brethren" in these two cities. McGarvey thinks that Timothy had already earned recognition as "a young preacher."[5]

MISSIONARY CALL

Impressed with Timothy's spiritual growth and his obvious talents for Christian work, Paul suggested to Silas and the local elders that the young man gave promise of making a good missionary. The suggestion was warmly sanctioned by the brethren of Lystra and Iconium, who spoke of his activities and Christian character in the highest terms. During a gathering of the local assembly, the Spirit of prophecy, speaking through His prophets, pointed out Timothy for special service, thus sanctioning Paul's desire to have Timothy "go forth with him" (Ac 16:3; 1 Ti 1:18).

But one fact impeded Timothy's usefulness as a member of Paul's party. The Jews in those parts knew that Timothy was uncircumcised (Ac 16:3), and this had always offended them. For one born of a Jewish mother not to be circumcised was in effect to reject his Jewish heritage. For Timothy, who had a Jewish mother and had received a Jewish education, to remain uncircumcised meant to be denied acceptance in any Jewish circle. If he had confined his ministry to his native area, the absence of circumcision would have made little difference in that predominantly Gentile territory; but it definitely did hinder Paul's method of working. Since Paul made it a practice to secure lodging in the Jewish quarters of a new city and begin work in the synagogue, his close association with one uncircumcised would have scandalized the Jews whom he wanted to win. It would also have barred Timothy from any work in the synagogue; most Jewish homes would have closed their doors to him. To remove this barrier, Paul "took and circumcised him" (Ac 16:3). That Timothy consented is obvious. It was a voluntary act, prompted by expediency. It was unrelated to the question of Timothy's own salvation or the necessity of circumcision for salvation. Timothy's circumcision was based upon principles entirely different from those which caused Paul to refuse to have Titus circumcised (Gal 2:3-5). Timothy's circumcision served to remove the prejudices of the unsaved Jews; Paul refused to circumcise Titus as a concession to the dogmatic demands of the Judaizers.

Although at the time of Christ, each town — at least in Palestine — had a man who specialized in the performance of the rite of circumcision, any Israelite might perform it.[6] Alexander says that Luke's expression "took and circumcised him" implies that Paul "performed the rite himself, as it was not a sacredotal act, but rather belonged to the father or his representative."[7] If so, Paul assumed the position of a natural father to his son in the faith.

Various estimations of Timothy's age at this time have arisen. In 1 Timothy 4:12, written fourteen or fifteen years later, Paul still spoke of Timothy's "youth," a term applied to men until the age of forty. How old Timothy was when he joined Paul's company no one knows. What age one assigns to Timothy largely depends on the chronology one accepts. Furneaux suggests that Timothy "at this time was about eighteen years of age." Lenski holds that he was at least twenty-one, while Pope was willing to allow the age of twenty-five.[8] An age somewhere between twenty and twenty-two seems most probable.

SECOND JOURNEY

Being accepted as a member of Paul's missionary party was an important event for young Timothy. It was the turning point in his life. His association with the big men with whom he had now cast his lot, stimulated and challenged him. He exchanged the quiet life of his provincial home for the bustle and strain of the road. His limited experiences of Christian service in his neighborhood found enlargement under the leadership of Paul, the missionary statesman.

Although he could not foresee the stirring events that lay ahead for him, Timothy well knew that the way before him would not be easy. Nor did he easily leave behind his beloved mother and gracious grandmother. But as one who felt the hand of God upon his life, Timothy resolutely gave himself to the challenging service that beckoned him as the privileged associate of his spiritual father in Christ.

Timothy's name is not mentioned in Luke's account of the exciting experiences of the missionary party in Philippi and Thessalonica. Perhaps, as Zahn and Lenski suggest, Timothy remained at Philippi when "Paul and Silas" left for Thessalonica (Ac 17:1-4) to assist Luke with the work in the Philippian church.[9] LaSor conjectures that Timothy did go along to Thessalonica but remained there when "Paul and Silas" were hurriedly sent to Berea after the riot (17:10), but this is quite uncertain. Whether Timothy remained at Philippi or went with the missionary party to Thessalonica, we do know that he was with Paul and Silas at Berea (Ac 17:14). When Paul had to flee from Berea to save his life, Timothy remained there with Silas to see the young church through the crisis caused by the Thessalonian Jews (17:13-14).

The Berean brethren who had conducted Paul to Athens, returned with instructions from Paul to "Silas and Timothy that they should come to him with all speed" (Ac 17:15). Luke did not record that Silas and Timothy went to Athens as requested by Paul, but from 1 Thessalonians 3:1-2 we infer that Timothy (apparently Silas also) did rejoin Paul at Athens. Upon arrival they brought Paul further information concerning the vicious activities of the Jews of Thessalonica in opposition to the gospel. Deeply concerned for the welfare of the Thessalonian believers (1 Th 3:1-5), the three missionaries decided that Timothy should return to Thessalonica to aid the believers in their trials. Since Satan hindered Paul's own efforts to return to Thessalonica (1 Th 2:18), Paul did the next best thing and sent Timothy back to that storm center. In reminding the Thessalonians of Timothy's mission to Thessalonica, Paul described Timothy as "our brother and God's minister in the gospel of Christ" (1 Th 3:2). This twofold description of Timothy reminded the Thessalonian believers of the true position of the one sent to them. In relation to Paul and Silas, Timothy was "our brother"; while in relation to God, he was "God's minister in the gospel of Christ." This stress upon Timothy's importance recalled the fact that no second-rate substitute had been sent to them. Paul's comment that he was thus "left behind at Athens alone" (1 Th 3:1) underlined his feeling that it had been no easy thing for him to deprive himself thus of the presence and assistance of Timothy.

Timothy returned to Thessalonica with a double assignment (1 Th 3:2-5). He was to ascertain and report to Paul the state of the Thessalonian church. He was further commissioned to perform an important service while at Thessalonica; that was, "to establish," to fix and make steadfast, "and to comfort" or encourage, the Thessalonian believers in their faith; so that they would not be swept away by the persecution. The assignment of such a mission to young Timothy demonstrated Paul's confidence in his abilities. It was the first separate mission assigned to him, and it gave his young co-worker valuable experience.

Timothy returned from Thessalonica while Paul was working at Corinth (Ac 18:5). Timothy's good report concerning the Thessalonian converts relieved Paul's anxiety, and he immediately wrote 1 Thessalonians (3:6). He dispatched a second letter to them a few months later. Both epistles were written in the name of "Paul, and Silvanus, and Timothy" (1 Th 1:1; 2 Th 1:1). As the youngest of the three men, Timothy's name properly stood last, but his inclusion testifies to his importance in relation to the Thessalonian church. He held an important relationship with that church because of the mission to them which he had just completed.

Alone, Paul began to preach the gospel at Corinth (Ac 18:4). But with the arrival of his associates, an intensive missionary campaign was launched at Corinth in which Silas and Timothy had an active part. Paul's words in 2 Corinthians 1:19, "For the Son of God, Jesus Christ, who was preached among you by us, *even* by me and Silvanus and Timothy," show that Timothy took an active part in the preaching of the gospel. Zahn, however, infers "that Timothy and Silas, who, according to I Cor., could have had no appreciable share in the founding of the local Corinthian Church, laboured successfully in the vicinity of Corinth."[10] Perhaps they made Corinth their headquarters but also engaged in missionary activities in the province of Achaia. That the preaching was not confined to Corinth is certain.

THIRD JOURNEY

Whether Timothy remained at Corinth when Paul left that city is not known. Timothy does not appear again in Acts until the time of Paul's ministry at Ephesus, during the third missionary journey (19:22). Ramsay holds that Luke's silence concerning Timothy "shows that he was understood by the author to have been attached to Paul's service during the intervening period, ready for any mission."[11] Lenski points out that Luke's description of Timothy as one of those "that ministered unto" Paul (Ac 19:22) indicates that he was "one of his steady assistants."[12]

During this Ephesian ministry of nearly three years (Ac 20:31), the gospel spread widely, so that "all they that dwelt in Asia heard the word of the Lord, both Jews and Greeks" (Ac 19:10). Obviously, Paul sent his assistants to various places to further the work. It would seem that Timothy had worked at Colosse and was well known to the church there. Paul associated his name with his own in the salutation to Colossians as well as in the private letter to Philemon.

With the establishment of the gospel in Asia assured, Paul began to make plans for the future (Ac 19:21). He accordingly "sent into Macedonia two of them that ministered unto him, Timothy and Erastus" (v. 22). Luke gave no indication of Paul's purpose in sending these two assistants ahead of him into Macedonia, but his mention of Paul's plans to visit Jerusalem (v. 21) makes it clear that they were sent into Macedonia in connection with the offering for the Jerusalem saints, which Paul was organizing at this time (Ac 24:17; 1 Co 16:1-4; 2 Co 8 – 9).

From 1 Corinthians we learn that Timothy had received instructions to go to Corinth also. That epistle was written shortly after Timothy's departure for Macedonia, and Paul expected that the epistle, sent directly by sea, would arrive at Corinth ahead of Timothy. The disorders in the Corinthian church, about which he had received information before Timothy left, convinced Paul that he must again give his Corinthian converts a reminder of how their father lived, so that they would become "imitators" of him (1 Co 4:16). Paul frankly told the Corinthians, "For this cause have I sent unto you Timothy, who is my beloved and faithful child in the Lord, who shall put you in remembrance of my ways which are in Christ" (4:17). His words are a beautiful tribute to Timothy. The Corinthians stood in the same relationship to Paul that Timothy did, being his children, but by their conduct they were showing that they had forgotten how their father lived. Timothy, as his "beloved and faithful child," would remind them of Paul's walk and teachings. Timothy was a faithful follower of his spiritual father, capable of revealing the father's ways to his Corinthian brothers. He stood in such close relation to Paul that he had become thoroughly permeated with his spirit and teachings. Paul's testimony to Timothy confirms the closeness of the ties between them.

Developments which led Paul to write 1 Corinthians, subsequent to the departure of Timothy, convinced him that the task confronting Timothy might be more difficult than they had at first anticipated. He feared that some haughty and puffed up members might be arrogantly prone to disregard or intimidate young Timothy. He therefore pointedly told them, "Now if Timothy come, see that he be with you without fear; for he worketh the work of the Lord, as I also do: let no man therefore despise him" (1 Co 16:10-11). Paul claimed their respect for Timothy because of his work; he identified Timothy with himself in gospel labors. He warned them against any temptation to consider Timothy unworthy of proper respect. The warning implies that Timothy was naturally somewhat timid and might allow himself to be browbeaten by some arrogant individual. Paul urged the Corinthians to send Timothy on his journey "in peace," without strife or controversy (16:11). Paul expected him, eagerly waiting for his report.

Timothy's actual arrival at Corinth is not recorded; although presumably, he did arrive there as directed. If he had not, it seems that some explanation of his failure to come would have been given in 2 Corinthians. From 1 Corinthians it seems that Paul expected Timothy to return to him at Ephesus from Corinth, since he planned to remain at Ephesus until Pentecost (1 Co 16:8). Whether Timothy returned before Paul left Ephesus is not certain, but we do know that he was with Paul in Macedonia when he wrote 2 Corinthians; Paul joined the name of "Timothy our brother" with his own in the salutation of that epistle (1:1).

When Paul left Macedonia and came to Corinth (Ac 20:2-3), Timothy apparently came with him. He was in the company of Paul when the apostle wrote the epistle to the Romans from Corinth. "Timothy my fellow-worker" was among those sending greetings to the Roman Christians (Ro 16:21). Not only was Timothy named first among them but he was also the only one in the group whom Paul designated as "my fellow-worker." It is another indication of how deeply Paul appreciated Timothy as his close companion and colaborer in the gospel.

In Acts 20:4, the name of Timothy appears in a list of seven men who were traveling with Paul. They were the bearers selected by the churches to accompany Paul to Jerusalem with the collection (1 Co 16:3-4; 2 Co 8:19-21). Luke mentioned that the seven awaited Paul's arrival at Troas (Ac 20:5). Since Paul had originally planned to sail for Palestine from Corinth (Ac 20:3), they had apparently all assembled at Corinth for the trip. When the discovery of a plot against Paul forced a change in plans, the group apparently divided, some going with Paul by way of Philippi, while the others crossed over to Troas, where they all reassembled. The entire group apparently journeyed all the way to Jerusalem with Paul, although only one of this group was later mentioned by Luke (Ac 21:29).

First Roman Imprisonment

For the next three years in Paul's life, there is no mention of Timothy. His activities during Paul's two-year imprisonment at Caesarea are unrecorded; nor did he make the journey to Rome with Paul. But from the prison epistles, we learn that he was with Paul at Rome.[13] How soon he rejoined Paul at Rome is not known. We do know Timothy was with the apostle when he wrote the letters to the Colossians and Philemon, because in the salutation of both letters, Paul mentioned the name of "Timothy our brother" (Col 1:1; Phile 1); but there is no indication that Timothy shared his imprisonment. He seems to have stayed close of his own free will to minister to Paul's needs and be his companion and helper.

When Paul wrote the letter to the Philippians during the latter part of his imprisonment, Timothy was still with him. Paul began that epistle with, "Paul and Timothy, servants of Christ Jesus" (1:1). Both served the same Master. Only that time did Paul use a designation in the salutation which placed another on a level with himself. Paul here avoided the use of *apostle* in order to associate Timothy with himself as an equal bondsman of Christ. But the salutation associated Timothy with Paul only as his fellow servant of Christ, not as the joint author of the letter. Paul at once proceeded to write in the first person singular. Timothy may have been his amanuensis.

The epistle to the Philippians contains a passage of high praise for Timothy (2:19-23). Paul informed the Philippians that he hoped to send Timothy to them as soon as he saw "how it will go with" him, when he learned the verdict of the imperial court (v. 23). Because of his solicitude for the Philippians, he would send Timothy to them. Timothy had the needed qualifications for the task. "For I have no man likeminded, who will care truly for your state" (v. 20). No one else available to him had the same genuine concern for the Philippians' welfare. The service of Timothy, unlike that of others, was free from all self-seeking. Paul appealed to the personal knowledge of the Philippians concerning his spiritual son in confirmation of his tribute to Timothy. "Ye know the proof of him, that, as a child *serveth* a father, *so* he served with me in furtherance of the gospel" (v. 22). Paul stressed the father-child relationship that existed between himself and Timothy, but he carefully avoided any suggestion that Timothy's service was merely that of a child serving his father; as a Christian worker, Timothy was jointly serving with him "in the furtherance of the gospel." This praise of Timothy leads Seekings to remark,

> Never did Paul allow himself such freedom in the praise of any of his co-workers as in this tender and generous outburst of feeling concerning one who had toiled with him in the holy work and whom he had come to esteem as a genuine son.[14]

POST-ACTS ACTIVITIES

Aside from a passing reference to Timothy in the epistle to the Hebrews, we must glean all further scriptural information concerning Timothy from the two epistles which bear his name as their recipient. The value attributed to the portrait of Timothy found in these epistles will depend upon the conclusion accepted concerning the much discussed question of their Pauline authorship.

Since the beginning of the nineteenth century, the pastoral epistles — the three letters addressed to Timothy and Titus — have constituted a fierce battleground of critical scholarship concerning their authenticity. Scholars are divided into three camps on the question. The radical camp denies their Pauline authorship entirely, holding that the historical allusions in them are inventions intended to give them the appearance of reality. Thus Kee, who regards the epistles as "pseudonymous writings from the third generation of the church's life," asserts, "The Pastorals are of no help in reconstructing the portrait of Paul's youthful associate, Timothy."[15] The mediating school of critics postulates that the epistles contain some genuine Pauline notes which were incorporated in the letters by a later admirer of Paul, but that the bulk of the letters is of non-Pauline origin. They generally believe that 2 Timothy contains the largest amount of these genuine Pauline fragments. Scott claims that these passages can be identified "by delicate linguistic tests,"[16] but the subjective character of the proposed tests is evident from the fact that no two scholars agree on the exact identity of the Pauline fragments. Thus any information in these epistles concerning Timothy which is to be accepted as authentic depends upon one's personal evaluation. The critical disagreements cast doubt upon the validity of any of the information. The conservative camp, refusing to surrender the epistles' authenticity, takes into account the problems that these epistles present.† The areas of difficulty relate to historical, ecclesiastical, doctrinal, and linguistic problems. Of these, most scholars consider the problem of linguistics as the most weighty. But the conservatives maintain that the Pauline authorship of these epistles is still the most tenable position. After a careful review of the problems, Guthrie concludes:

> The traditional view that they are authentic writings of the apostle cannot be said to be impossible, and since there are greater problems attached to the alternative theories it is most reasonable to suppose that the early Church was right in accepting them as such.[17]

With this conclusion, I fully agree; I accept these epistles as authentic information concerning Timothy.

By common consent, the dates of the epistles to Timothy must follow the time of the story of Acts. They provide pertinent information concerning the activities of Timothy after Paul's release from the imprisonment recorded in Acts 28. When 1 Timothy was written, Timothy was laboring in Ephesus at Paul's personal request. Paul's remark, "As I exhorted thee to tarry at Ephesus, when I was going into Macedonia" (1:3), indicates that the two men had been together at Ephesus. Paul's visit there after his release soon convinced him that much work needed to be done in the churches in that region. When

---

† *Against* Pauline authorship see: Barrett, *The Pastoral Epistles in the New English Bible*, pp. 4-12; Goodspeed, *An Introduction to the New Testament*, chap. 21; P. N. Harrison, *The Problem of the Pastoral Epistles;* Werner Georg Kümmel, *Introduction to the New Testament*, pp. 258-272; Scott, "The Pastoral Epistles," in *The Moffatt New Testament Commentary*, pp. xvi-xxiii. *For:* Guthrie, *New Testament Introduction*, pp. 584-622; William Hendriksen, "Exposition of the Pastoral Epistles," in *New Testament Commentary*, pp. 4-33; J.N.D. Kelley, "A Commentary on the Pastoral Epistles, in *Harper's New Testament Commentaries*, pp. 3-34; R. D. Shaw, *The Pauline Epistles*, pp. 435-487; E. K. Simpson, *The Pastoral Epistles*, pp. 1-23.

Paul left for Macedonia, he urged Timothy to remain and supervise the work in his absence. That Timothy had been reluctant to accept the assignment, appears from the verb "exhorted" which may also be rendered "urge, request, entreat." Paul had assigned him the task of seeking to check the evil influences being exerted by certain false teachers (1:3-7), to promote the spiritual welfare of the saints through positive teaching, and to give guidance in public worship and congregational organization and life. It was a difficult task, but Timothy had the courage to undertake it at the urging of Paul. Paul was confident that Timothy, because of his years of experience, was able to take care of the difficult situation.

Much misunderstanding has often obscured Timothy's position at Ephesus. He was not the pastor of the Ephesian church, for that church was organized under the leadership of its own elders long before Timothy was stationed there (Ac 20:17-35). Nor was Timothy a bishop with ecclesiastical jurisdiction over the churches in that area. Such a position became a later ecclesiastical development. Rather, Timothy was stationed at Ephesus as the personal representative of the apostle Paul during his absence. As the apostolic representative, his work did not affect the local organization of the churches. We may liken his work to that of a modern missionary superintendent, commissioned to exercise supervision over a group of national churches.

Paul had communicated his charge orally to Timothy when he left, hoping to return before long. When it appeared that he might be detained longer than he had expected (1 Ti 3:14-15), Paul wrote the letter to Timothy to encourage and instruct him. He anticipated that Timothy would face opposition from the heretical teachers and would require written credentials from Paul investing him with the proper authority. The epistle thus provided Timothy with the needed "documentary proof of St. Paul's agreement with himself, and condemnation of the opposing doctrines."[18] Being solicitous for Timothy's effectiveness, Paul also included personal instructions and guidance for Timothy.

An illuminating ray falls upon the picture of Timothy in Paul's passing advice to him, "Be no longer a drinker of water, but use a little wine for thy stomach's sake and thine often infirmities" (5:23).

This bit of fatherly advice reveals that Timothy had a delicate consti-
tution and was battling with recurrent physical infirmities. Conscious
of the impact of his own example, Timothy had been practicing strict
abstention from the use of wine. Concerned for his physical fitness,
Paul gave Timothy this dietary advice: instead of drinking only water,
which is often contaminated, for the sake of your stomach, use a little
wine. This advice illustrates the personal intimacy that existed between the apostle and his dear young associate.

Timothy was apparently still, or again, working at Ephesus when
2 Timothy was written. Again we find Paul imprisoned in Rome
(1:17) and being treated as a dangerous criminal (2:9). The
Neronian persecution was running its fiery course, and, humanly
speaking, the church was trembling on the brink of extinction. Paul
was well aware that Timothy stood alone and awfully exposed in that
hour, needing all the encouragement Paul could offer him. The epistle
was intended to undergird and encourage Timothy in that dark hour.
It is characteristic of both men that in such circumstances, the words
of encouragement and cheer were spoken by the older man, facing
imminent martyrdom, rather than by the sorrowing young friend.

In the loneliness of his dark dungeon, Paul craved to have his
devoted and sympathetic young friend with him again. He therefore
urged Timothy to come to him speedily, giving diligence to "come
before winter" (4:9, 21). Paul's deep yearning for fellowship with
Timothy in the face of impending death also eloquently illustrates the
strong attachment that existed between them. Whether Timothy arrived before Paul's execution is not known.

One last fleeting glimpse of Timothy comes in Hebrews 13:23,
where we read, "Know ye that our brother Timothy hath been set at
liberty; with whom, if he come shortly, I will see you." Due to various unresolved questions concerning the epistle to the Hebrews, the
precise situation revealed in those words is uncertain. The place,
cause, and duration of Timothy's imprisonment, no one knows. But
the words do reveal that Timothy had remained steadfast to the point
of personal imprisonment. The Scriptures do not reveal what finally
happened to Timothy.

CHARACTER OF TIMOTHY

Timothy had a singularly attractive character, as set forth in the

Scriptures. He was a devoted and loveable person, warmhearted, tender, and affectionate. Deeply devoted to his spiritual father and guide, he was happy to work under Paul's wise guidance and instructions. He lacked Paul's bold aggressiveness, and did not have his commanding personality. He evidently was inclined to be timid and somewhat retiring, a feeling increased by his youthfulness (1 Co 16:10-11; 1 Ti 4:12) and his lack of robust health (1 Ti 5:23). But he proved himself a faithful and loyal worker.

Certain interpreters, seizing upon some expressions in the letters to Timothy, especially the second, have attributed certain weaknesses of character and even definite failings to Timothy. Paul's admonitions to him have been taken to mean that he was weak-willed, full of indecision, and prone to be cowardly in the face of danger. They infer from certain statements and admonitions in 2 Timothy, that when Paul wrote, he was no longer quite sure of Timothy. Thus Alford claimed that "there is throughout this Epistle an altered tone with regard to Timothy — more of mere love, and less of confidence, than in the former."[19] It is held that Paul's admonitions indicate that Timothy had experienced a moral declension in the years that he had worked alone and that Paul now felt it necessary to warn him against the temptations of the flesh, the love of money, and a cooling zeal. It is asserted that in the second letter we have echoes of Paul's disappointment in Timothy because "the cement of Timothy's character seems never to have really set."[20]

While no one would claim exceptional strength of character for Timothy, surely such a view misreads the purpose of Paul's fatherly admonitions to his beloved son. Paul's appeals were meant to be preventive rather than corrective measures. They were timely and pertinent in view of the dark future. To encourage our children in the face of difficulty and grave danger, does not necessarily mean that we have lost confidence in them; rather it indicates that we are aware of the dangers they face and desire them to be on guard constantly against the wiles of the devil. That Timothy did have his shortcomings no one denies. But Paul's esteem for Timothy certainly indicates that Timothy was faithfully striving against them and was overcoming them through the grace that is in Christ Jesus.

8

TITUS

2 Corinthians 2:12-13; 7:6-7, 13-14; 8:6, 16-17, 23; 12:17-18
Galatians 2:1-3
Titus 1:5
2 Timothy 4:10

THE NAME OF TITUS is familiar to all Bible readers as one of Paul's young companions and the personal recipient of one of Paul's canonical epistles. Although Titus was considerably younger than the apostle, a close and affectionate relationship existed between the two men. From the difficult tasks that Paul assigned to him, it is clear that Paul considered Titus a capable and trustworthy colaborer, possessing a forceful personality. He was capable, energetic, tactful, resourceful, skillful in handling men and affairs, and effective in conciliating people. Naturally more aggressive than Timothy, he could not only take orders but also take the initiative in the face of challenging circumstances. He breathed the spirit of Paul, and in his conduct, manifested the same unmercenary attitude that characterized Paul. Titus has variously been characterized as "the bridge-builder," "the conciliator," and "a successful trouble-shooter."[1]

The scriptural references to this outstanding man among the companions of Paul are surprisingly rare. His name appears in only four of Paul's epistles and not at all in Acts. The absence of any mention of Titus in Acts has perpetually puzzled the commentators, and they have advanced various hypotheses to account for the silence. Perhaps the most probable suggestion, advanced by Ramsay, Souter, and others, is that Titus was the brother of Luke, the author of Acts.[2]

114

A spirit of self-suppression would lead Luke to omit all mention of his brother's name, even as he did his own, from his history. This attractive suggestion, older than Eusebius, coincides with the conclusion commonly drawn from Colossians 4:10-14 that Luke was a not a Jew. The suggestion finds illustration in the fact that John never mentioned the name of his brother James, and veiled the identity of his mother under the title "his mother's sister" (Jn 19:25). But it must remain a conjecture. The Greek of 2 Corinthians 8:18 cannot properly be appealed to as establishing this view. Lees overstates the evidence when he asserts that it is "plain in the Greek" and renders, "With Titus I sent *his* brother."[3] The Greek, "the brother," may have that meaning, but it is equally probable that it simply designated him as a fellow Christian. Lightfoot's proposed solution that Titus simply was not important enough to deserve mention by Luke,[4] does not commend itself in view of the references to him by Paul in his epistles.

Our rather meager scriptural information concerning Titus conveniently centers around several geographical designations.

ANTIOCH

The first mention of Titus, chronologically, connects him with Syrian Antioch. In Galatians 2:1, Paul wrote, "Then after the space of fourteen years I went up again to Jerusalem with Barnabas, taking Titus also with me." It is commonly held that this visit in Galatians is the same as the trip to Jerusalem for the Jerusalem Conference mentioned in Acts 15:1-4. Some scholars like Bruce, Blunt, and Duncan, equate the visit in Galatians 2:1-10 with the famine visit of Acts 11 — 12.[5] But this makes the burning question of circumcision emerge in acute form long before Acts 15. These scholars have little evidence to marshal, and from the general situation as recorded in Acts, the very idea is improbable.

The controversy which occasioned the Jerusalem Conference originated in Syrian Antioch, and the trip to Jerusalem was made from that city. Thus Titus was a member of the Antiochene church at the time. Since at the time the church considered him old enough to be a "select" representative to the conference, he must have been an active young Christian at Antioch. One may naturally assume that he was a native of Antioch and accepted Christ there as a lad. Paul's designation of Titus as "my true child after a common faith" (Titus 1:4) suggests that he was one of the apostle's converts. The same designation was also applied to Timothy (1 Ti 1:2). Paul's use of the term *child* points to his affectionate regard for Titus, while the adjective *true* or *genuine* acknowledged that Titus ran true to his spiritual parentage. Humphreys' suggestion, that Titus was converted as a lad during the remarkable revival at Antioch under Barnabas and Saul (Ac 11:25-26), is ever probable.[6] Paul kept an eye open for young believers who showed promise of usefulness in Christian service, and the spiritual maturity of his young convert must have delighted him when he and Barnabas returned to Antioch at the close of the first missionary journey (Ac 14:26-28).

JERUSALEM

When the Antiochene church decided to submit to "the apostles and elders" at Jerusalem the vexing demand that Gentile believers must be circumcised, Paul, Barnabas, and "certain others" were appointed to carry the matter to Jerusalem (Ac 15:1-3). From Galatians 2:1-3 we learn that Titus was among those "certain others". Paul's words, "taking Titus also with me," indicate that he was responsible for the inclusion of Titus in the party. Paul deliberately selected Titus because he was "a Greek" (Gal 2:3), an uncircumcised believer in Christ. Paul intended to use him as a test case for his doctrinal position that Gentiles could become good Christians without being circumcised. As LaSor remarks, "Titus was 'Exhibit A' — evidence that could be examined; living proof that a Gentile who had not come under the Law of Moses could still demonstrate the fruits of the Spirit that were the sign of a regenerate man in Christ."[7] There were numerous other uncircumcised believers in the Antiochene church, but the fact that Paul singled out Titus indicates that he was a good specimen of his class.

The presence in Jerusalem of "Titus who was with me" (Gal 2:3) as a member of the party from Antioch, was specially offensive to the Judaizers and stimulated their demand for the circumcision of Gentile believers. Paul's assertion, "But not even Titus who was with me, being a Greek, was compelled to be circumcised," indicates that heavy pressure was exerted to that end. It was demanded by the

Judaizers and favored by compromising brethren who wanted to smooth things over. But Paul steadfastly refused to yield to the pressure, recognizing that "the truth of the gospel" for the Gentiles was involved (v. 5). It would have compromised his position that the Gentiles were saved solely on the basis of faith in Christ without the necessity of submitting to the ritual of the Mosaic law. Thus, the case of Titus provided a specific test for Paul's position, and his view was vindicated by the decision of the Jerusalem Conference not to impose the Mosaic law upon Gentile believers. The significance of this victory, as personified in Titus, can hardly be overestimated for the progress of the gospel among the Gentiles.

Paul's language in Galatians 2:3-5 is quite involved, and the construction is broken. Men have interpreted his words in different ways. Some of the church Fathers understood the passage to mean that Titus was circumcised.[8] The confusion as to its meaning is reflected in the fact that a few manuscripts omitted the negative in verse 5, reading "to whom we yielded the subjection for an hour." This interpretation is advocated by certain modern scholars like Farrar and Duncan,[9] who hold that Paul meant Titus was not "compelled" to be circumcised but that it was done voluntarily, "not an abandonment of principle, but a stretch of charity."[10] But that seems a very forced interpretation of Paul's language. It is out of harmony with the context and contrary to the thrust of the entire epistle. Would Paul have made such a concession on the very point for which he was contending? Thus to surrender to allay controversy would not be a victory.

This view cannot justly be supported by an appeal to Paul's circumcising Timothy at Lystra a short while later (Ac 16:3). Paul circumcised Timothy as a matter of practical expediency, and it involved no concessions to doctrinal principles (see pp. 102-103). But the demand that Titus be circumcised had a strong doctrinal motivation. Involved was the principle of the freedom of the Gentile Christian from the yoke of the Jewish law. Moe remarks.

> If Titus really had been circumcised, it would not afterwards have been easy for the apostle to prove that he had not been forced to take this step. And we can hardly imagine that the clear-thinking Paul out of sheer amiability should have overlooked the likelihood of such a consequence.[11]

EPHESUS

Nothing further is heard concerning Titus for some eight years, until the time of Paul's work at Ephesus during the third missionary journey. Perhaps Titus had continued to work in the church at Antioch, where he had "grown into a man of rare fidelity, reliability and courage."[12] Why Titus does not appear earlier among the active helpers around Paul, is not clear. Ramsay thought that Paul did not actively use Titus during these years because of his "thankless policy of conciliating the Jews."[13] If so, Paul definitely abandoned that policy during his third missionary journey. We have evidence from 2 Corinthians (8:23) that Titus was one of Paul's valued co-workers during the nearly three years of busy ministry at Ephesus (Ac 19:10; 20:31). Just when and where this close association in labor began, we do not know. Paul may have taken Titus along from Antioch at the beginning of the third missionary journey. That Titus had visited the Galatian churches with Paul during the second missionary journey does not necessarily follow from the mention of his name in the Galatian epistle. While Humphreys and others conclude that Paul's mention of his name indicates that Titus was well known to the Galatians, Ramsay asserts that he was "a stranger to the Galatians, whose Greek birth had to be explained to them."[14] Titus anonymously belonged to that group that "ministered unto" Paul (Ac 19:22) during his work at Ephesus.

CORINTH

Titus comes into prominence as an active Christian worker associated with Paul in connection with the church at Corinth. Paul sent him to Corinth as his representative on more than one occasion. Efforts to place in precise chronological sequence the varied contacts of Paul and Titus with the Corinthian church as reflected in 2 Corinthians, meet with difficulty. Proposed reconstructions of the sequence of events have produced great variety. It seems most probable that Titus took three separate trips to Corinth.

During the third missionary journey, a project that occupied much of Paul's thought and effort was the raising of a collection in his Gentile churches for the poor saints at Jerusalem (1 Co 16:1-3; 2

Co 8 — 9; Ro 15:25-28). About a year before the writing of 2 Corinthians, Paul had sent Titus to inaugurate the collection at Corinth (2 Co 9:2; 12:18). Paul's instructions to the Corinthians in 1 Corinthians 16:1-3 indicate that the collection had already been inaugurated at Corinth when that epistle was written. Since the collection had been begun "a year past," when 2 Corinthians was written, clearly only a few months elapsed between the writing of our two Corinthian epistles.[15] Thus apparently Titus made his visit to Corinth to introduce the project of the collection several months before Paul found it necessary to write our 1 Corinthians.

Possibly, Paul sent Titus back to Corinth as the bearer of 1 Corinthians, but it seems more natural to hold that it was taken back by the delegation from the Corinthian church that visited Paul at Ephesus and formed the immediate occasion for the writing of the letter (1 Co 16:17-18). Apparently Titus made a second visit to Corinth at the request of Paul a short time after the writing of 1 Corinthians. Information received at Ephesus concerning further developments in the Corinthian church caused Paul deep concern. He had learned that opponents at Corinth were fomenting active opposition to him in the church (2 Co 10:12-18; 11:22-23; 13:1-3). Paul sent Titus to deal with the trouble. Their plans called for Titus to rejoin Paul at Troas, since Paul planned to engage in missionary work there (2 Co 2:12-13).

When Titus failed to come to Troas as planned, Paul became deeply disturbed and anxious about the Corinthian situation. Because of his anxiety, he had no heart to enter into the opportunity that opened to him at Troas. Anxious to meet Titus, he terminated his stay at Troas and went into Macedonia (2 Co 2:12-13). There, after some further anxiety (2 Co 7:5), he met Titus coming from Corinth with the good news that his mission had been successful, causing Paul's anxiety to be replaced with joy and praise (2 Co 7:6-9). Paul found joy not only at the good news of Titus that the Corinthian church had been brought to repentance and a renewed willingness to acknowledge Paul's apostolic authority (2 Co 7:8-11), he also found encouragement and joy in the joy of Titus himself at the response of the Corinthians (2 Co 7:13-14). Their response had confirmed the hopeful predictions he had made to Titus in sending him. The Corinthians had refreshed the heart of Titus, and he had fallen in love with them. The glad report of Titus was the occasion for the writing of 2 Corinthians.

When Paul requested Titus to return again to Corinth with the letter he had just written and take in hand the completion of the collection which had become stalled at Corinth, Titus accepted the assignment (2 Co 8:6). Not only was he willing to accept the assignment, but Titus was eager to carry out the mission (8:16-17). Two other workers went with him to assist in the completion of the collection before Paul arrived (8:18-22).

In sending this delegation to Corinth, Paul gave Titus, its leader, a strong recommendation. "Whether *any inquire* about Titus, *he is* my partner and *my* fellow-worker to you-ward" (8:23). Anticipating the question of some contentious Corinthian, Paul took care to give Titus his full backing. He was no less than Paul's "partner," his associate in toil and work on behalf of the Corinthians, his "fellow-worker," engaged with Paul in the furtherance of the gospel. Such a man could be trusted not to take any advantage of them (2 Co 12:18). Their past associations with Titus had given them ample reason to trust him. Pointedly Paul reminded the critical Corinthians that Titus was motivated by Paul's own spirit. Like Paul, he too had refused to be maintained by the Corinthians (12:18).

When Paul arrived at Corinth and "spent three months" there (Ac 20:3), the collection had been completed and the difficulties of the church had been resolved. During his stay there, Paul felt free to devote his attention to the writing of his important letter to the church at Rome. But apparently Titus was no longer at Corinth when Paul wrote Romans, for his name does not appear among the group of Paul's fellow workers who sent greetings to the church at Rome (Ro 16:21-23). Neither does his name appear among the delegates chosen by the churches to travel with Paul to deliver the collection at Jerusalem (Ac 20:4; 2 Co 8:19-21). Again for some five years we hear nothing further concerning Titus.

CRETE

Titus again comes before us in connection with the letter that bears his name. We accept the letter as an authentic communication from Paul to Titus. Kee regards the letter as pseudonymous and asserts that the portrait of Titus in the epistle "varies so markedly from the vigorous, resourceful, strong right arm whom Paul pictures in Galatians and II Corinthians" that the letter cannot be accepted as authentic.[16] But such a conclusion seems quite unwarranted from the fact that Paul directed Titus to use "his authority in ecclesiastical, doctrinal, and moral matters"[17] in dealing with the situation on Crete. The epistle was written to Titus to confirm the oral commission Paul had given him, as indicated by the phrase "as I gave thee charge" (1:5). The letter supplemented his oral instructions and formally invested Titus with written authority to act as Paul's agent in the work.

Paul's remark, "For this cause left I thee in Crete" (1:5) clearly indicates that Paul had worked with Titus on that island. Since Luke's account of Paul's activities in Acts leaves no room for this joint work on Crete, the reference must be to a time subsequent to Paul's release from his first Roman imprisonment. Just how long Paul worked on Crete is not known. When he found it necessary to leave, Paul commissioned Titus to remain behind to "set in order the things that were wanting, and appoint elders in every city" (1:5). It was not an easy field of work, because the Cretans' general moral level was deplorable. In his work, Titus must take cognizance of these characteristics (1:6-7, 12-14). He also had the unpleasant task of silencing the deceptive work of the false teachers (1:10-11). In circumstances far from congenial, Titus was directed to use his authority to establish a worthy ministry, overcome opposition, and teach sound doctrine.

The position of Titus on Crete was that of a temporary apostolic legate. Titus was not "the first bishop of the church of the Cretans," as the unauthoritative subscription added to a few late manuscripts has it. For sure, he had only a temporary appointment there, since Paul planned to send a replacement for Titus (3:12). Titus' position might more nearly be compared to that of a modern missionary superintendent appointed to exercise supervision over a number of national churches in a given area. His presence and authority did not alter the organizational setup of the Cretan churches. One of his duties was to help complete and make effective that organization in each church (1:6-10).

The epistle also served to give Titus some personal information. He learned that Paul contemplated sending another worker to replace him on Crete and asked Titus to rejoin him at Nicopolis, apparently the city situated on the southwest promontory of Epirus in Greece. The place would provide a good base of operation from which to launch further missionary work. Paul's request to Titus to come to him there indicates that Paul was formulating further plans for the services of Titus. That Titus came to Nicopolis as requested may be safely assumed.

DALMATIA

We catch our last glimpse of Titus in a passing phrase in 2 Timothy. Paul informed Timothy, "Demas forsook me, having loved this present world, and went to Thessalonica; Crescens to Galatia, Titus to Dalmatia" (4:10). Since Paul was writing from prison in Rome (2 Ti 1:16-17), the natural implication is that Titus had been with Paul during his second Roman imprisonment. That Titus had been with Paul at Rome has generally been taken for granted, but Bourdillon insists that "there is nothing whatever to show that Titus went with Paul to Rome."[18] But he bases his assertion on the uncertain assumption that Paul was arrested at Nicopolis and from there went to Rome as a prisoner.

Paul informed Timothy that Demas had deserted him. Clearly Demas had acted unworthily. But the absence of a separate verb has raised the question whether the censure also extends to Crescens and Titus. Had they also left for an unworthy motive, or did Paul send them? It is highly doubtful that all three men were guilty of the same act of cowardice. Any suggestion that Titus had deserted Paul is so inconsistent with all the previous notices of his character that we can confidently assume that he had courageously gone to Dalmatia at the call of Christian duty. And so we lose sight of this capable and energetic servant of Christ while still actively carrying on the work for his Lord in Dalmatia, modern Yugoslavia.

Part 2

LESSER LIGHTS

9

ANANIAS of DAMASCUS

Acts 9:10-19; 22:12-16

ANANIAS OF DAMASCUS has the distinction of being Paul's first Christian friend and assistant. We hear of him only in connection with one crucial event in Paul's life. On the third day of Saul's fasting and heart-searching prayer which followed his arrest by the Lord on the Damascus road, Christ sent Ananias as His apostle to the future apostle to the Gentiles. Ananias appeared suddenly in that crisis hour to render a vital service to Saul of Tarsus and again as suddenly retired in complete obscurity. It was a favor which Paul deeply appreciated and never forgot.

His Identity

The name Ananias, meaning "Jehovah has been gracious," was common among the Jews and in its Hebrew form, Hananiah, is frequently found in the Old Testament.

Luke simply introduced him as "a certain disciple at Damascus" (Ac 9.10). He made his home in the city of Damascus which had enough Jews residing there to have several synagogues (9:2). That Ananias was not one of the refugees who had fled from Jerusalem because of the violent persecution under Saul, we ascertain from his statement that he had "heard from many" about Saul's activities.

How he came to faith in the Lord Jesus as the Messiah, Luke did not indicate. He may have been one of the Pentecostal converts or may even have been converted during the ministry of Jesus. Paul's

125

insistence in Galatians upon his independence from the apostles agrees with the view that Ananias was converted independently of the ministry of the twelve. Later tradition makes him one of "the seventy" (Lk 10:1), but there is no scriptural evidence for this.

Ananias was not the only Christian in Damascus (Acts 9:14, 19); however, there is no evidence that he was the presbyter of the Christians in the city, as Augustine and others have assumed. There is no indication that he held any official position among the believers at Damascus.

Although a disciple of Christ, Ananias so lived as to hold the full approval of the Jews at Damascus. In his speech to the fanatical mob at Jerusalem, Paul described Ananias as "a devout man according to the law, having a good report of all the Jews which dwelt there" (Ac 22:12, KJV). Paul's description of him tactfully laid emphasis not on his Christian but on his Hebrew character. He was a devout Jew "according to the law," meeting all the Jewish standards for a faithful observance of the Mosaic law. He showed his piety in a blameless observance of the law. This evaluation of his spiritual character was confirmed by all the Jews at Damascus; they esteemed him a most faithful Jew. This picture of Ananias leads Morgan to conclude that he was a Hebrew and not a Hellenist.[1]

Apparently, at Damascus a division between the synagogue and the disciples of Christ had not yet taken place. As earlier in Jerusalem, the followers of Christ still worshiped in the Jewish synagogue. In asking the high priest for letters of authorization to "the synagogues" at Damascus (Ac 9:2), Saul the persecutor still viewed them as Jews. Though they attended the synagogue, like the early Christians in Jerusalem, they maintained Christian fellowship among themselves (cf. 9:19). Ananias seems to have known the identity of the "saints" in Damascus who would feel Saul's wrath. Though he remained faithful to the Mosaic law, Ananias sincerely followed Christ and lived in personal fellowship with his Lord.

When Christ commissioned Ananias to go to the stricken Saul, the two men had not had any previous personal acquaintance. From his objections, it is clear that he knew of Saul only through the reports of others (9:13). Saul's vision of "a man named Ananias" coming to him (9:12) likewise indicates that they were unacquainted.

His Commission

Ananias received his orders "in a vision" (9:10). It may have come in a dream or while he was awake; since no mention is made of sleep, he apparently was awake (cf. Ac 10:3). When the Lord called him by name, Ananias made a quick and ready response, "Behold, I *am here*, Lord." He was on speaking terms with his Lord and at once recognized the divine voice. His reply indicates a readiness to hear and a promptness to obey. The Lord then gave Ananias explicit instructions on where to go and what to do. Ananias had heard of the coming of the notorious persecutor with authority to carry on the grim work at Damascus. He was probably deliberating the prospects with considerable anxiety when he was suddenly told to go to the man himself.

The Lord at once revealed two things to Ananias to encourage him to obey this startling command. He could be sure that a great change had taken place in the persecutor, "for behold, he prayeth." He was now a humble supplicant of divine grace. The Lord further encouraged Ananias to go because He had already prepared Saul for his coming. "He hath seen a man named Ananias coming in, and laying his hands on him, that he might receive his sight" (9:12). This revealed to Ananias that the man was now blind and needed his help. This beautifully illustrates the Lord's practice of working in triangles. While preparing Saul for the coming of Ananias, He was also preparing Ananias to go; but it would take the obedience of Ananias to complete the triangle.

His Difficulty

Christ's commission to him at once raised difficulties for Ananias. He was hesitant and understandably reluctant to venture forth on such an assignment. Unfortunately he knew only too well the fearful notoriety of this man Saul. He had heard from "many" of the fugitives from Jerusalem concerning "this man" and all the evil he had done to Christ's "saints at Jerusalem." He knew further that even "here" in Damascus he had authority to take captive those that called upon Christ's name in worship. Even without modern means of communication, rumors and news spread rapidly in the East. McGarvey suggests that the apostles in Jerusalem "had sent runners ahead of Saul's company to warn the Damascus disciples of the impending danger."[2] A natural dread to meet such a man made Ananias cautious and hesitant.

Ananias frankly laid his difficulty before the Lord, implying that it would be foolish for him to walk deliberately into such a trap. Kelly points out that the freedom of Ananias thus to voice his objections is an exquisite example "of the free intercourse which grace has now opened between the heart of the Master in heaven and that of the servant on earth."[3] Ananias' reaction makes it clear that no word had yet reached him concerning Saul's experience on the road near Damascus. "While evil tidings have swift wings, good news travels slowly."[4]

The reluctance of Ananias was overruled by the Lord. He was told, "Go thy way," although the use of the present tense ("just be going") softened the command. But with the command, the Lord calmed the troubled mind of Ananias by taking him into His confidence in revealing to him the divine purpose concerning Saul's future. He was a divinely chosen instrument who would be greatly used to carry the Lord's name "before the Gentiles and kings, and the children of Israel" (9:15). But his great ministry would be connected with great suffering. "Ananias called attention to 'how much evil' Saul had done to Jesus' saints, Jesus calls attention to 'how much' suffering he will experience in behalf of Jesus"[5] Ananias must have had a magnanimous spirit to overlook the past offenses and go to Saul in his need.

His Ministry

Assured through the Lord's revelation concerning His purposes with Saul, Ananias obediently went to the designated house on Straight Street to carry out his mission. Upon being admitted to Saul's chamber, certainly in the presence of some of the members of the home, Ananias first of all laid his hands on Saul. This act, in fulfillment of the vision granted to Saul, together with his words of address, removed all doubts and misgiving for Saul, and assured him that his prayer was being answered. His words of address, literally, "Saul, brother," manifest the magnanimity of the heart of Ananias. His gracious heart reached out to the now penitent and changed persecutor in the use of the Aramaic form of his name, "Saoul," while his use of the term *brother* with love and tenderness welcomed him as a fellow Christian. He stated his authorization and mission to Saul in clear and precise terms. The Lord Jesus who had appeared to Saul on the way to Damascus had commissioned Ananias to come to him for a double purpose, "that thou mayest receive thy sight, and be filled with the Holy Spirit" (9:17).

The authenticity of his message was confirmed by the immediate restoration of Saul's sight. The fulfillment of the second phase of his announced mission to Saul, a spiritual and inner experience, is not recorded in so many words. That he did receive the filling of the Spirit, the needed equipment for service, is obvious.

After recovering his sight, Paul received, according to his own account of the events (Ac 22:14-15), his apostolic commission from Christ through Ananias. As the Lord's spokesman, Ananias told him, "The God of our fathers hath appointed thee to know his will, and to see the Righteous One, and to hear a voice from his mouth. For thou shalt be a witness for him unto all men of what thou hast seen and heard." The three points of this commission — to know God's will, to see Christ the Righteous One, and to receive God's message for communication to all men — found fulfillment in the ministry of the apostle to the Gentiles.

Following Ananias' urging (Ac 22:16), Saul straightway "arose and was baptized" (Ac 9:18). Plumptre remarks, "It is clear that both Saul and Ananias looked on this as the indispensable condition for admission into the visible society of the kingdom of God. No visions and revelations of the Lord, no intensity of personal conversion, exempted him from it."⁸ The neglect or disparagement of baptism did not characterize the early church. While not explicitly stated, it seems obvious that Ananias baptized Saul.

Through Ananias there was also opened to Saul the door to the fellowship the new Saul craved and found with the Christians at Damascus. "And he was certain days with the disciples that were at Damascus" (9:19b). This fellowship must have delighted both Saul and Ananias. And so Ananias discovered that God is able to turn a dreaded, unpleasant task into an occasion of personal joy and a means of blessing for the world.

Paul's appreciative reference to Ananias more than twenty years later and his vivid description of the man and his ministry to him (Ac 22:12-16), bear eloquent testimony to Paul's undying gratitude to this man who became his first friend as a Christian. It seems clear that Paul must have formed a close friendship with Ananias during the early days of his preaching in Damascus as a zealous young convert (Ac 9:20-22).

10

ANDRONICUS and JUNIAS

Romans 16:7

OF ANDRONICUS AND JUNIAS we have no information other than that contained in Paul's brief but remarkably rich greeting to these two saints living in Rome (Ro 16:7). The meagerness of our information leaves several questions concerning them.

At once, the question confronts us of the exact relation of these two saints to each other. Are they two men or a man and a woman? The problem arises from the fact that the second name may be that of either a man or woman. If the name was "Junia" (KJV), it belongs to a woman, but if it was "Junias" (ASV), it refers to a man. The confusion arises from the fact that both names in the Greek have the same form in the accusative case, as here.

If the name was Junia, she probably was the wife or sister of Andronicus; if it was Junias, the two men were probably brothers. Either is possible, but the joint description of them in the remainder of the verse makes it more probable that Paul sent his greetings to two esteemed men.

Andronicus is a Greek name, but since Paul indicated that he was a Jew, it apparently was a second name in addition to his Jewish name. The name of the second individual is Latin and likewise seemingly was a second name borne by this person. The use of such non-Jewish names was common for Jews of the dispersion. Schnackenburg has little doubt that they were Hellenistic Jews of the Diaspora, and remarks that even if we assign them to the early Jerusalem church, they must be counted "among the 'Hellenists', as their names suggest and their later activity as missionaries confirms."[1]

In sending them his greetings Paul identified Andronicus and Junias in four points, but these are not enumerated in their historical sequence.

KINSMEN

Paul first identified them as his "kinsmen." The term makes it clear that, like Paul, they were of Jewish descent. But it is debatable whether Paul used the term in the narrow sense of his relatives or in the broader sense of his fellow countrymen.

In Romans 9:3, Paul employed the term in its broad meaning when he spoke of "my kinsmen according to the flesh," his fellow Jews. In chapter 16 he applied the term *kinsmen* to six different individuals (vv. 7, 11, 21). Did he simply mean that they were Jews, or was he using it in the narrow sense of his relatives?

Advocates of the narrow meaning point out that Aquila was a Jew (and perhaps also others in this chapter), but Paul did not call him a kinsman. Liddon insists that "the narrow meaning of 'relations' is more natural (S. Mark vi.4; Acts x.24), as also implying a distinction which Jewish birth alone would hardly give."[2] Accepting the view that "kinsmen" means his blood relatives, Miller remarks, "Paul seems to have had a powerful family. Had it been otherwise, he hardly would have been taught by Gamaliel."[3] Of Paul's designated blood relatives, we hear elsewhere only in Acts 23:16.

Advocates of the broader meaning insist that Paul could hardly have had as many relatives in Rome (Ro 16:7, 11) and in Macedonia (v. 21) as this interpretation implies. Thus Zahn asserts, "It is exceedingly improbable that Jason of Thessalonica, Sosipater of Beroea, cf. Acts xvii. 5-9, xx.4, and a certain Lucius (ver. 21), Macedonians sojourning in the neighbourhood of Paul at Corinth, also Herodion (v. 11), Andronicus and Junias (v. 7), were all relatives of Paul."[4] He further argues that the claimed emphasis upon family kinship would have no weight here, that "the uniform lack of particularity in describing the various ties of kinship (Col. iv.10; Acts xxiii.16) would be singular," and that "the separation of the names of the relatives living in Rome (xvi.7, 11) would be incomprehensible."[5] Denney further argues for the broad meaning of the term by insisting that it would be natural for Paul in writing to a church that was mainly Gentile to distinguish those in its membership who were connected with him by bonds of nationality.[6]

It does not seem probable that the term kinsmen should here be used by Paul in the narrow sense of his blood relatives. Nor does the broad interpretation that they were simply members of the Jewish nation seem to account sufficiently for the tenderness and depth of feeling with which Paul applies the designation.

Conybeare proposed that we steer a middle course and "suppose the epithet to denote that the persons mentioned were of the tribe of Benjamin."[7] Ramsay used his vast knowledge to support his view that these "kinsmen" in Romans 16 were members with Paul of the same Tarsian civic tribe to which the Jewish citizens of that city belonged.[8] He felt that such a view adequately accounted for the pride and tenderness with which Paul referred to this relationship.

FELLOW PRISONERS

Paul next identified Andronicus and Junias as "my fellow-prisoners." The term is to be taken literally and implies that somewhere they shared imprisonment with Paul for their faith in Christ. Paul counted it a glorious reminiscence that they had thus suffered with him. His own sufferings for the Lord in the line of duty made him deeply appreciate what it meant.

Paul's terminology pictures their imprisonment under the figure of captives of war. As soldiers of Christ, they had shared the hardships of gospel warfare and suffered capture for His cause. Paul indeed regarded it as a high distinction, "as the most glorious crown of these men."[9]

We have no information as to when and where their imprisonment with Paul occurred. Sanday and Headlam insist that Paul's statement does not necessarily indicate that they had suffered imprisonment at the same time with Paul.[10] But Denney thinks that this is the natural implication of his words.[11] The end of the verse may indicate that it was during the time before Paul began his missionary tours. Zahn suggests that Andronicus and Junias had fled to Syrian

Antioch as refugees from Jerusalem (Ac 11:19) and while active in the mission there with Paul, had been cast into prison with him.[12]

ESTEEMED PEOPLE

Paul further characterized Andronicus and Junias as belonging to that class of people "who are of note among the apostles." This somewhat ambiguous statement concerning their distinguished position has been interpreted in two ways. It may mean that they themselves were distinguished apostles, or that they were highly respected among the apostles.

The former view takes the term *apostles* in its wide meaning as messengers sent forth or commissioned. Barrett, who accepts this view as "much more probable," renders "who are notable in the ranks of the apostles."[13] Sanday and Headlam support this view with three arguments: 1) it was so taken by all patristic commentators; 2) it best agrees with Paul's words, "who are of note among the apostles;" 3) it is in accordance with the wider use of the term.[14] That the term *apostles* was used of others beside the twelve is clear from Acts 14:4, and 14, where it is used of Barnabas.

According to this view, Andronicus and Junias belonged to the primitive Christian community and had apparently received their commission from the Lord Himself, perhaps being among the seventy.[15] They were among the early preachers of the gospel and had won distinction among this larger group of gospel messengers.

Others insist that Paul does not designate Andronicus and Junias as apostles, but means rather that they have received special commendation from the apostles themselves. Paul's cautious use of the term *apostle* makes it difficult to believe that he thought of a class of people who were called apostles, large enough to include two otherwise unknown persons like Andronicus and Junias. Lenski contends that it is unwarranted to imagine such a large host of "apostles" and then put these two notable members in that group.[16] Zahn asserts that "'the apostles' alone means, in Paul's mouth, the original twelve (Gal. i.19; 1 Cor. xv.7)."[17] When Paul used the term of others, he added a qualifying genitive (2 Co 8:23; Phil 2:25). When used of Barnabas in Acts 14:4 and 14 it retains its basic meaning of "one commissioned and sent," with Paul for missionary work by the Antioch church.

Paul's use here of the term *the apostles* seems rather to point to the well-known group of the twelve, while his expression "in the circle of the apostles" (*en tois apostolois*) indicates quite naturally the circle where Andronicus and Junias had received recognition. They had won this recognition and prominence by their active cooperation with the apostles. This seems the more probable view.

EARLY CONVERTS

Paul's last note of distinction concerning these two esteemed friends is that they "also have been in Christ before me." As early converts they had come to be "in Christ" before him. Paul's expression instructs us concerning the essence of being a Christian. "The Christian life is conceived of, not simply as an assent to the doctrine of Christ, but as incorporation with — existence in — Christ, as the sphere of the New Life."[18]

Paul never mentioned when Andronicus and Junias became converted. They may have accepted Christ at Pentecost. Surely they were already Christians while Paul was still furiously active in persecuting believers in Jerusalem. Stifler thinks that Paul must have recalled the bitterness of spirit he felt when, as persecutor of the saints, he learned that these two kinsmen of his had accepted Christ.[19]

Because of their association with the church at Jerusalem from very early times, Andronicus and Junias were among the "early disciples" (cf. Ac 21:16), and therefore held venerable places in the eyes of the believers. Paul gladly ascribed this distinction to them. Yet it seems that as he wrote that, Paul envied them. Maggs thinks that "there came to him a sinless envy of their priority."[20] Paul now realized that being "in Christ" was the most enviable human condition and regretted his blind failure to see it sooner. He now rejoiced that these two kinsmen of his had chosen early the blessedness of a life of love and service for the Lord Jesus.

11

ARISTARCHUS

Acts 19:29; 20:4; 27:2
Colossians 4:10
Philemon 24

ARISTARCHUS, an intimate and valued companion of Paul, faithfully shared his labors, travels, and hardships. His name, meaning "best-ruling," is a common Macedonian name. It occurs five times in the New Testament, each time of a close companion of Paul. Assuredly, the references all relate to the same man. Our few glimpses of him reveal an attractive individual of whom we might wish that we knew more.

IMPERILED WORKER

Aristarchus first enters the scene in Acts 19 in connection with Luke's graphic account of the riot of Ephesian silversmiths under the instigation of Demetrius (vv. 23-41). When the aroused but confused mob rushed into the theater, they forcibly took with them "Gaius and Aristarchus, men of Macedonia, Paul's companions in travel" (v. 29). Just where the silversmiths seized the two, we do not know. They may have been seized at their lodgings when some of the mob went in search of Paul, but more probably they accosted them on the street. Obviously they were recognized as Paul's companions. The crowd's purpose in apprehending them is anyone's guess, but clearly it was a dangerous situation for the two men. Fortunately, they were not harmed by the confused, leaderless mob (v. 32).

Luke appended a twofold identification in naming the men. He referred to them as "men of Macedonia," which was the first of the two Roman provinces in which Paul worked on the second missionary journey. According to Acts 20:4 and 27:2, Aristarchus came from Thessalonica. He apparently was the fruit of Paul's ministry in that city, clear evidence of the permanent results that had been achieved. It is a curious fact that each time Luke mentions him in Acts, he is identified as a Macedonian (19:29), a Thessalonian (20:4), or as both (27:2). It may suggest that he was a well-known individual in that area.

Luke further described the two men as "Paul's companions in travel" (v. 29), although he did not precisely define the term. Ramsay held that it pointed forward to 20:4, "as we have no reason to think that either Gaius or Aristarchus had hitherto been companions of Paul on a journey."[1] But Plumptre holds that the designation implies "missionary activity beyond the walls of Ephesus, in which they had been sharers."[2] These two men had probably traveled in various parts of the province of Asia spreading the gospel under Paul's direction (cf. 19:10), but there is no evidence that Paul had traveled with them in this work.

COLLECTION BEARER

In Acts 20:4, Aristarchus is named in a group of seven men who traveled with Paul. They were the appointed representatives of the various churches, chosen at Paul's request to travel with him in taking to Jerusalem the collection his churches gathered during the latter part of the third missionary journey (Ac 24:17; 1 Co 16:1-4; 2 Co 8 — 9). That Aristarchus and Secundus represented the Thessalonian church indicates that Aristarchus was a trusted and esteemed member of the assembly in Thessalonica.

While not expressly stated, it may be assumed that the entire delegation traveled with Paul all the way to Jerusalem. This agrees with the fact that Luke's "we" section, of which this list of names is a part, continues until Paul's arrival in Jerusalem (Ac 20:4 — 21:17). Then Aristarchus personally observed the stirring events in Jerusalem which culminated in Paul's arrest and imprisonment.

MARITIME TRAVELER

Nothing is known concerning Aristarchus during the two years that Paul was a prisoner in Caesarea (Ac 24:27). Probably he was among the friends who ministered to Paul during that time (24:23). When the governor decided to send Paul to Rome for trial before the imperial court (Ac 25:12), Luke and Aristarchus began the long sea journey with him from Caesarea (Ac 27:2). Clearly they were not fellow prisoners, but their precise status in making the trip with Paul has provoked much discussion. Ramsay, as the chapter on Luke brought out, says that they went along as Paul's slaves, thus enhancing Paul's importance in the eyes of the Roman centurion. David Smith warmly supports the suggestion. Bruce comments that Ramsay's suggestion "merits the respect due to his great knowledge of social history in the Roman Empire of the first century A.D." But Carter replies that "it might be suspected that Ramsay unconsciously read into the narrative more of the aristocratic cultural influence of the British society of his day than the known facts of the case would warrant." Lenski pointedly asks whether Paul would have stooped to such a pretense to gain a standing in the eyes of the centurion and insists that the two companions would be permitted to accompany him without such a pretense; the treatment accorded Paul by the two Roman governors clearly showed "Paul's importance and standing in the eyes of the Roman authorities."[3] Farrar thinks that these two men traveled with Paul at their own expense or with money provided "for that purpose by Christians, who knew how necessary was some attendance for one so stricken with personal infirmities as their illustrious Apostle."[4] In any case, Paul deeply appreciated the presence and fellowship of these men on the trip.

The presence of Aristarchus is not further noted at any point during the entire journey to Rome. Lightfoot suggests that he probably departed from the group at Myra on his way home to Thessalonica.[5] But the concensus is that Aristarchus, like Luke, went all the way to Rome with Paul. Since both he and Aristarchus receded into the background during this journey, Luke found no occasion to make special mention of Aristarchus during the trip.

PRISONER'S COMPANION

Aristarchus spent with Paul at least part of the time that he was a prisoner in Rome. Paul included the name of Aristarchus in the circle of friends who sent their greetings to the Colossian church (Col 4:10-14) and to Philemon (vv. 23-24). In Colossians, Aristarchus' name stands first, "Aristarchus, my fellow-prisoner saluteth you" (4: 10); and to Philemon, Paul wrote, "Epaphras, my fellow-prisoner in Christ Jesus, saluteth thee; *and so do* Mark, Aristarchus, Demas, Luke, my fellow-workers" (vv. 23-24).

In grouping Aristarchus with Mark, Demas, and Luke as his fellow-workers" (Phile 24), Paul gratefully acknowledged his active cooperation in the extension of the gospel through personal effort. He stood loyally with Paul in his aggressive propagation of the message of the gospel.

Paul's designation of Aristarchus as "my fellow-prisoner" (Col 4:10) is high commendation. Did Paul mean that Aristarchus was also physically a prisoner? If so, the incident in Acts 19:29 does not explain the designation. Lightfoot suggested that "the most probable solution would be, that his relations with St Paul in Rome excited suspicion and led to a temporary confinement."[6] But this seems remote, since in the letter to Philemon, written at about the same time, Paul does not apply the title to Aristarchus but uses it of Epaphras instead. What probably happened was that Aristarchus and Epaphras voluntarily alternated sharing Paul's confinement. Then the title expressed Paul's grateful recognition of the restrictions they voluntarily endured for his sake.

This honorable designation for these two companions probably arose out of Paul's view of the Christian life as a spiritual warfare. His use of the prefix *sun*, rendered "fellow," united them with him in that warfare. Nowhere else did Paul use the term here rendered "prisoner" of his own imprisonment, but always *desmios*, "a prisoner in fetters." The term here, used strictly, means a captive taken in war, which was literally true neither of Paul nor his two co-workers. Thus he probably used the term metaphorically to denote that jointly they were soldiers in the army of Christ, enduring the consequences of their aggressive offensive against the enemies of Christ.

Paul's grouping of the men in Colossians 4:10-14 raises the question of the racial background of Aristarchus. Was he a Jew or a Gentile by birth? In verses 10-11 Paul grouped Aristarchus with Mark and Jesus called Justus, and added "who are of the circumcision." The most natural reading of the passage is that Aristarchus was a Jew. If he was not a Jew, it would have been more logical to group him with the three Gentiles named in verses 12-14. But Norris figures that the designation "who are of the circumcision" must be restricted to the last two men, if this Aristarchus is also the Aristarchus of Acts.[7] He feels that Luke's identification of Aristarchus as a Macedonian means that he was a Gentile. That Paul had two such intimate companions named Aristarchus is highly unlikely. It would seem that Luke's designation implies that Aristarchus was a Gentile. The factors do not readily agree. Possibly Luke's stress upon the fact that he was a Macedonian may mean that Aristarchus' connection with that province was well known, without indicating his racial background. Perhaps he was born a Gentile and became a Jewish proselyte before becoming a Christian.

12

DEMAS

Colossians 4:14
Philemon 23-24
2 Timothy 4:10

DEMAS IS A RARE INSTANCE of those around Paul whose name has had a lasting stigma attached to it because of his tragic failure. And because his case is so singular, his name is well known, although it appears only three times in the New Testament. Demas' name is typically Greek, and is probably a shortened form of the name Demetrius. From Paul's grouping of the names of his companions with him when he wrote the letter to the Colossians (4:10-14), we assume that Demas was a Gentile and not a Jewish believer.* Probably, he came from Thessalonica.

Demas appears in the Pauline circle only during the latter part of Paul's life. He was among the companions of Paul during the apostle's first Roman imprisonment as well as the later imprisonment seen in 2 Timothy.†

FELLOW WORKER

The presence of Demas as a companion of Paul comes out in two of the prison epistles, which are commonly accepted as having been written during Paul's first Roman imprisonment. He sent greetings with other Pauline associates in the letters to the Colossians and to

---

* See pp. 64-66.
† On the evidence for the two different Roman imprisonments see Hiebert, *Introduction to the Pauline Epistles*, pp. 311-312; 319-324.

Philemon. In Philemon 24, "Mark, Aristarchus, Demas, Luke, my fellow-workers" send their personal greetings to Philemon. Naming Demas between Aristarchus and Luke indicates that he was an accepted member of that intimate circle around Paul whose presence cheered Paul in his imprisonment. The further fact that he was included in the designation "my fellow-workers" indicates that Paul acknowledged Demas as actively engaged with him in the service of Christ.

In the letter to the Colossians, written about the same time as the letter to Philemon, Paul wrote, "Luke, the beloved physician, and Demas salute you" (4:14). Many diligent readers have noted that in verses 10-14, Paul named six men who sent greetings, but that Demas was the only one of the group to whom Paul did not apply any epithet of commendation. David Smith saw in this a sign of Paul's "evident coldness" toward Demas, and Ramsay concluded that it revealed Paul already doubted the "thorough trustworthiness" of Demas.[1] Such conclusions from the absence of any commendation for Demas are ingenious but conjectural; these scholars read into the situation an inference based on something that occurred some three years later. Lenski objects to such an inference concerning Paul's attitude toward Demas, with the remark that it is "decisively excluded by Philemon 24, his name there even appearing between Aristarchus and Luke."[2] One suggested explanation for the absence of any commendation for Demas is that he acted as Paul's amanuensis when Paul dictated the letter to the Colossians. After penning the greetings from the others, Demas may have asked to add his own greetings; and when Paul approved the request, he simply added the words "and Demas." This too is an ingenious conjecture that cannot be proved. Note that in both letters Paul mentioned Demas next to Luke. Clearly, Paul thought of the two men side by side. If Paul already harbored suspicions concerning the trustworthiness of Demas, it is difficult to understand why he would name Demas in the same breath with Luke.

Act of Desertion

Nothing further is known of Demas until about three years later. The tragic last mention of Demas occurs in 2 Timothy, which Paul wrote shortly before his death while again a prisoner in Rome (1:17;

2:9). In this last letter to Timothy, Paul requested him to come to him at Rome (4:9) and at once explained his reason for his request, "For Demas forsook me, having loved this present world, and went to Thessalonica; Crescens to Galatia, Titus to Dalmatia. Only Luke is with me" (4:10-11). Paul needed Timothy, because, except for Luke, he was all alone. The poignant words, "Demas forsook me," make it clear that Demas had been with Paul at Rome during the earlier part of his imprisonment. The verb "forsook," in the aorist tense, simply stated the historical fact but left no doubt that Paul was keenly disappointed in the action of Demas and felt that it was unjustified. The compound verb carries the idea of abandoning someone amid adverse circumstances. Demas had let Paul down, left him in the lurch. The explanatory statement to Timothy arose out of a heart that yearned for companionship in his dark dungeon. (According to tradition, Paul was confined in the underground Mamertime Prison.)

Paul grieved at Demas' departure because of his motive, "having loved this present world." The ingressive aorist indicates that Demas had "fallen in love with this present world," the present age with its alluring pleasures and treasures, standing in contrast to the invisible, future world as centered in the hope of the returning Christ. Paul remarked that Demas had come to love this present age, probably intending to mark the contrast between Demas and those "that have loved his [Christ's] appearing" (2 Ti 4:8).

Paul's statement did not charge Demas with having forsaken Christ; his action was interpreted in his relation to Paul personally. Nor do his words form a sure foundation for the idea that Demas lapsed into apostasy, as tradition later asserted. More likely, Demas temporarily fell from his steadfastness; his courage failed to face the dangers that seemed inevitable if he continued in close association with Paul in that hour. Although Paul had escaped immediate condemnation during his first appearance before the imperial court (2 Ti 4:16-17), the attitude of the court assured Paul that he could not expect acquittal. Demas immediately saw the implications for himself. "Paul was a dangerous friend to company with. Nero had burst forth into mad fury, and the Christians bore the brunt of his murderous mania."[3] Concerned for his own safety and lacking the personal fortitude to face the dangers resolutely with Paul, Demas decided to leave

Paul and the city of Rome. He determined to escape the undesirable consequences of an uncompromising stand with Paul as the servant of Christ. The weight of such a cross was more than he felt that he could bear. His concern for security in the present world had blurred his vision of that glorious future kingdom, for which Paul willingly endured the severest afflictions.

Having decided to break his ties with Paul, Demas "went to Thessalonica." He may have gone there for various reasons. It may well have been his home; he felt that he would be safer there than in Rome. On the basis of the fact that the name Demetrius occurs twice in the list of politarchs at Thessalonica, Boyd indeed conjectured that Demas abandoned "the hardships and dangers of the Apostle's life and returned to Thessalonica, where his family may have held positions of influence."[4] Kelly more realistically surmised that he went there "to carry on Christian work in a region where a more friendly reception could be expected."[5] The view that he went to Thessalonica to take advantage of its inviting commercial opportunities rather than to continue Christian work is a conjecture connected with his assumed apostasy.

The known story of Demas closes with this dark blot on his name. We have no evidence that he later overcame his tragic weakness and failure. Some have indeed suggested that he may have have been the Demetrius whom John commended as having "the witness of all *men,* and of the truth itself" (3 Jn 12), but this seems doubtful. Both the name and the time interval are against the charitable suggestion.

The desertion of Demas stands in striking contrast to the unwavering loyalty of Luke, who in that dark hour steadfastly remained at Paul's side. Demas had the wonderful opportunity of showing himself a staunch friend to the most worthy of friends in this crisis, but he failed to stand the test. He lacked the stuff of which heroes are made, and so he failed Paul in his time of deep need. "There is no place of honour for Demas; he will ever bear the odium of the fickle, but Luke has gained the distinction of the loyal!"[6]

13

EPAPHRAS

Colossians 1:7-8; 4:12-13
Philemon 23

Among all the friends and co-workers of Paul, Epaphras holds the unique distinction of being the only one whom Paul explicitly commended for his intercessory prayer ministry. With Paul he had entered into a vital realization of the tremendous possibilities of working by prayer. So aggressively did he devote himself to this work while with Paul at Rome, that even Paul, the apostle of prayer, was impressed. Colossians 4:12-13 may well be called his diploma of success in this ministry.

All that we know about Epaphras comes from references to him in the apostle's twin letters, Colossians and Philemon, sent to the city of Colosse by the hand of Tychicus. His name occurs but three times in these letters (Col 1:7; 4:12; Phile 23), and only five verses in all have reference to him. Yet these limited references provide an attractive picture of this prayer warrior. They reveal that his Christian character and faithful pastoral labors eminently qualified him for his intercessory ministry.

WORK AT COLOSSE

In Colossians 1:7, Paul named Epaphras as the one through whom the Colossian believers had first heard the wonderful message of the grace of God. He was the first messenger of the gospel to them, "even as ye learned of Epaphras." The word *also* (KJV) lacks adequate textual support and is best omitted. Epaphras did not merely add to the story which they already knew; he was the original messenger from whom they came to learn the truth of God's redeeming grace. People were won to faith in Christ through his ministry, and the Colossian church was founded.

Paul was not directly involved in the founding of the church at Colosse (2:1), but its origin appears to be directly related to the time of his ministry at Ephesus during the third missionary journey. From Acts 19:10 we learn that the work of evangelization, which had its center at Ephesus, spread throughout the province of Asia. As the metropolis of Asia, visitors from all parts of the province thronged Ephesus, coming for business, worship, and pleasure. Many of these visitors while in Ephesus came into contact with the gospel, were saved, and carried the message of salvation back to their homes. Paul's assistants went into various parts of the province to further and consolidate the victories of the gospel.

It would appear that Epaphras, while on a visit to Ephesus, came into personal contact with Paul, heard the glorious message of the gospel, and accepted Christ as his own Saviour. Epaphras revealed himself an eager and apt pupil of Paul and won the apostle's love and esteem. Having come to know personally the wonderful story of salvation in Christ, Epaphras soon felt that he must share it with his neighbors and friends at home. Soon he found himself back again among his old friends but with a new message of salvation on his lips.

In Colossians 4:12, Paul referred to Epaphras as "one of you." The expression, identical with that used of Onesimus in verse 9 above, indicates that Epaphras was a native, or at least a permanent resident, of Colosse. He had the grace and the courage to witness faithfully to his own people. His preaching resulted in the formation of the Colossian church, apparently also the churches in the neighboring cities of Laodicea and Hierapolis (4:13). But apparently he was careful to make it clear that he had received his knowledge of the gospel from Paul and was himself dependent upon Paul for instruction and guidance. Since they were thus his spiritual grandchildren, Paul felt a deep interest in and responsibility for the believers at Colosse.

PAUL'S APPROVAL

Paul's references to Epaphras made it clear to the Colossians that he fully approved and supported the teaching and work of Epaphras. Paul described the one through whom they had heard the gospel as "our beloved fellow-servant, who is a faithful minister of Christ on our behalf" (1:7). Paul's double designation described Epaphras in relation to himself and to Christ. Personally he gladly acknowledged Epaphras as "our beloved fellow-servant." Paul warmly loved Epaphras, who was zealously engaged with Paul in the service of their Master. Paul placed Epaphras on a level with himself as equally the servant of Christ, belonging to Him and doing His bidding.

Paul further characterized Epaphras as "a faithful minister of Christ on our behalf." The manuscripts vary between "our" and "your," but the reading "on our behalf" is much better attested and more significant. It clarifies why Paul had such a deep personal interest in the work at Colosse. Epaphras had not undertaken an independent enterprise; he had gone with the full support of Paul and as his representative. Since Paul had felt that he could not leave his fruitful work at Ephesus, he had commissioned Epaphras to minister on his behalf. In his work there, he had shown himself "a faithful minister of Christ." He had proved himself "a faithful minister," rendering voluntary service to others for their benefit. Above and beyond Paul's commission was the fact that Epaphras belonged to Christ and actively furthered His cause.

Apparently Epaphras continued on as the shepherd of the flock at Colosse. He thus stood in an intimate relationship with the Colossian believers; he was the founder and spiritual teacher of the church there. As such he had the hearty approval and support of Paul.

CONFERRING WITH PAUL

When Paul wrote to the Colossians, some five years or so had passed since the founding of that church. In the meantime, Paul had been taken a prisoner while in Jerusalem, and he was now a prisoner in Rome. Recently an insidious new teaching had begun to manifest itself in Colosse. It was a subtle teaching, which puzzled and lured the believers, threatening to make havoc of the work that had been accomplished. The new teaching claimed to be Christian but was undermining the gospel by robbing Christ of His unique nature and authority. Epaphras felt himself unable to refute this heresy effectively. Naturally he had a strong desire to present the problem to Paul and seek his able guidance. Undaunted by the long journey that was demanded, he made his way to Rome, and in due course found himself again in the company of his beloved teacher.

In making his report to Paul, Epaphras gave a favorable account of the general conditions of the church. As he had been faithful in declaring to them the truth as he had learned it from Paul, so now he faithfully presented the situation at Colosse to Paul. Thus Paul assures them that Epaphras "declared unto us your love in the Spirit" (1:8). He reported the spiritual growth of the members and their steadfastness (1:6; 2:5-6). But his report also contained information about the new teaching at Colosse which filled the mind of Paul with deep anxiety for them (2:1-4), an anxiety which Epaphras fully shared with him. Having informed himself concerning the true nature of the new teaching as described to him by Epaphras and having given himself to earnest prayer and thought about it (1:9; 2:1-3), Paul determined to write his letter to the Colossian church. That letter was the fruit of the pastoral concern of Epaphras for his people.

GREETING HIS PEOPLE

The letter to the Colossians was taken to its destination by Tychicus (4:7). As the letter was being concluded, Epaphras eagerly joined Paul's other companions in sending his personal greetings to his people at home (4:12). Although he was absent from them, his love for them had not diminished; he had a deep spiritual affinity with them. It was that very pastoral concern for them that explained his presence with Paul at Rome.

Clearly Epaphras did not return to Colosse with the letter. Different explanations for his continued stay in Rome have been suggested. Some think he did not stay voluntarily but that he had been temporarily imprisoned. In Philemon 23, Paul referred to Ephaphras as "my fellow-prisoner." Robertson holds that the phrase is best understood literally and suggests that because of his close relations with Paul at Rome, Epaphras "fell a victim to the Roman hostility to Paul."[1] But in Colossians 4:10, this honorable title was withheld from Epaphras and given to Aristarchus, while in Philemon 23 Aristarchus was simply called a fellow worker. Perhaps the two men voluntarily alternated in sharing Paul's confinement. Very likely Paul used the title "my fellow-prisoner in Christ Jesus" in a metaphorical sense. In using this title of Epaphras, Paul indicated that both of them were soldiers in the army of Christ and were enduring the hardships involved in their warfare for Christ.

In appending the greeting of Epaphras, Paul again paused to give him an honorable designation, "a servant of Christ Jesus" (Col 4:12). His stay in Rome did not mean that he no longer served Christ. The designation paid a high tribute to Epaphras. It is a title that Paul several times used of himself, and he used it once of Timothy in conjunction with his own name (Phil 1:1). Epaphras is the only other individual whom Paul called "a servant of Christ Jesus." He belonged to Christ as His "servant," literally, "bondservant." The term implies not the compulsory service of a slave but rather the fact that he had wholly given himself to do his Master's will. Significantly, in all three places where his name occurs, it is always employed in direct relationship to Christ.

Having come such a long distance to confer with Paul, Epaphras apparently wanted to stay longer with Paul to learn more from him, to be better able to serve his people upon his return. In the meantime, he was engaged in a very significant service for them.

INTERCEDING FOR SAINTS

While absent from his beloved brethren in Christ at Colosse, Epaphras continued to remember them in his prayers. "The best scene of memory is at the throne of grace."[2] The fact that he gave himself to prayer for them while absent from them was the true index of his spiritual concern. His activity was prompted by his love for them. Love finds its highest employment in praying for those it loves. Prayer is the noblest service that Christian love can render.

Epaphras was quite unable to write the epistle to the Colossians refuting the error that threatened them, but he could earnestly pray for them. Paul gratefully told the Colossians that Epaphras was serving them through the potent ministry of prayer. He was "always striving for you in his prayers" (4:12). "Always" assured them that it was not just an occasional, listless asking. Ceaselessly he bore them up before the throne of grace. He carried a constant burden of intercession, "always striving for you in his prayers." "Striving" stresses that it was a strenuous and costly activity. The term comes from the athletic arena and pictures the intense effort and energy of the athlete in contending for a prize, like a wrestler grappling in all earnestness with his opponent. It is the verbal form of the noun *agony*, which Luke used to describe Christ's prayer in Gethsemane (Lk 22:44). Epaphras engaged in "a mighty and continual wrestling of heart."[3] The expression makes clear the difficulty of effective intercessory prayer. "True prayer is the intensest energy of the spirit pleading for blessing with a great striving of faithful desire."[4]

His praying was definite, "always striving for you." Epaphras knew exactly for whom he was praying and what he wanted for them. He had the Colossian saints prominently on his heart, and he kept them prominent in his prayers. He was aware of the dangers that threatened them, and he prayed accordingly. Although separated from them, his pastoral heart constrained him to continue to pray for them.

Behind this exertion lay the high ideal of his pastoral hope, "that ye may stand perfect and fully assured in all the will of God" (Col 4:12). This result Epaphras expected from his prayers. He well realized the possible disastrous results if the heretical teaching at Colosse went unchecked. But Paul's statement of the prayer aim of Epaphras indicated that he was not merely concerned with their preservation from error but rather for the positive, balanced development of their Christian character.

Epaphras prayed for the establishment of the Colossians. His desire for them was that they "may stand perfect and fully assured." "May stand" is more literally "be made to stand," or "be established." Threatened as they were by the attacks of heresy, it was important that they be strengthened spiritually, so that they would be able to stand unharmed in spite of the snares of the false teachers and the open opposition of the forces of evil.

Such stability would increase as they became spiritually mature and fully assured of the truth of the gospel. His concern was for their maturity of Christian character and their thorough understanding of God's will. "In all the will of God" marks the area in which their stability would manifest itself. Lightfoot translates the phrase "in everything willed by God."[5] He desired that each separate detail of the will of God would be the object of their attentive consideration and implicit obedience. Beet comments,

> Epaphras prayed that his converts might know without doubt whatever God would have them do and be, that every element of His will might be realized in their spiritual growth, and that thus they might maintain their spiritual position.[6]

Epaphras' high aim for his people reveals the high level of his spiritual life. His costly intercessory labor for them manifested his true attitude toward them. "Souls are precious in the sight of the pleader when for their sake he counts not the pain of such intercession too great a price to pay for their perfecting!"[7]

TESTIMONY OF PAUL

Having described the prayer ministry of Epaphras, Paul added his own testimony confirming the reality of that ministry. "For I bear him witness, that he hath much labor for you, and for them in Laodicea, and for them in Hierapolis" (Col 4:13). Paul wanted to unveil the heart of Epaphras to his people to assure them that their leader had their highest interests at heart. It confirmed the fact that he had left them to consult with Paul about their situation only because of his deep concern for them. It would allay suspicions and assure them that they were right in following Epaphras in taking a stand against those teaching heresy.

Ever since Paul had heard about the condition of affairs at Colosse, he too had given himself to definite intercession on their behalf (1:9; 2:1). Epaphras had fully entered into that prayer struggle with Paul. He "was Paul's true scholar in the school of intercession."[8] The apostle delighted to witness Epaphras' prayer labors and gladly testified to their reality.

Paul's testimony touched both the strenuousness and the scope of the prayers of Epaphras. Their strenuousness Paul set forth by the comment that "he hath much labor for you." The word rendered "labor" occurs only here in the writings of Paul. (The rendering "a great zeal" in the KJV is based on an inferior variant reading.) The word carries the idea of great effort, toil, or strenuous exertion. Trench remarks that it denotes "labour such as does not stop short of demanding the whole strength of a man; and this is exerted to the uttermost, if he is to accomplish the task which is before him."[9] Paul knew from personal experience that effective praying is hard work.

The scope of his prayers was stated in the words, "for you, and for them in Laodicea, and for them in Hierapolis" (4:13). He prayed not only for the Colossian believers but also for those in the neighboring cities. All three cities were located in the Lycus valley, had close contacts with each other, and could all be visited in one day. All these believers faced the same insidious heresy, and Epaphras felt an equal concern for them all. The churches in all three cities were apparently the fruit of his labors, and he felt himself responsible for them. This also manifests the true shepherd's heart of this man of prayer.

Someone has pointed out the remarkable fact that he had never seen a church dedicated to St. Epaphras. Does that not bear sad witness to the fact that only too few Christians have adequately realized the tremendous posibilities of intercessory prayer, and consequently have failed to appreciate and follow his example?

14

EPAPHRODITUS

Philippians 2:25-30; 4:18

We know Epaphroditus only through a few weighty sentences in Paul's letter to the Philippian church concerning one of their own number. They give a deft portrait in miniature of this gallant Macedonian co-worker of Paul. His name means "charming," and he well deserved his name.

Background

Epaphroditus may have come from a pagan background. The name, a common one in the Roman period, is formed from the name Aphrodite, the Greek goddess of love and beauty.* It may well be that his parents were devotees of the cult of Aphrodite.

The name offers another instance of a Christian continuing to be known by his pagan, pre-Christian name. Apparently the early Christians felt it unnecessary to drop such names because of their associations with idolatry. They were more intent upon the spiritual realities of life. When and how Epaphroditus was converted is not known. That he came to Christ through Paul is a good guess.[1]

"Epaphras" was a common, contracted form of "Epaphroditus." But there is no valid reason to identify the Epaphroditus of the Philippian epistle with the Epaphras of Colossians (Col 1:7; 4:12). Beside their different backgrounds in Scripture, the name in either form was too common to warrant such an identification.

---

* Jews who assumed Greek names carefully abstained from such names as directly involved the titles of heathen gods.

153

The precise status of Epaphroditus in the Philippian church is not mentioned. That he was a recognized and trusted member of the assembly we can ascertain from the assignment given to him. But did Epaphroditus hold ecclesiastical office? Moe accepts that he was "probably a bishop or deacon (cf. Phil. 1:1)."[2] Farrar calls him "a leading presbyter of the Church of Philippi."[3] And quaint old John Trapp, speaking of the return of Epaphroditus, adds, "It is not meet that a pastor be long absent from his people. A godly minister when he is abroad is like a fish in the air; whereinto if it leap for recreation or necessity, yet it soon returns to his own element."[4]

But no positive evidence exists that Epaphroditus was one of the presbyters of the church (1:1). The view cannot be substantiated from Paul's designation of him as "your apostle" (Phil. 2:25, Gr.). Paul's use of the term in the context only identified him as the official messenger of the Philippian church.[5] Kennedy further points out that Paul's designation of him as his "fellow-worker" does not prove that he was even in the ministry.[6]

We may assume that the church recognized Epaphroditus' spiritual leadership, but that he held an ecclesiastical office cannot be proved. Stevenson thinks that Epaphroditus "was apparently not a leader but just one of the members of the Church at Philippi, chosen for this mission to Paul because of his zealous desire to be of service to his fellow-believers and to the apostle."[7] Whatever his exact status, it is certain that Epaphroditus was a trusted and zealous member of the Philippian church.

COMMISSION

When the Philippian saints learned of Paul's imprisonment in Rome, their thoughtfulness toward him blossomed anew, in that they prepared to send him another offering (4:10, 15-16). When the question of the transmission of the collected funds arose, Epaphroditus doubtless volunteered to make the long and arduous journey to Rome to deliver them. Fully aware of the integrity and dependability of the man, the church gladly accepted his offer. But Epaphroditus was not allowed to go simply as a private agent; he was solemnly commissioned by the whole church as their "messenger and minister" to Paul's need (2:25).

The position of Epaphroditus in the mission, in relation to the church, is indicated by Paul's designation of him as "your messenger and minister" (2:25). The word rendered "messenger" is literally "apostle"; but it was used here in its wider sense to denote him as their commissioned representative through whom the whole church spoke and acted[8] (cf. 2 Co 8:23). The word *messenger* (*leitourgos*) denotes one who performs a public service, usually of a religious nature, such as the ministries of a priest.[9] His use of the term indicates that Paul thought of Epaphroditus as performing a priestly service on behalf of the Philippian church in conveying their sacrificial gift. Herklots justly concludes, "The language suggests that Epaphroditus was specially and solemnly commissioned by the Philippian Church before he left as their envoy to St. Paul."[10]

Paul's high view of the Philippians' gift brought by Epaphroditus is fully expressed in 4:18 where he acknowledged it. He assured them that he had "received from Epaphroditus the things that came from you, an odor of a sweet smell, a sacrifice acceptable, well-pleasing to God." He regarded their gift as an offering laid upon the altar of God, as wholly acceptable and well-pleasing to Him. Such a gift from his beloved church brought by such a man as Epaphroditus deeply touched Paul's heart.

In informing them that he had received their gift in full, Paul mentioned only Epaphroditus as its bearer. So, most writers generally assumed that he came alone. But Lenski contends that in harmony with the customary practice in transmitting funds, Epaphroditus would be accompanied by companions in travel.[11] He thinks that Paul sent his official thanks back to the Philippian church by these companions when they returned home. This would seem to explain why Paul did not mention their gift until the end of the letter.

Paul's language concerning Epaphroditus makes it clear that there was a further phase of the commission given him by the Philippian church. Not only was he sent with the money but was commissioned to remain with Paul in Rome as his personal attendant as long as he might be needed. That Epaphroditus was expected to remain with Paul is evident from Paul's statement, "I counted it necessary to send to you Epaphroditus" (2:25). Although they had intended for him to stay with Paul, Paul informed them that he was returning at Paul's initiative. "Hence, Epaphroditus had been sent both to *bring* a gift, and *to be* a gift from the Philippians to Paul."[12] The service of Epaphroditus was to be an official and sacred service, not only to Paul but also to God. It was for the church a means of continued "fellowship in the furtherance of the gospel" (Phil 1:5).

Having presented to Paul the offering from the church, Epaphroditus zealously gave himself to the second phase of his commission. Not only did he seek to provide companionship to Paul in his confinement but also aggressively assisted him in "the work of Christ" (2:30) at Rome. He thus became the personal bond between the apostle and his beloved Philippian church. As their representative, he sought to do what they would gladly do for Paul if they were able. His presence made up for Paul the one deficiency he felt in their gift, the lack of their personal presence (2:30).

SICKNESS

But even the most unselfish plans of God's devoted saints may go awry. The zealous Epaphroditus fell sick, prostrated by a sickness that proved nearly fatal. Its seriousness Paul indicated in his report, saying that he was "sick nigh unto death," being for a while literally "alongside of death as a neighbor" (2:27). For a while, death camped at his side, and the fate of Epaphroditus hung in the balance.

The nature of the sickness, we never find out, but Paul indicated its ultimate cause by saying, "Because for the work of Christ he came nigh unto death, hazarding his life to supply that which was lacking in your service toward me" (2:30). Certainly we could not accuse Epaphroditus of indifference or laziness in carrying out his commission.

Precisely what Paul meant to include in the expression "the work of Christ" is not certain. Some think that this refers to the long, hazardous, exhausting journey he made to Rome. More probably it refers to his zealous activities at Rome. His sickness apparently was the result of imprudent overexertion in the work there. But the journey very probably contributed to the undermining of his physical resources. The messenger incurred sickness in the course of the aggressive performance of duty. Lightfoot concludes that his "illness was the consequence not of persecution but of over-exertion."[13]

Paul's reference to Epaphroditus as "hazarding his life" is a strong expression. It occurs only here in the New Testament. (The reading in the KJV, "not regarding his life," is based on a different reading in the Greek manuscripts.) It is a gambler's word, denoting the taking of venturesome risks for the sake of possible gain. "He hazarded his life, risking his health with the reckless prodigality with which a gambler risks his gold."[14]

RECOVERY

The recovery of Epaphroditus from his prostrating sickness came gradually. His words express Paul's recognition of "man's helplessness in sickness and God's complete control of sickness and recovery."[15]

Paul saw in the recovery not only God's mercy to Epaphroditus but also to himself. God granted it that Paul "might not have sorrow upon sorrow" (2:27). The death of his beloved friend would have been a further sweeping wave of sorrow overwhelming a heart already grieved at the sufferings of Epaphroditus. As Calvin remarks, "He does not boast of stoical apathy as if he had been insensible and exempt from human affections."[16] The Scriptures never hint that it is spiritual for a believer to look coldly and with aloof detachment upon the sufferings and death of friends.

The slow recovery of Epaphroditus indicates that Paul could not perform miracles of healing at will. If he did, he certainly would have healed his afflicted friend. "Even in that charismatic era the apostles could not perform miracles whenever they felt so inclined. *Their* will was subject to *God's* will."[17] Such miracles were granted as confirmation of the divine nature of the apostolic message (Heb 2:3-4) and were not given indiscriminately. The apostles seem never "to have considered themselves at liberty to exercise them in their own immediate circle, or for any ends of personal happiness."[18] A survey of the New Testament evidence leads Stewart to point out that Paul "never healed a Christian; he used that power always for the Gentiles, barbarians, the unsaved."[19] Vine further remarks, "The theories that God wills that believers should have strong healthy bodies, and that failure to obtain healing is necessarily a sign of lack of faith, or of yielding to evil spirits, or that sickness is always caused by sin, are all refuted by the case of Epaphroditus."[20]

RETURN

Paul spoke in glowing terms of Epaphroditus, whom he was sending back to Philippi. He declared his own close relations to him by
calling him "my brother and fellow-worker and fellow-soldier" (2:25).
His "my" goes with all three terms which are united under one article
in the original. Arranged in an ascending scale, the three picture an
ideal Christian relationship. "Brother" unites them in a fellowship of
faith, for they are brothers in the Lord; "fellow-worker" unites them
in a partnership of toil, working in the furtherance of the gospel; and
"fellow-soldier" unites them as comrades in arms, jointly engaged in
combat with the forces of evil. With this honorable testimony to him,
Paul set forth the essence of the high ministry for which Epaphroditus
enlisted in coming to Rome. Paul said nothing finer of any of his
other companions in toil.

Paul indicated three reasons for his decision to send Epaphroditus
back home. The first relates to Epaphroditus himself. He had decided
to send him back "since he longed after you all, and was sore troubled,
because ye had heard that he was sick" (2:26). His decision was
prompted by his personal solicitude for Epaphroditus.

News of the sickness of Epaphroditus had reached his home
church and had occasioned deep concern for him. "This feeling on
their part," Howson observes, "was a sure indication that he was
worthy of their love and esteem."[21] (The past tenses in vv. 25, 28 are
epistolary aorists, the writer placing himself at the time the readers
will read the letter.) And Epaphroditus in turn was well aware that
they were anxious about him. It deeply distressed him that his trouble
was troubling them. He realized that his sickness disappointed them,
since it made him unable to help Paul as they had intended in sending
him. In fact, he must have felt he was an added burden on Paul's
hands and therefore longed to be home again. Paul's statement that
Epaphroditus "was sore troubled, because ye had heard that he was
sick" (Phil 2:26) does not require that a messenger from Philippi had
returned to report their reaction, as is often assumed. Paul knew that
the report had reached Philippi, either through companions who had
come to Rome with Epaphroditus or through some other companion.
Reicke holds that "Paul did not have to wait for confirmation of their

having received this news, but rather counted on the speedy circulation of such news by faithful brethren."[22] And Epaphroditus keenly anticipated what their reaction to that report would be.

Since Epaphroditus had sufficiently recovered to make the return trip, Paul determined to send him back "the more carefully," better, "more quickly," sooner than he would have otherwise. A verdict in Paul's case by the imperial court was impending (2:23), so that the much appreciated services of Epaphroditus would not be needed much longer.

Paul's second reason for the return of Epaphroditus was his concern for the Philippian church. Knowing their own anxious feelings about their ailing representative, he was sending him back "that, when ye see him again, ye may rejoice" (2:28). His return would cause their hearts to rejoice that the recovered Epaphroditus was again safely in their midst.

Paul mentioned his own consideration as a third reason for the return. He was bidding his valiant helper to return home in order "that I may be the less sorrowful" (2:28). The relief experienced by the Philippians because of the presence of Epaphroditus, as well as their joy at the good news which he would give them of Paul's impending release, would give him a feeling of relief. He could not say that the return of this devoted helper made him rejoice, but it would make his own burden lighter, leaving him "less sorrowful."

To assure for Epaphroditus a hearty reception by the church, Paul requested the Philippians, "Receive him therefore in the Lord with all joy; and hold such in honor" (2:29). Purposefully, Paul sent him back in the triumphal dress of his own personal esteem and hearty recommendation. They were to receive him in the spirit in which Paul sent him and give him a cordial welcome.

Paul seemed to be carefully forestalling any criticism of Epaphroditus for returning. There was no reason for any feeling of chagrin or resentment at his return; rather, he had earned a right to the warm esteem of the saints. He deserved not only a warm welcome but the appropriate honor due those who have rendered hazardous service in the cause of the Lord (2:30).

Epaphroditus apparently felt reluctant to act upon Paul's suggestion that he return, feeling that he had not fully carried out his commission. But Paul firmly overruled all his objections by insisting that he return and that he take a message to them from Paul. And so Epaphroditus became the happy bearer of Paul's precious letter of love and friendship to the Philippians. And Epaphroditus himself was a worthy representative of the warm relationship that existed between Paul and his devoted Philippian friends.

15

ERASTUS

Acts 19:22
Romans 16:23
2 Timothy 4:20

THE NAME ERASTUS occurs three times in the New Testament, each time as that of a companion of Paul. Each occurrence relates to a wholly distinct occasion in the apostle's life. The name, which is Greek, was quite common. It means "beloved" or "lovely."

ASSISTANT TO PAUL

Acts 19:22 says that near the close of his work at Ephesus on the third missionary journey, Paul "sent into Macedonia two of them that ministered unto him, Timothy and Erastus." He sent them on ahead of him so that they could assist the churches in making up the collection before Paul's arrival. First Corinthians 4:17 and 16:10-11 implies that Paul intended that Timothy at least should proceed on to Corinth. His recorded plans do not include Erastus.

Erastus is described as being among those "who ministered unto" Paul. The term *ministered* denotes the performance of any kind of service to another; the present tense indicates an habitual service. Erastus thus was one of Paul's steady assistants in the work, ready to carry out any assignment given him. In thus performing necessary tasks, he served Paul in the execution of his missionary endeavors.

THE CITY TREASURER

In concluding his letter to the Romans, written from Corinth on the third journey, Paul named "Erastus the treasurer of the city" (Ro

16:23) as sending greetings. The designation indicates that Erastus held an office in the city of Corinth. It implies that he had a fixed residence in Corinth, and thus belonged to the Corinthian church.

Paul's identification of Erastus as "the chamberlain" (KJV) or "the treasurer of the city" (ASV) (*ho oikonomos tēs poleōs*), indicates that his friend's office carried managerial responsibility of some sort in connection with the public affairs of Corinth. When used in connection with a private estate, the term (*oikonomos*) referred to the steward or manager who supervised his master's affairs (Lk 16:1).

Erastus was the steward or manager of Corinth's business affairs. Robertson calls him "the city manager."[1] The rendering "the treasurer" (ASV) places him in charge of the financial transactions of the city. Vincent thought that he probably was "the administrator of the city lands."[2] Whatever his precise assignment, Erastus obviously held a position of importance and dignity.

Paul's designation marked Erastus as a man of some political and social distinction in Corinth. His membership in the Corinthian church confirms Paul's statement in 1 Corinthians 1:26 that there were some of the upper classes in the church (cf. Ac 18:8). Haldane remarked that this reference to his office "shows us that Christians may hold offices even under heathen governments, and that to serve Christ we are not to be abstracted from worldly business."[3]

In 1929, archeologists working at Corinth uncovered a Latin inscription on a reused paving block, dating from the first century, which read, "Erastus, commissioner for public works [aedile], laid this pavement at his own expense." While agreeing that this Erastus may be Paul's friend, Bruce points out that the two public offices were not the same. He suggests that Erastus "had presumably been promoted to the city treasureship from the lower office of 'aedile' by the time Paul wrote" Romans.[4]

Is "Erastus the city treasurer" (Ro 16:23) the same man as Paul's assistant (Ac 19:22)? Views differ. McGarvey accepts the identification without question and remarked that Paul had sent Erastus as well as Timothy as far as Corinth "because, being the treasurer of Corinth, that was his home."[5] But this is highly improbable since the Erastus of Acts 19:22 was a constant attendant upon Paul; while the city official would scarcely be able to absent himself thus for a long time from his work.

Liddon seeks to support the identification by suggesting that Erastus had "given up his civil office, in order to devote himself to the Apostle, and is called *oikonomos tēs poleōs,* as having occupied the office in former years."[6] But no evidence remains that he had resigned his office when Paul wrote Romans. The context rather indicates that he held the office at the time of writing.

Duncan proposes to identify the two men with the suggestion that Erastus had become treasurer of Corinth since he had been sent to Corinth by Paul by way of Macedonia.[7] But such a rapid rise to influential office in the city of Corinth by a traveling Christian preacher is highly unlikely. Since Erastus was quite a common name, there is no need to resort to such expedients in the attempt to identify the two men. Paul's assistant (Ac 19:22) is best distinguished from the city treasurer of Corinth (Ro 16:23).

PAUL'S TRAVEL COMPANION

A third occurrence of the name Erastus is found in 2 Timothy 4:20. Writing from his Roman dungeon, Paul informed Timothy of the men who had been with him as his companions. He said, "Erastus remained at Corinth." The reference is to Paul's movements just prior to his second Roman imprisonment.

The companion referred to was the same as the Erastus of Acts 19:22. Since he is mentioned without any further identification, we may assume that Timothy would know at once that Paul meant his well-known companion in travel.

Only a hasty assumption would make the city treasurer of Corinth this man also, simply because Paul said that he remained at Corinth. If he were one and the same, the remark becomes quite pointless. We could accept the identification only on the unlikelihood that the city treasurer had later given up his office and associated himself with Paul as his close companion in travel.

16

EUODIA and SYNTYCHE

Philippians 4:2-3

EUODIA AND SYNTYCHE, two prominent and energetic ladies in the church at Philippi, are known to us because Paul appealed to them to be reconciled. "I exhort Euodia, and I exhort Syntyche, to be of the same mind in the Lord" (4:2). The form "Euodias" in the King James Version transforms the first name into that of a man,* but both names are clearly those of women. This is required by the use of the feminine pronoun "them" (*autais*) in verse 3, which must refer to the two people named in verse 2. The rendering "those women" in the King James blurs the reference.

Euodia and Syntyche were influential, of high character, and well known in the Philippian church. That they were deaconesses, like Phoebe (Ro 16:1), is an unsupportable guess. They had rather common but beautiful names. Euodia means "prosperous journey" and Syntyche "fortunate."

STANDING DISAGREEMENT

Unfortunately, misunderstanding and disagreement had developed between these two Christian women. For some unstated reason, open differences had developed and harmonious relations between them no longer prevailed. No doctrinal matters which demanded Paul's corrective action were involved. Gibb surmises, "They may have represented different types of piety, or may have differed on

---

* In the accusative case in the Greek, as here, the masculine "Euodias" and the feminine "Euodia" have the same form.

some question of church life."[1] As aggressive individuals, they apparently failed to understand each other's viewpoint; perhaps they disagreed on their methods of service. Apparently it was essentially a clash of strong personalities.

Whatever the cause for their disagreement was, it had become chronic, being of long standing and of common knowledge in the church. Their bickering had cast a shadow over the life of the church. But in a church as pure and wholesome as the Philippian church, even such a comparatively minor matter would be noticed. Epaphroditus, the bearer of the Philippian offering (4:18), had informed Paul about the trouble.

The needed admonition which Paul addressed to these two women was kindly and considerate. His verb of appeal (*parakaleō*), which literally means "to call alongside of," is here perhaps best rendered "appeal to" (Berkeley) or "urge" (NASB). Moule pointed out that "exhort" (ASV) was not tender enough while "beseech" (KJV) was rather too tender.[2] Paul's repetition of the verb with each name avoided the slightest appearance of favoritism and placed them on the same level. But it implied that they were both responsible for the estrangement, although both might not have been equally guilty. Paul endeavored, as it were, to confront each woman personally with his appeal. "So to speak, he takes one by his right hand, and the other by his left, in order to draw them together in Christian reconciliation."[3]

Paul avoided all elaboration of the nature of their difficulty, nor did he resort to negative commands. His earnest appeal to them "to be of the same mind in the Lord" sought rather to solve their difficulty by taking it into the solemn sanctuary of the Lord's presence, where they would find the true secret of Christian accord. "Paul does not desire a union of minds *apart from* Christ."[4] Their quarrel would dissolve itself if they brought it into His presence, and as their Master, gave Him His proper place in their relations with each other.

ASSISTANT NEEDED

Paul realized that the relations between Euodia and Syntyche had come to a place where outside help was needed. He therefore appealed to a third party to "help these women" (v. 3). He was to come to their aid and assist them in effecting a reconciliation. Robertson remarks that the verb, which strictly means "to take hold together with," clearly implies "that Euodia and Syntyche wanted to lay aside their differences, but found it somewhat embarrassing to make a start."[5] Paul treated their disagreement as an infirmity that needed help rather than a grievous fault to be roundly condemned.

PAST LABORS

Paul stressed that these women eminently deserved the assistance he was asking for them. While deploring their present quarrel, he remembered their past brave service. They belonged to that worthy group of believers who had been his co-workers in the past. He recalled that "they labored with me in the gospel, with Clement also, and the rest of my fellow-workers." The rendering "labored" does not adequately bring out the force of the original, which implies united action in the face of opposition and strife. This metaphor emerged from the arena, and pictures these women as having served as Paul's fellow soldiers in the battle to establish the gospel at Philippi. They rendered effective and much appreciated service in the spread and confirmation of Christianity there. That does not mean that they preached, but they were of special assistance in the furtherance of the work among their own sex. Women had a prominent place in the Macedonian churches.

Paul deplored the present failure of Euodia and Syntyche to work together in harmony. They were not maintaining their past record. His reminder that in the past they had worked in splendid cooperation with him and his other fellow workers implied that with a little assistance they would again be able to work in cooperation and harmony. Their present disagreement unfortunately blemished their otherwise excellent record.

17

GAIUS

Acts 19:29; 20:4
Romans 16:23
1 Corinthians 1:14

THE NAME GAIUS was the Greek form of the Latin Caius, a very common name among the Romans. "So common was it that it was selected in the Roman law-books to serve the familiar purpose of John Doe and Richard Roe in our own legal formularies."[1] The name Gaius appears in the New Testament referring to four separate individuals, three of whom were companions of Paul. (The Gaius to whom 3 John was addressed had no known connections with Paul.)

GAIUS OF CORINTH

Chronologically, the first occurrence of this name in connection with Paul is 1 Corinthians 1:14. There Paul mentioned that he had personally baptized Gaius, a member of the Corinthian church. It was a departure from Paul's usual practice not to baptize his converts himself (1 Co 1:14-17). Since he was mentioned in the same breath with Crispus, the converted "ruler of the synagogue" (Ac 18:8), the implication is that Gaius was a convert of some importance. Goodspeed identified Gaius with the Titus Justus of Acts 18:7, whose home Paul used as a preaching center after the synagogue was closed to him. Bruce thinks that "there is much to be said in favor of" this identification.[2] Thus Gaius became an important friend of Paul during the apostle's work at Corinth on the second missionary journey.

When Paul wrote the letter to the Romans from Corinth during the third missionary journey, he was lodging with a fellow Christian named Gaius (Ro 16:23). Since this Gaius was an established resident of Corinth, it seems obvious that he was the same man whom Paul had baptized. When Paul returned to Corinth, he gladly opened his house to the apostle.

In conveying the greetings of Gaius to the Roman Christians, Paul identified Gaius as "my host, and of the whole church" (16:23). This brief comment illustrates Paul's ability to characterize a man accurately in a single sentence. Paul pictures Gaius as a man noted for his liberal and extensive Christian hospitality. If Gaius was an elder in the Corinthian church, he admirably fulfilled the requirement that elders must be "given to hospitality" (1 Ti 3:2). It also presupposes that he had some wealth. Clarke well observed that Gaius "must have been a person of considerable property to be able to bear this expense; and of much piety and love to the cause of Christ, else he had not employed that property in this way."[3] That the Gaius to whom 3 John was addressed had this same characteristic is not sufficient ground for any identification of the two. Surely such Christian hospitality was not that rare. The time interval between them makes the identification improbable.

Paul paid tribute to the hospitality of Gaius by his double designation, "my host, and of the whole church." The precise significance of the second phrase has received various interpretations. Perhaps he opened his home as the assembly place for the Corinthian church. Arnold thought that this was "the most natural interpretation of these words."[4] Others think it may mean that Gaius graciously opened his home to the large concourse of Christian visitors who flocked to his house while Paul was there.[5] Still others think that it referred to his well-known practice of showing hospitality to Christian travelers whenever they came through Corinth. Then Paul was "alluding, with graceful hyperbole, to the hospitality which he was always ready to exercise."[6] As the personal recipient of his gracious hospitality, Paul deeply appreciated its practice by Gaius as so often commended in his writings.

Gaius of Macedonia

Acts 19:29 mentions in passing a Gaius who associated with Paul during the latter part of his work at Ephesus on the third missionary journey. When the devotees of Artemis (Diana) were stirred to mob action by Demetrius, before rushing into the theater, they seized two Christians, "Gaius and Aristarchus, men of Macedonia, Paul's companions in travel." Whether they seized these men when they encountered them on the street or seized them because they could not find Paul, is not indicated.

"Men of Macedonia," literally, "Macedonians," designates them as to their place of origin. Both men were doubtless the fruit of Paul's previous missionary labors in that province. Following the reading of a few late manuscripts, some scholars suggest that the term *Macedonians* should be singular and limited to Aristarchus.[7] Such limiting would make it possible to identify this Gaius with "Gaius of Derbe" (Ac 20:4), but it lacks manuscript authority.

"Companions in travel" is an expression found elsewhere in the New Testament only in 2 Corinthians 8:19, where it designates the delegates appointed by the churches to travel with Paul in the matter of the collection for the poor saints at Jerusalem. Its use here in Acts 19:29 may anticipate Acts 20:4, where the delegates are named. But at the time of Acts 19:29, the Macedonians had not yet made their collection (2 Co 8:1-4; 9:2-4) or appointed their delegates. Probably the expression generally denotes Paul's companions on his varied journeys. But we have no information that Gaius had previously traveled with Paul.

GAIUS OF DERBE

Among the seven men mentioned in Acts 20:4 as traveling with Paul was "Gaius of Derbe." They were the church-appointed bearers of the collection that Paul had asked his Gentile churches to raise during the preceding two years. Apparently the entire group went with Paul all the way to Jerusalem, but this is not certain. The problem phrase "as far as Asia" (Ac 20:4) is omitted by some ancient manuscripts. When retained, it has various interpretations.[8]

"Gaius of Derbe" links this companion in travel with the province of Galatia (Ac 14:20-21); so we must distinguish him from the Gaius of Macedonia (Ac 19:29). This has raised difficulty for interpreters, since most of them feel that the two men should be the same. This feeling is even reflected in the variant readings of the manuscripts.

One attempted harmonization suggests that the text should be repunctuated to make Gaius one of the Thessalonians (with Aristarchus and Secundus), joining "of Derbe" with Timothy.[9] In favor of this is the fact that in Acts 19:29, Gaius was associated with Aristarchus as a Macedonian. But to be natural, this suggestion would require a change of conjunctions in the original, which is unwarranted. Furthermore, in Acts 16:1, Timothy seems clearly associated with Lystra rather than with Derbe.

Others accept as the right reading that found in Codex D, "a Doberian."[10] Doberus, a Macedonian town, lay about twenty-six miles from Philippi. This would bring Acts 20:4 into harmony with 19:29 as referring to a Macedonian. As the more unusual reading, some have considered it the original, but it lacks the weight of manuscript authority, and is best regarded as an ancient scribe's attempt to harmonize the text. The accepted text thus connects this Gaius with the town of Derbe, where Paul and Barnabas preached on the first missionary journey (Ac 14:21). He may well have been Paul's convert there.

18

LYDIA

Acts 16:13-15, 40

LYDIA MAY APTLY be characterized as a businesswoman with an open heart and an open house. "The open heart reveals her receptivity; the open house her generosity."[1] Both aspects are prominent in Luke's brief account of this remarkable woman. She was a shrewd and sagacious businesswoman whose deepest interests extended far beyond her commercial transactions and the material things of life. Due to her keen interest in religious matters, her contacts with Paul brought her into a vital knowledge of spiritual things. She became one of Paul's enthusiastic supporters.

Lydia's name appears in Scripture only in connection with Paul's initial missionary work in the province of Macedonia. She was his first convert at Philippi. Luke introduced her as "a certain woman named Lydia, a seller of purple, of the city of Thyatira" (Ac 16:14). It has been suggested that her name originally was an adjective, "the Lydian woman."[2] In Philippi she may have gone by this designation, since she came from a city located in the ancient kingdom of Lydia. But more probably, Lydia was her personal name.

That it was a common female name in Latin literature[3] explains Luke's introductory formula, "a woman named Lydia," as well as the fact that he named Thyatira as her place of origin. Her name offers no valid basis for the conjecture of Rackham that Lydia "may have been a freed woman."[4]

171

BUSINESS ACTIVITY

Lydia had established a successful business in Philippi when Paul and his missionary party arrived there. She was "a seller of purple, of the city of Thyatira." Luke joined the mention of her business with her native city because the two were closely connected. Thyatira, located in the Roman province of Asia, was famous for its purple dyeing. Inscriptions mention its guild of dyers. The costly purple dye was obtained from the shellfish *Murex trunculus.* The dyed woolen fabrics were in great demand among the rich in the ancient world. The official toga of Rome and its colonies was made of this material. As a "seller of purple" Lydia dealt in the bright purple material imported from Thyatira. As a Roman colony (Ac 16:12), Philippi offered a brisk market for her goods. These costly purple fabrics apparently constituted her chief item of business, but she probably also sold less expensive materials.

Lydia obviously was a woman of considerable wealth. She had a house in Philippi which was large enough to accommodate four missionaries in addition to her own household. A number of her employees probably resided with her. Also, Lydia's business would require a considerable financial investment.

Besides being an intelligent and capable businesswoman, Lydia was an active and influential individual in the community, as well as the head of her own household. She may have been single, but more probably she was a widow carrying on the business of her deceased husband. Her position and influence evidence the comparative freedom enjoyed by women in Macedonian society.[5]

RELIGIOUS INTERESTS

Although successful in business, Lydia had deep religious interests. Luke identified her as "one that worshipped God" (Ac 16:14). It is Luke's usual expression for Gentiles who had been drawn to the worship of the God of Israel. This devout woman "had recognized the insufficiency of paganism, and had found a measure of contentment in Judaisms's pure and lofty monotheism."[6] Since no strong Jewish colony had formed in Philippi, her commitment to the God of Israel must have dated back to her earlier life in Thyatira. That city had a strong

Jewish colony, while the pagan practices there were notoriously cor-
rupt. Lydia's yearning for religious truth and purity drew her to the
Jewish synagogue, where she became convinced that the teaching of
Judaism revealed the true God. Wholeheartedly, she gave herself to
follow the light that she had found there.

When business took her to Philippi, Lydia did not lay aside her
religious commitment to the true God. Faithfully she identified herself with the few worshipers of the God of Israel residing in the city.
Loyally she closed her place of business on the Sabbath day to join
with a few others at the "place of prayer" (v. 13). They met outside
the city on the bank of a stream, apparently the Gangites river, about
a mile west of the city.[7] The word rendered "place of prayer"
(*proseuchē*) often designated a synagogue building.[8] But that does
not seem to be its connotation here. Every *proseuchē* was not necessarily a synagogue. Jewish regulations required the presence of at
least ten men for the organization of a synagogue. Luke's reference
to "the women" who had assembled implies that the needed men for
an organized synagogue were not available. The place where the
women assembled may have been a hall, an enclosure open to the sky,
or even a grove at the edge of the river. Perhaps they selected the
place out by the riverside because of its convenience for their ceremonial ablutions.

Of the women assembled, Luke identified only Lydia. Some of
them may have been Jewish women married to Gentiles, but probably
most of them were proselytes like Lydia. Some of the women gathered
may have been in her employment. Since they had no synagogue to
attend in Philippi, they assembled at their "place of prayer" for prayer
and fellowship.

Very probably Lydia led this group. She faithfully lived up to
the spiritual light that she had. That fact opened the way for her to
receive God's full revelation. Paul found her "not in the market place
or house of business, but rather in the place of prayer."[9]

PREPARED HEART

The arrival of the missionary party at the place of prayer must
have surprised the women. But when the visitors made known their
status and purpose, the women welcomed them and gave them an

opportunity to speak to the group. Luke's remark that "we sat down, and spake unto the women" (v. 13) suggests that no formal synagogue service was attempted. It was an informal discussion meeting in which the various members shared. "Spake" is the imperfect tense and pictures the conversation in progress. "At first all took part, but by-and-by the interest centered in the words of Paul."[10]

Something in Paul's message sharply drew Lydia's attention. She "heard us" — continued to listen with keen interest. She had a sincere interest in religious things, and the message unfolded by Paul appealed to her mind. But more was needed to bring her to an experiential knowledge of the gospel message. As she listened, "the Lord opened" her heart. This implies that the natural heart is blind to the spiritual realities of the gospel and that its spiritual illumination is exclusively the work of God. The divine work in her heart made the message attractive and vital to Lydia, and she eagerly drank in the facts presented by Paul. All innate resistance to a personal commitment to that message was overcome as the conviction of the truth gripped her very being. In faith she committed herself to Christ, as instructed by Paul. The renewal in her heart was the work of the Spirit of Christ, but the means used was the faithful presentation of the Word of God by the missionaries. In leading human hearts to saving faith in Christ, God's messengers must never resort to any other means to bring about that result.

PUBLIC TESTIMONY

It is not certain that Lydia was converted during that first meeting of the missionaries, although that seems very probable; but there does seem to have been a definite time interval between her conversion and her baptism. This is inferred by the fact that following her baptism, Lydia appealed to the fact that the missionaries had considered her "faithful to the Lord." "This judgment was formed either tacitly or openly on the ground of the whole conduct of Lydia even before her baptism."[11] In subsequent meetings, the nature and significance of Christian baptism was presented. Lydia doubtlessly expressed her desire to identify herself openly with the Christ whom she had accepted by faith. She gladly bore public testimony in baptism

to her new experience of having been united with Christ by faith in
His death and resurrection (Ro 6:1-4).

But Lydia was not baptized alone. "She was baptized, and her
household" with her. "So genuinely converted and so influential was
her life that her entire household followed her in baptism."[12] As the
head of her home, she set an example that made it easy for the others
to follow. The spiritual blessing that her conversion had brought to
her heart permeated every area of her domestic life.

GRACIOUS HOSTESS

Following her baptism, Lydia at once urged the missionaries to
accept the hospitality of her home. Luke preserved the very formu-
lation of her request, "If ye have judged me to be faithful to the Lord,
come into my house, and abide there" (Ac 16:15). Her conditional
statement of the request reflected delicate modesty, but the assumed
reality of the condition used contained a challenge. She challenged
them to accept her hospitality as proof that they had regarded her
faithful to the Lord in baptizing her. If she was fit to be baptized,
was she not fit to be their hostess? To refuse her hospitality would be
to cast doubt upon the reality of her conversion.

Her offer of hospitality was based on the fact of her personal relationship to Christ Jesus. Providing a home for the missionaries gave
her an opportunity to serve Christ. It would enable her to demonstrate her own gratitude to the Lord in good works. "She had always
been busy, she would remain so. But now the things of the kingdom
would come first."[13] She had a heartfelt yearning to serve those who
had brought the blessings of the gospel into her own heart and home,
and thus assist them in their missionary work.

Luke's comment, "She constrained us," makes it clear that Paul
was reluctant to accept the offer. His reaction was prompted by higher spiritual considerations. "For the sake of the freedom of the gospel
S. Paul was very reluctant either to lay himself under obligation to
his converts or to expose himself to the charge of interested motives."[14]

But Lydia insisted. "She constrained us" quite literally means,
"She forced us." It was the compulsion of vehement, love-prompted
entreaty. She would not accept a refusal of her hospitality. Her
gratitude and love made her determined to have the privilege of mak-

ing "her house a resting place and an asylum for the missionaries of the Cross."[15] She desired to unite herself with the movement of Christianity not only through personal acceptance of its message but also through active cooperation with its messengers.

Paul's acceptance of Lydia's hospitality was highly unusual on his part. He could not bring himself to follow his established rule in her case. "She was so evidently one of those generous natures who have learnt how far more blessed it is to give than to receive, that Paul did not feel it right to persist in his refusal."[16] Lydia's hospitality relieved him of the necessity of working for his living while at Philippi, as he did elsewhere. Due to the intimate relations existing between him and the Philippian church, Paul also accepted gifts from the church after leaving Philippi (2 Co 11:8; Phil 4:15-16). No doubt, Lydia was the moving force behind the offerings sent to him while working at Thessalonica and at Corinth. Paul thus permitted the Philippian church to do for him what he would not permit at Corinth (2 Co 11:7-12).

Lydia's enthusiastic offer of hospitality did not grow threadbare after the novelty wore off. Luke's reference to "many days" in verse 18 makes it clear that their stay extended over a considerable period. Her faithfulness to the Lord was proved by her continued faithfulness in assisting the work of the missionaries.

PARTING GLIMPSE

The last mention of Lydia's name occurs at the close of Paul's stay at Philippi. Following his vivid account of the arrest, imprisonment, and release of Paul and Silas (16:19-39), Luke recorded that they "entered into *the house of* Lydia: and when they had seen the brethren, they comforted them, and departed" (v. 40). Clearly, the believers at Philippi, upon hearing of the imprisonment of Paul and Silas, had gathered at Lydia's house to pray. Apparently her house had become the accustomed place of assembly for the young church, and thus her home had become the center for Christianity in Philippi.

When Paul and Silas, with their backs painfully lacerated, returned to the home of Lydia, her compassionate heart employed every means available to her to relieve their discomfort. "They comforted them" suggests that the realization that Paul and Silas were leaving them, especially in their needy physical condition, grieved Lydia and the other believers.

It is remarkable that Lydia was not mentioned in Paul's letter to the Philippian church. Either she had died in the years since the founding of the church, or she had returned to Thyatira. It may be conjectured that she returned to Thyatira to use her influence in the establishment of a church in that city (Rev 2:18).

The idea that Lydia was not her personal name has led to the suggestion that she was either Euodia or Syntyche named by Paul in Philippians 4:2. This view is founded on a double conjecture. Others, indeed, have suggested that Lydia was the "true yokefellow" to whom Paul appealed to help Euodia and Syntyche to reconcile their disagreement (4:3). In pursuance of this suggestion, it has further been conjectured that Paul had married Lydia; hence he could appropriately address her as his "true yokefellow." But this ingenious suggestion is ruled out by the fact that the adjective "true" is masculine rather than feminine in the original.

Lydia's generous hospitality demonstrated the practical character of her new faith. Certainly her infectious spirit did much to stamp the young church at Philippi with its known spirit of liberality (2 Co 8:1-5). Paul deeply appreciated their missionary spirit and gratefully paid tribute to their "fellowship in furtherance of the gospel from the first day until now" (Phil 1:5).

19

ONESIMUS

Colossians 4:9
Philemon 10-21

EVERYONE REMEMBERS Onesimus as the fugitive slave befriended by
Paul and for whom the apostle interceded in a letter to his master.
Onesimus appears during the time of Paul's first Roman imprisonment.
He is known to us only from the twin letters to the city of Colosse:
Colossians and Philemon. His story must be gathered from the letter
to Philemon.

BACKGROUND

Onesimus, whose name means "profitable," bore a common slave
name. He belonged to Philemon, a Christian householder of some importance residing at Colosse. The novel theory of Knox that Archippus
rather than Philemon was the owner of this slave, has not commended
itself to most modern scholars.[1] Under what circumstances Onesimus
became the slave of Philemon is not known. He may have been
purchased by Philemon from a former owner or as the unfortunate
captive of war, or he may have been born of slave parents in the
household of Philemon.

Paul's remark to the Colossians that Onesimus "is one of you"
(Col 4:9) indicated that he was a native of Colosse, at least that
Colosse was his rightful place of residence. He was thus apparently
a native Phrygian. That would place Onesimus in that class of slaves
who by common estimation were of poor quality. "A Phrygian slave

178

was a byword for rascality."[2] The common proverb had it, "A Phrygian is the better and the more serviceable for a beating."[3]

FLIGHT

Onesimus lived up to the evil reputation of the Phrygian slave. He absconded from his master's house after either robbing him or doing him some other "wrong" (Phile 18). In his effort to escape apprehension by the slave catchers, who were always on the outlook for fugitive slaves, Onesimus made his way to the city where Paul was then a prisoner. The traditional view has been that Paul was a prisoner in Rome (Ac 28:30) when he wrote the epistles to the Colossians and Philemon. That Onesimus should flee the long distance to Rome is understandable. He would naturally feel that there among its teeming masses he had the best chance of escaping detection. It was a common practice for evil men to flock to Rome, which the historian Sallust called the "common cesspool of the world."[4]

Some recent scholars consider it unreasonable to think that Onesimus would hazard the long and expensive trip to Rome. Thus Duncan thinks it unlikely that a fugitive from justice would have "undertaken over unknown and dangerous roads a journey of a thousand miles by land, together with two sea voyages extending over some five days."[5] Two alternative locations have been advocated. Some like Meyer and Dibelius and Kümmel[6] have favored Caesarea, being nearer and more easily reached. Reicke argues for this view since it allows for "the assumption that the runaway slave, Onesimus of Colossae, had come to Palestine on foot."[7] But Caesarea would offer considerably less security against detection than Rome. As a prisoner at Caesarea, Paul was confined in Herod's palace (Ac 23:35; 24:23), and it seems highly improbable that Onesimus would be bold enough to come into contact with Paul there. Others, like Duncan, feel that Onesimus would probably flee to Ephesus, which was comparatively near at hand and was "a city with which he was no doubt already familiar."[8] But the very fact that Colosse stood in close communication with Ephesus would have exposed Onesimus to ready recognition and apprehension in that city. Duncan's view is part of his theory that the prison epistles were written from Ephesus. While the non-Roman origin of these epistles has met with considerable scholarly favor in recent years, Moule concludes that "the case for Rome is still a strong one, and on the whole more plausible than the others."[9] I accept the common view that Paul sent Colossians and Philemon from Rome, as no one has yet established that the long flight for Onesimus, which this view requires, was impossible. Thompson reminds us that "it is easy to underestimate the facilities for travel in the ancient world."[10]

How did Onesimus come into contact with Paul in Rome? Several interesting suggestions have been advanced. Did one of Paul's co-workers, Epaphras or Tychicus, by chance encounter Onesimus somewhere in Rome and, recognizing him, bring him to Paul? Or perhaps Onesimus found himself in dire want in that large city and, recalling that before he left Colosse he had heard that Paul was in Rome, as a last resort, visited him "if haply he might extend to him a dole of charity."[11] Or maybe the memory of some words of the gospel, heard at Colosse in the home of Philemon, haunted his tortured soul and drew him to Paul to unburden his heart to him. Whatever the occasion or motive that brought Onesimus into contact with Paul, the apostle eagerly grasped the opportunity to share the gospel.

Transformation

Paul's contacts with Onesimus soon resulted in the conversion of the fugitive slave. Through the work of Paul, he became a new-born babe in Christ. With joy Paul called him "my child, whom I have begotten in my bonds" (Phile 10). In accepting as a worthy member of the family of God, the runaway slave, who had no rights in the eyes of the Roman law and was regarded as little more than a living tool, Paul "freely conceded his humanity, his moral worth" as a believer.[12] Under Paul's love and care, the new nature which had begun in the heart of Onesimus, soon began to unfold in the development of a lovable and attractive character. A strong attachment sprang up between Paul and his spiritual child. When he sent Onesimus back to his master, Paul found it difficult to part with him and spoke of it as sending "my very heart" (v. 12).

Onesimus faithfully devoted himself to ministering to Paul in his imprisonment (v. 13). So capable and useful did Paul find his service that he even considered keeping Onesimus with him to take the place of Philemon, his master. But he resolutely refused to do so without the knowledge and free consent of the slave's owner (v. 14).

Paul bore glowing testimony to Philemon concerning the transformation that had taken place in his errant slave. Making a play upon the meaning of the name of Onesimus, he informed him that Onesimus "once was unprofitable to thee, but now is profitable to thee and to me" (v. 11). Formerly, Onesimus had not lived up to the meaning of his name, but now he did. Paul had personally experienced that Onesimus had become profitable, and he cheerfully assured Philemon that Onesimus now was profitable to him also.

RETURN

While Paul rejoiced in the spiritual transformation that had taken place in Onesimus, he keenly realized that something more was necessary in his case. Onesimus had received the forgiveness of his heavenly Master, but he still needed to be forgiven and restored by his earthly master. Paul felt that the slave must return to his master in accordance with the demands of Roman law. In order to clear himself, Onesimus must go back to Philemon with his confession of wrong and place himself at his master's disposal without reserve. Paul did not believe that the fact that Onesimus had become "the Lord's freedman" (1 Co 7:22) permitted Onesimus to disregard his social obligation to Philemon. Paul's letter to Philemon makes it clear that Onesimus recognized his obligation to return and expressed his willingness to do so. But in doing so, he must have been well aware of the possible consequences to himself. Lightfoot remarks,

> Roman law, more cruel than Athenian, practically imposed no limit to the power of the master over the slave. The alternatives of life or death rested solely with Philemon, and slaves were constantly crucified for far lighter offenses than his.[13]

Thus the willingness of Onesimus to go back was eloquent testimony to the transformation that had taken place in him.

In returning Onesimus to his master, Paul thoughtfully took care not to expose his spiritual child to unnecessary danger. He knew that it would be unwise to send Onesimus back alone. There would be danger that he might be arrested by the slave catchers before he reached Colosse. He determined to do all he could to assure a safe return and that the desired reconciliation between master and slave would be effected. When circumstances demanded that Tychicus be dispatched to Colosse with Paul's letter to that church, all concerned recognized that the opportune time to return Onesimus had arrived.

Paul felt it expedient to write a letter to Philemon personally explaining the situation and entering his own plea for Onesimus. The resultant letter to Philemon is unique among the writings of Paul that have come down to us. It gives a remarkable illustration of Paul's ability to identify himself sympathetically with both parties and to draw them together skillfully on the basis of higher spiritual considerations. Paul urged Philemon to forgive his slave and to receive him as he would the writer himself (v. 17). Paul bore warm testimony to the transformed character of the one being returned, placed the best possible construction upon the entire unpleasant past, pointed out the new spiritual relationship between master and slave that the conversion of Onesimus had established, and personally pledged himself to make good any loss that Philemon had sustained. The brief letter reveals exquisite tact and delicacy and breathes the spirit of true Christian courtesy. Paul was a master of sanctified psychology.

Paul also took care to smooth the way for Onesimus as a new member of the Colossian church. He did so by adding a warm commendation of Onesimus in his epistle to the church (Col 4:9). Paul informed them that Tychicus, the bearer of the letter, was accompanied by "Onesimus, the faithful and beloved brother, who is one of you." As one who was at home at Colosse, Paul assured them that Onesimus was fully worthy of being received as a brother in their fellowship. He assured them that the former no-good was now a changed man. He was a "faithful and beloved brother." While they knew Onesimus as a disloyal and dishonest slave, Paul assured them that as a Christian brother he had already proved himself to be faithful and worthy of Christian love. Paul did not mention the slave status of Onesimus, for that was a matter of indifference in the Colossian church. Both masters and slaves were among its members.

Paul further remarked, "They shall make known unto you all things that *are done* here" (Col 4:9). His "they" tactfully placed Onesimus on the same level as Tychicus; both could give them reliable information concerning Paul's affairs at Rome. Each man would have his own story to relate. Onesimus would be able to provide some information beyond that given by Tychicus. MacLeod points out that Paul's commendation of Onesimus to the Colossians shows that "Paul has every confidence that they will indeed receive Onesimus with forgiveness and complete reconciliation."[14] Paul trusted Onesimus and Philemon, as well as the Colossian believers, to do what was right, and his words challenged them to rise to the level of his expectation.

Many people believe that Onesimus was given the letter to Philemon to deliver to his master personally. But since Onesimus traveled under the protection of Tychicus, it is much more probable that Paul entrusted both letters to Tychicus. Upon his arrival at Colosse, Tychicus would not only speak for Onesimus whom he was returning to his master, but as Paul's personal representative, would present his letter to Philemon. Thus Tychicus wisely served as the personal mediator between the master and his returning slave.

As to the actual outcome of Paul's plea for Onesimus, we have no definite information, yet there need be no doubt as to its success. It is highly improbable that Philemon would have permitted Paul's letter to survive if he deliberately rejected his appeal. Paul's expectation that Philemon would respond favorably is clear from his words in Colossians 4:9.

Philemon probably did more than Paul specifically asked of him (Phile 21); perhaps he even gave Onesimus his freedom.

Varied traditions concerning Onesimus have been preserved, among them that he became an active Christian leader, eventually attaining the status of bishop. Knox conjectures that Onesimus, the freed slave of Philemon, is the same as the bishop of Ephesus with that name in the time of Ignatius, about A.D. 110.[15] While this proposal cannot be proved, it has merit. It would provide a beautiful sequel to the biblical picture of this friend of Paul.

20

ONESIPHORUS

2 Timothy 1:16-18; 4:19

ONESIPHORUS was an Ephesian Christian who, true to the meaning of his name, proved himself a "profit-bringer" to Paul during the dark days of his second Roman imprisonment. Except for his courageous ministry to Paul in a time of desperate need, we would never have heard of this exceptional man. He appears briefly only in the second epistle to Timothy.

COURAGEOUS ACTION

Paul's reference to Onesiphorus in 2 Timothy 1:16-18 placed his noble example in striking contrast to the cowardly conduct of the two men mentioned in the preceding verse. Paul's heart welled up in gratitude and prayer, as he recounted the story to Timothy. He painted the picture of Onesiphorus' courageous ministry to him with a few graphic strokes. He reversed the historical order of events and listed them in the order in which he learned of them.

Gratefully Paul recorded, "He oft refreshed me" (1:16). The verb *refreshed*, occurring only here in the New Testament, conveys the picture of providing a cool, refreshing breeze for a man about to faint. In the papyruses, it was used with the meaning of giving relief and relaxation. The hostile atmosphere and threatening circumstances under which Paul found himself at Rome had left him feeling stifled. The fact that he had been left all alone to defend himself at his first appearance before the imperial court (4:16) had exhausted and discouraged him. Although he had escaped immediate condemnation (4:17), he had been remanded to prison with no prospect of an ultimately favorable verdict. During his time of desperate need, Onesiphorus came to him with his ministry of refreshing.

Although we need not exclude the thought, we must not think that he refreshed Paul merely with food and drink or with a gift of money. What Paul most appreciated was the fact that Onesiphorus by his presence repeatedly "braced his morale with his fellowship."[1] "Oft" points to Paul's deep appreciation of the fact that the refreshing ministry was not confined to one visit. Repeatedly he visited Paul in his cell, causing the prisoner to breathe more easily in the oppressive environment of his dark dungeon.

Paul deeply valued these visits because of the loyal attitude thus displayed toward him. His visits proved beyond question that he "was not ashamed of my chain" (v. 16). "My chain" here must be taken literally to indicate that Paul was chained, as though a dangerous criminal. The fact that they treated him as a malefactor (2:9) was humiliating to Paul and a source of embarrassment to him. This evoked the cowardly action of other men toward him, but Onesiphorus showed that he was not ashamed to be identified with his dear friend when in chains. It took courage to identify himself with Paul under those circumstances. Stevenson comments, "There is no stigma in being the friend of Christians who enjoy as good or better social standing than ourselves; but only true godliness will befriend the despised and the desolate."[2]

Paul traced the persistent, courageous effort that led to those visits. "But, when he was in Rome, he sought me diligently, and found me" (v. 17). "But" marks the contrast between what Onesiphorus might have done and what he did do. He might have hunted up Luke (4:11) and given him his message of sympathy and encouragement for Paul, or he might have contented himself with one visit, feeling that he had fulfilled the obligations of friendship. But Onesiphorus refused to resort to such easy and safe expressions of personal friendship.

From 2 Timothy 1:18 and 4:19, we know that Onesiphorus lived at Ephesus. We do not know what had brought him from Ephesus to Rome. "When he was in Rome" simply recorded his presence there.

It is generally assumed that his business had demanded his coming to Rome. Scott states that the language implies this.[3] Being in Rome, his love compelled him to look Paul up. De Welt says that he came to Rome "to testify in defense of the Apostle."[4] But this does not agree with Paul's statement that he was alone at his first defense (4:16). "Was" denotes that he was no longer with Paul.

"He sought me diligently" indicates that it was no easy thing for Onesiphorus to locate Paul. Earnest, persistent efforts were necessary to gain information concerning the place of Paul's imprisonment. It required courage for Onesiphorus to continue with his inquiries, since the government regarded Paul as a dangerous individual and kept him in close confinement. It doubtless involved making repeated inquiries of the very military leaders who were holding Paul in custody. His "eager searching involved greatest peril, for it implied an acknowledged identification with one who was accused as a teacher of heresies and a traitor to the emperor."[5] Even more dangerous was the fact that Onesiphorus persisted in making repeated visits to this notorious prisoner.

Paul's use of the aorist tense "sought" implied that the search was successful, while the added verb "and found me" recorded the happy result for Paul himself. After Onesiphorus discovered where Paul was confined, he did everything necessary to be permitted to see Paul personally. It must have been a glad surprise to Paul when Onesiphorus appeared personally in his dark cell.

Previous Ministry

As Paul recounted the courageous ministry of Onesiphorus in Rome, his mind went back to his previous experiences with the services of this dear friend. His action at Rome was in keeping with his past beneficent conduct as "the climax of a consistent loyalty."[6] The words "unto me" in the King James Version rest on insufficient manuscript evidence and should be omitted. The ministries of Onesiphorus at Ephesus had not been limited to Paul. He had rendered valuable services to the cause of Christ. Those ministries had been performed under Timothy's personal observation; Timothy knew them "very well," better than Paul could describe them to him.

Paul did not mention the precise status of Onesiphorus in the

Ephesian church, since Timothy would know it already. Some have thought that the verb rendered "ministered" (*diakoneō*) denoted his position as a deacon, but probably the term means helpful services of any kind. More often scholars regard him as an elder of the Ephesian church. This is entirely possible, but Paul's picture of him does not require his holding an office of any kind. His was a free and voluntary service prompted by love.

PRAYER WISHES

Paul's gratitude for the gracious ministry of Onesiphorus to him at Rome was reflected in the fact that he breathed a prayer wish both before and after telling Timothy about it. He began his story with the devout wish, "The Lord grant mercy unto the house of Onesiphorus" (v. 16), and concluded with the prayer wish, "The Lord grant unto him to find mercy of the Lord in that day" (v. 18). Lenski remarks, "Like two arms these wishes lay before Timothy and the Lord what this man did for Paul."[7]

Onesiphorus extended mercy to Paul in his hour of need, and Paul knew that he would never be able to repay him for what he had done. He therefore turned his heart Godward and expressed his devout desire that he and his family might be the recipients of God's mercy. Paul well knew that his gracious ministry to him did not release Onesiphorus and his family of their need for God's benevolence. God's favor is not merited by deeds of kindness to others, but is freely given by God to the believing heart because He is a God of mercy.

Paul began with his prayer wish for the "house of Onesiphorus" because he well realized that they were deeply involved in what Onesiphorus had done. The service he had rendered Paul entailed expense and personal risk, and the entire family was vitally concerned with the expression and possible outcome of the action. Paul's mention of the "house" may have been prompted by his knowledge that Onesiphorus was still away from home. But his words need not mean that he was thinking of the family apart from its head. The household and its head were inseparably linked, in Paul's thoughts. In 1 Corinthians 16:15, Paul mentioned "the house of Stephanas" where the head of the house was absent at the time but was clearly included in the designation. The entire family of Onesiphorus was involved in the cost of his service, and Paul yearned that all of them might receive God's blessing because of it.

In his prayer wish for Onesiphorus personally, Paul added an eschatological note, that he will "find mercy of the Lord in that day" (v. 18). "That day" looks forward to the future day of judgment. His prayer does not relate to the time between death and resurrection but to the time of Christ's return.

MYSTERIOUS OMISSION

The fact that Paul did not send greetings to Onesiphorus personally but rather to his house (4:19) and expressed a prayer wish for the household (1:16) has led many to infer that Onesiphorus was dead when Paul wrote.[8] If so, then the prayer in 1:18 is a New Testament instance of prayer for the dead. In support of this view, 2 Maccabees 12:43-45 provides Jewish precedent for such a practice. Plummer strongly supports the implication that the words of Paul are consistent with the practice of prayer for the dead; he holds that both reason and tradition support the practice and asserts that the practice in the primitive church is confirmed by the "chain of Christian writers beginning with Tertullian in the second century, and also of early inscriptions in the catacombs."[9]

But other scholars insist that the assumption that Onesiphorus was dead is unwarranted and unnecessary.[10] Paul's somewhat cryptic language provides no basis for the questionable doctrine of prayer for the dead. Guthrie properly cautions that "it is precarious to base a doctrine, which finds no sanction anywhere else in the New Testament, upon the mere inference that Onesiphorus was already dead."[11] If Paul knew that he was dead, it seems "strange that not a word is mentioned concerning the death of this hero."[12] Then it would have been in order for Paul to send a word of comfort and encouragement to the bereaved family instead of his simple greeting (4:19). Furthermore, then the two prayers would more naturally have been reversed, first the prayer for Onesiphorus himself and then for his bereaved family. Fausset further maintains that "if the master were dead the household would not be called after his name."[13]

The view that Onesiphorus was still alive is quite consistent with the eschatological nature of Paul's prayer for him personally. Paul did at times offer such prayers for those still alive. In 1 Thessalonians 5:23 Paul certainly expressed an eschatological prayer wish for people still alive.

But even if one might naturally infer from Paul's words that Onesiphorus had died, they still offer no sure basis for prayer for the dead. Scott remarks that Paul's words were "only the expression of a very natural feeling. As he thinks of this good friend, Paul is convinced that God in the end will reward him."[14] Since Paul's prayer wish looks forward to the future eschatological "day" of judgment, there is no valid reason for connecting it with prayers asking for the deliverance of loved ones from purgatory.

Paul's brief words concerning Onesiphorus present a pleasing portrait of a greathearted man who proved himself a true friend in need. Unfortunately, this beautiful character has often been lost sight of because his name has been entangled in this unwarranted theological controversy.

21

PHILEMON

Philemon 1-25

WE KNOW about this beloved Christian because his slave ran away and met Christ through his encounter with the great apostle. The conversion of Onesimus caused Paul to send Philemon the brief letter, preserved in our Bible, when returning his slave. The absconding of Onesimus must have given Philemon an unpleasant experience which he would have preferred to forget; but under the providence of God, it became the occasion for the preservation of his name for posterity. All sure knowledge concerning Philemon must be gathered from the warm and tactful little letter which Paul directed to the master of the converted slave.

HISTORICAL SITUATION

The recipient of Paul's letter resided in Colosse (Col 4:9; Phile 11). He was a man of mature years, if we accept the common assumption that Archippus was the son of Philemon and Apphia (Col 4:17; Phile 1). He was evidently a prominent and well-to-do Colossian householder, and he probably owned other slaves beside Onesimus. We have further proof of his social prominence and possession of material means from the fact that he had a house large enough to serve as a place of assembly for the believers at Colosse (v. 2), and that he ministered benevolently to an extended circle of fellow believers (vv. 5, 7). The conjecture of Burrell that he had a prominent weaving establishment has no basis beyond the fact that weaving was a common industry at Colosse.[1] Whatever his business, he had connections which often took him to Ephesus, the metropolis of the province of Asia.

Philemon was a Christian and a treasured friend of the apostle Paul. Paul's comment in Philemon 19 probably means that Philemon had been converted under Paul's personal ministry. The likeliest place for Philemon to hear Paul was Ephesus, during Paul's work in that city on the third missionary journey (Ac 19:9-10). Perhaps while on a business trip to Ephesus, Philemon heard Paul preach in the school of Tyrannus and believed.

Further contacts between Paul and Philemon ripened into a warm, personal friendship. Paul's affectionate regard for Philemon shows through in his letter. Scott observes, "Paul speaks repeatedly of his warm attachment to Philemon (vers. 7, 17, 21), but even apart from these references we can gather from the cordial and informal tone of the letter that he is writing to an old friend."[2] Paul addressed Philemon as "our beloved and fellow-worker" (v. 1). Paul loved Philemon as a brother in Christ and also because he found him a lovable man. In calling Philemon his "fellow-worker," Paul deliberately united him with himself in the service of their common Master. Lightfoot saw in the designation "a noble testimony to his evangelical zeal."[3] The precise significance of Paul's term *fellow-worker* raises questions. Perhaps, following his conversion, Philemon assisted Paul in his ministry at Ephesus, and then he continued his evangelistic labors upon returning home. Paul did use the term of preachers of the gospel (2 Co 8:23; Phil 2:25; Col 4:11), but that does not prove that Philemon was a preacher. Later traditions do represent him as a presbyter, bishop, or deacon, all harmless guesses.

What Paul probably had in mind in calling Philemon his "fellow-worker," were other, more private modes of cooperation on the part of his dear friend, such as the beneficent ministries of Philemon mentioned in verse 7. The designation suited Philemon, "because he opened his house for public worship, and in various ways was so benevolent and active in ministering to the wants of the disciples of Christ."[4] Scott views Philemon as "a warm-hearted Christian man who preferred to remain in the background," and thinks that he did not have an active part in the leadership of the local church, "but was always at hand when there was need for practical helpfulness."[5]

The commonly accepted interpretation that Onesimus was the slave of Philemon has recently been challenged by Knox in his reconstruction of the story behind this letter.[6] According to him, Archippus, rather than Philemon, owned Onesimus. But this view does not coincide with the fact that Philemon is the first person addressed in the letter, and that following the additional names in the salutation, he is the one person addressed throughout. The reconstruction advocated by Knox has commended itself to few modern scholars.[7]

PAUL'S PETITION

Paul's purpose in writing the personal note to Philemon was to assure him of the writer's high regard for both the master and his slave, and to induce Philemon to receive, forgive, and reinstate Onesimus. Paul based his request on the crucial fact that Onesimus' conversion had established a new relationship between master and slave. He asked Philemon not to treat Onesimus as a chattel but as a Christian brother, even though he occupied the social status of a slave.

Paul desired that Philemon would receive Onesimus with the same affection that he would show to Paul personally (v. 17). As his spiritual father, Paul obligated himself to Philemon to make good any loss that the master had sustained through the action of Onesimus (v. 19). Paul closed his appeal with a statement of his confidence that Philemon would do even more than Paul asked of him (v. 21). This has generally been taken as a hint to Philemon that Paul expected him to free Onesimus. Thus Hackett says, "Having asked everything short of that already, nothing but that seems to remain as the something which he has not asked."[8] Knox adds that Paul's real purpose was "to secure the slave for his own service,"[9] trusting that Onesimus would be sent back to him. But verses 15-16 imply that Onesimus would remain in the company of Philemon. If Paul did suggest that Onesimus was to be freed, he thought of him as a freedman voluntarily remaining in the service of Philemon, which freedmen often did.

Others however prefer that Paul's remark in verse 21 was simply intended as a general compliment to Philemon's character, an expression of confidence that Philemon would readily do all that was right in the case, and that he would show the returning slave, freely accepted as a Christian brother, even greater kindness than had been asked for. Clogg holds that "Philemon is not bidden to release Onesimus, but to love him — a far harder thing."[10]

Paul's desire for the loving restoration of Onesimus was motivated by his concern not only for the welfare of the young man but also for the highest spiritual development of Philemon. Paul hoped that his request would challenge Philemon to give a still higher demonstration of his beneficent activities toward the saints (v. 7). Paul prayed that Philemon's faith would become effective in carrying out the request in keeping with his knowledge of all the good things Philemon had received in Christ (v. 6). Philemon would never be a truer follower of the one who prayed, "Father, forgive them; for they know not what they do" (Lk 23:34), than in receiving the fugitive Onesimus to his heart and welcoming him back as a beloved member of the household.

What Paul knew of the kindly heart and beneficent activities of Philemon made him confident that his request would be granted. Barclay remarks, "Philemon was clearly a man from whom it was easy to ask a favour."[11] It was a compliment to Philemon that Paul felt free to make his difficult request. Paul's passing remarks reveal that Philemon possessed "in no common degree some of the finest and most distinctive Christian graces."[12] These included a living faith in the Lord Jesus that revealed itself in active love and good deeds toward the saints (vv. 4-6). Concerning Philemon, Hackett remarks, "His character, as shadowed forth in this Epistle, is one of the noblest which the sacred record makes known to us."[13]

Whatever Philemon understood Paul to mean, he undoubtedly carried out Paul's request to the fullest extent. Paul's commendation of Onesimus to the Colossian church (Col 4:9) clearly shows that he expected his appeal to be successful. Certainly the preservation of this personal letter to Philemon bears eloquent testimony to that outcome.

MORAL ISSUE

For the modern reader, this letter raises the problem of slavery as a moral issue. That such a noble Christian as Philemon should

own slaves may well seem strange to us today, but for Philemon it
was not a conscious moral issue. The institution of slavery was an
integral part of Roman society and was accepted without question as
an indispensable element of the social structure of life. Angus remarks, "The Greeks and the Romans saw no more wrong in having
slaves than we see in having domestic servants."[14]

Not infrequently both the master and his slave were members of
the same church (1 Ti 6:1-2). Their diverse social status raised no
barrier in recognizing that both were brothers in Christ. Kelly remarks,

> It was the burning conviction of these early Christians that, through
> their fellowship with Christ, they had entered into a relationship
> of brotherhood with one another in which ordinary social distinc-
> tions, real enough in the daily round of life in the world, had lost
> all meaning (Gal. iii. 28; I Cor. xii. 13; Col. iii. 11; Phm. 8-18). . . .
> They were not so much concerned with natural ethics as with the
> ethics of the redeemed community.[15]

Yet the hard reality of their social diversity led Paul to give definite
instructions to both slaves and masters concerning their practical relations to each other (Eph 6:5-9; Col 3:22 — 4:1). Paul stressed not
personal liberty but individual responsibility and duty, insisting upon
justice and equality. He aimed at fostering humane relationships
rather than at destroying existing institutions.

Paul's reaction to slavery was conditioned by the Old Testament
concept of slavery. Hebrew laws permitted slavery, but the laws regu-
lating it were very humane, and made strong demands to prevent
cruelty to the slave. Paul was fully aware that Roman slavery operated
under a wholly different concept than that inculcated in the Hebrew
laws. He well knew the prevailing cruelty and injustices that existed
under the Roman system. Yet in keeping with the Old Testament
view of slavery, Paul did not make a frontal attack upon the institution
as such. To have openly advocated and supported the forceful aboli-
tion of slavery in the Roman empire could only have resulted in a
bloody revolution on the part of the slave classes, which would have
ended in their being fiercely suppressed, and added suffering and op-
pression for slaves generally. Paul keenly realized that to change the

political status of the slave did not change the slave or necessarily promote his spiritual welfare. Paul knew that the better way was to inculcate a spirit of love and consideration by spiritually transforming the attitudes of both master and slave in their relations to each other. As Longenecker observes, "The apostle's approach to this crucial social problem of his day was to work from a 'Christ consciousness' in the individual to a 'Christian consciousness' in society."[16] In keeping with his own character as a Christian, Philemon was asked to treat Onesimus as a human being and a Christian brother, while Onesimus was expected to show himself profitable to his master. Such a spirit removed the sting of slavery and introduced a power which ameliorated and ultimately abolished the institution of slavery.

The letter to Philemon provides a beautiful illustration of the operation of the gospel of Christian reconciliation. The vexing case of Onesimus was brought to a glorious solution because the grace of God had wrought spiritual renewal in the lives of each of the three principle characters in the story, resulting in a new relationship of love. Neil's apt words beautifully paint the picture:

> An ex-Jewish rabbi, to whom all Gentiles were once untouchables; a wealthy Gentile patrician, to whom an itinerant Jewish preacher in a Roman prison would normally be an object of contempt, and to whom a runaway thieving slave was a dangerous animal to be beaten or put to death; a rootless slave without hope of human sympathy, or even human justice — in all conscience, humanly speaking, an impossible trio, yet all three are caught up through their common allegiance to Christ into an entirely new relationship, where each acknowledges the other as one of God's adopted sons, and a brother for whom Christ died.[17]

22

PHOEBE

Romans 16:1-2

ONLY IN PAUL's BRIEF but beautiful commendation of Phoebe in Romans 16:1-2 do we catch a glimpse of this worthy Christian woman. That Paul placed his appeal for her at the head of this chapter, which is devoted to friendship matters, indicates that she had a special connection with the letter. It is commonly assumed that Phoebe carried the letter to its Roman destination. Meyer calls it "a supposition which there is nothing to contradict."[1] In support of this assumption, her arrival apparently was simultaneous with the arrival of Paul's letter; also, no one else in the letter was given a similar commendation.

Since only Roman officials and their friends were permitted to use the imperial postal service, Paul happily availed himself of the opportunity to have his letter taken to Rome by this esteemed Christian lady. In faithfully performing this valuable service for the apostle, she indeed rendered a noble deacon service to the church of Christ. As Renan remarked with plausible exaggeration, "She bore in the folds of her robe the whole future of Christian theology."[2]

Some critics have postulated that Romans chapter 16 was originally a letter sent to Ephesus and by mistake became attached to the letter to the Romans. This hypothesis has enjoyed considerable favor but the arguments in its favor are insufficient to overthrow the claims of the traditional view that the chapter is a true part of Romans.*

---

* See pages 43-44 and the literature there cited.

Her name, which means "bright" or "radiant," implies that Phoebe was a convert to Christianity from paganism. Phoebe in Greek mythology was the name of Artemis, goddess of the moon. Since loyal Jews avoided the names of pagan deities, it seems obvious that her parents were non-Jewish. But her name also makes it clear that Gentile converts did not feel impelled to renounce such pre-Christian names, for they had lost for them their pagan religious significance. Furthermore, the etymology of such names was probably then as little recalled in the case of proper names as now.

Paul in thus writing a letter of recommendation for Phoebe was employing a common practice in the ancient world. Papyrus evidence shows that the use of letters of recommendation was "not rare" among non-Christians.[3] The use of such letters was likewise a characteristic feature of the apostolic church (Ac 18:27; 2 Co 8:18-24; 3 Jn 9, 12). They were valuable means of fostering the union and communion between the various churches and were a practical protection against impostors and false teachers. Denney points out that the possession of such a letter "was equivalent to a certificate of church membership."[4]

Paul's letter of recommendation for Phoebe served the double function of introducing and recommending her to the believers at Rome. The penning of this tribute was no empty conventionality for Paul but a sincere expression of genuine appreciation for the sterling worth of the one thus introduced, whom he considered reliable and trustworthy.

IDENTIFICATION

In commending Phoebe to the Roman church, Paul gave her a double identification. He introduced her as "our sister, who is a servant of the church that is at Cenchreae" (Ro 16:1). The first designation marked Paul's own relationship to Phoebe, while the second stated her relationship to the local church at Cenchreae.

"Phoebe our sister" not only indicated her Christian status but also the close spiritual kinship Paul felt toward her. *Sister* points to that intimate family relationship between believers, springing from their oneness in Christ, while his use of *our* stressed Paul's own strong sense of that kinship. Phoebe is the only woman among all of Paul's

friends whom he called *"our* sister" (*tēn adelphēn hēmōn*).† Elsewhere Paul applied this personal pronoun (either singular or plural)
to fellow workers to whom he was under obligation for personal
service.‡ In verse 2, Paul also expressed his grateful sense of obligation to Phoebe.

Paul connected Phoebe with the local church at Cenchreae, the
eastern seaport of Corinth, some nine miles distant. It was a flourishing town. We have no record of the founding of the church there,
but obviously it was an extension of the church at Corinth. It illustrates the diffusion of Christianity throughout the province during
Paul's eighteen months of work at Corinth on the second journey (Ac
18:11).

Paul's designation of Phoebe as "a servant of the church" has resulted in disagreement as to her exact status in the Cenchreaen church.
This disagreement arises out of the double meaning of the term translated "servant" (*diakonon*). As a general designation, it denotes a
helper or attendant, one who carries out the directions of another; the
term views the worker in relation to his beneficent work, without
stressing its specific character. As a technical term, it denotes a church
officer, the deacon.§ Did Paul here employ the term to denote the
fact of Phoebe's free ministries as a member of the church, or did he
use it in its official sense? Were her services privately assumed, or
did she minister under official appointment?

That Phoebe showed her fitness and ability for such ministries
through her voluntary services is obvious; from such willing workers
the early leadership of the churches was drawn. But Howson comments that Paul's statement clearly implies that Phoebe was "no mere
volunteer, acting outside of all ecclesiastical arrangements."[5] Paul
called her not a servant *"in* the church" but *"of* the church." This
would indicate that the ministries of Phoebe were no mere private
effort, but were carried on under the approval and authorization of
the church.

---

† The ASV uses "our sister" of Apphia also (Phile 2), but the Greek is simply
"the sister" *(tē adelphē).*
‡ Cf. 2 Co 2:13; 2 Co 8:22; Phil 2:25; 1 Th 3:2.
§ *Diakonon* appears a total of 30 times in the New Testament, under 3 different
renderings (KJV, ASV): "servant," 6 times in the gospels, only once in the
epistles; "minister" twice in the gospels, 18 times in the epistles (all by Paul); and
"deacon" 3 times, all in the epistles.

But did Phoebe belong to an official order of deaconesses in the church? That the term *diakonos* might already carry an official meaning when this letter was written seems implied from Paul's use of *diakonia* (ministry) in 12:7. Phoebe would then belong to the class there designated as having a ministry. In addressing the Philippian church only a few years later, Paul clearly used the term in a technical or official sense (1:1). Dodd asserts, "We may assume that, whatever the 'deacons' were at Philippi, that Phoebe was at Cenchreae."[6] If so, this is the first mention of the office of deaconess in the New Testament.

No one has yet raised a plausible argument against the idea that deaconesses could have served as early as this in the Christian church. Deacons were early appointed in the Jerusalem church to attend to the needs of the poor among its members. In carrying out their ministries to the poor, the orphans, and the sick, it would soon become obvious that certain ministries could more fittingly be discharged by godly women than by men, however pure-minded and respected they were. After the appointment of deacons, the appointment of deaconnesses follows as the next logical step. We are not informed when they took that step.

In Greece and other parts of the East, the seclusion in which women were kept would necessitate such an order of female workers. Since the women lived very much apart, and were almost inaccessible except by members of their own sex, deaconesses would be essential for the well-being and progress of the churches.

Some have questioned the appointment of deaconesses in the churches as early as Paul's letters. But Lenski contends that "the way in which Paul introduces this deaconess to the Romans indicates that the fact that women served in this office was no novelty, but something then already known."[7] Newell argues that we should not shun the implication that Phoebe was an official deaconess, and reminds us that Dorcas "was full of good works" (Ac 9.36), yet she is not called a deaconess.[8]

That Phoebe held the office of deaconess in the church at Cenchreae seems the most probable interpretation of Paul's statement. Her appointment to the position testified not only to her ability and diligence but also to her acceptance as worthy of such appointment by the church. Paul deeply appreciated her active ministries, and his commendation of her stressed that fact. "It was her work for the Lord that was stressed rather than her connection with a church, for in the early Church much was made of service, little of position."[9]

PAUL'S REQUEST

Having identified the person he was recommending, Paul made a double request of the Roman believers on her behalf.

His first request was, "That ye receive her in the Lord, worthily of the saints" (Ro 16:2). They were urged as a definite act to welcome her into their midst while she visited their city. Two expressions in his statement indicate the manner and motive of the requested reception. They were to receive her "in the Lord." He did not want them merely to open their homes to her; rather they were to welcome her as one who shared their union with the Lord. "She was no alien to be debarred from spiritual intimacy."[10]

Paul wanted her reception to be "worthily of the saints." He instructed them to receive her with the kindness becoming to saints.

Paul's request contains no indication that Phoebe "was moving to Rome at this time," as Shepard asserts.[11] If she were, Paul would have written, "Receive her into your midst." Furthermore, his identifying her as *being* also a deaconess of the church in Cenchreae" (Greek) indicates that he regarded her as still a member of the church at Cenchreae. Paul simply asked an appropriate welcome for her during the time that she remained in Rome, which might of necessity be drawn out.

Paul further requested that they "assist" or stand by her to aid her, "in whatsoever business she hath need of you" (KJV). Such assistance would require their time and effort, yet he was confident that as Christians they would readily do this for this worthy Christian woman. Stifler comments, "What a charitable free-masonry existed in the church! Her 'business' was her own, but Paul does not hesitate to call on the whole Roman brotherhood to stand by her in it."[12] Sadly, such practical assistance to the saints is often lacking today. They may be given a warm welcome in the assembly on Sunday, but blandly left to shift for themselves during the week.

The nature of Phoebe's business in Rome is not known. That she felt it necessary to make the long and dangerous trip to Rome indicates its importance.

Some have surmised that the trip was in connection with her office and work as a deaconess. But it seems hardly probable that the early church would use women to travel thus in the discharge of official business. Certainly, some personal business matters necessitated her trip.

From the legal terms used, Conybeare concluded that "the business on which Phoebe was visiting Rome was connected with some trial at law." But Vincent stamps this as "mere fancy." Moule conjectured that her business "concerned property, and involved enquiries and directions about law."[13] If so, the more intimate knowledge of Roman believers would greatly assist her.

Whatever comprised her business, she did the right thing by going there to take care of it herself. She had Paul's full approval in making the trip. Bourdillon remarks, "It is no part of Christian duty to neglect our worldly affairs. On the contrary, discredit has often come upon religion through such neglect on the part of those actively engaged in religious work."[14]

EXPLANATION

Paul explained his appeal for their assistance to Phoebe from her own service record. "For she herself also hath been a helper of many." She deserved their help because she herself had helped "many." By his use of that one word *many*, we have "a large amount of brave and active service revealed to us."[15]

The translations "helper" (ASV) or "succourer" (KJV) do not give the full force of the original term (*prostatis*). It may be rendered "protectress, patroness, or guardian," and presents the picture of a woman who stands before others to protect them by caring for their affairs and aiding them with her own resources. The term fits in well with the view of her official status as deaconess. In her work at Cenchreae, Phoebe had shown herself as a champion of needy believers, proving herself a benefactor of many. No doubt part of that work consisted of aiding needy believers who landed at the port of

Cenchreae. Hunter suggests that the church at Cenchreae may have met in the home of Phoebe.[16]

The term implies that in all probability Phoebe was a woman of some wealth and position. This would enable her to act as the protector of the small and struggling Christian community at Cenchreae. Clearly she was a woman of mature years who had proved herself thoroughly competent to perform such beneficial services on behalf of the brethren.

Phoebe was probably a widow and as such was capably managing her own business affairs. Conybeare asserts that according to Greek manners, Phoebe could not have acted in the independent manner here indicated if her husband was still living or if she had never married.[17]

Since Paul did not mention anyone as traveling with her, we may infer that Phoebe made the trip to Rome without any official companions. But Lenski insists that Phoebe "could not have travelled alone in those days; and this means that she most likely travelled with her servants."[18] Rhys supports this implication of Phoebe's position of wealth and prominence by pointing out that "in the ancient world the only women who travelled much were wealthy."[19]

Among the many who had been the recipients of Phoebe's ministries Paul gladly numbered himself, "and of mine own self." When Phoebe thus ministered to Paul is not recorded. Lenski calls the remark "another unwritten incident."[20] Hamilton thinks that she "entertained Paul with generous hospitality on his trips to Cenchreae." But others like Gifford and Smith surmise a reference to a more specific event.[21] They think this probably refers to Acts 18:18, and figure that Phoebe nursed Paul during a serious illness at Cenchreae before he left Greece on the second missionary journey. Phoebe is often referred to as the patron saint of the nursing profession.

Whatever kind ministries he had received from Phoebe, Paul could not fail to express his own warm gratitude to her for them. Amid his many sufferings in the service of the Lord, Paul always deeply appreciated the services of those who contributed to his relief.

23

STEPHANAS

1 Corinthians 1:16; 16:15-18

STEPHANAS AND HIS FAMILY were active and worthy workers in the Corinthian church. Paul highly appreciated this fine Christian family. Though only briefly mentioned in 1 Corinthians, Paul referred to their eminence as a family, their voluntary services to the saints, and urged the Corinthians to give them appropriate recognition.

FAMILY EMINENCE

Paul affectionately described "the house of Stephanas" as "the firstfruits of Achaia" (1 Co 16:15).* This abides as the honor of this family. "The Greek always says 'house' for family."[1] Paul thus identified them as the first family to be won to Christ in the province of Achaia. But the description of this family in the Corinthian church as "the firstfruits of *Achaia*" (not Corinth) raises a historical difficulty. Technically the term *Achaia* included Athens, and since Paul had already made some converts at Athens (Ac 17:34), we would have expected the expression to be applied to these Athenian converts. Different suggestions in explanation have been offered.

Moffatt thinks that by Achaia, "Paul probably means Corinth." Waite feels that Paul used the term in "its early restricted sense" to denote the immediate neighborhood of Corinth.[2] On the other hand, a study of Paul's practice in the use of various geographic names leads Zahn to conclude that "Paul never uses any but the provincial names

---

* The true reading in Ro 16:5 is "the firstfruits of *Asia*," not Achaia (KJV).

for districts under Roman rule, and never employs territorial names which are not also names of Roman provinces."[3] As the great missionary statesman to the Roman empire, Paul seems to have thought consistently in terms of Roman provinces in relation to his missionary activities. It thus seems unsatisfactory to hold that he would here employ the provincial name, Achaia, in such a restricted sense.

While strongly supporting the position that Achaia included Athens, Ramsay seeks to remove the difficulty by supposing that the few persons in Athens who "believed" only took the first step in the process of conversion and did not go on to the second step of "turning to the Lord" in an open identification with Christianity in receiving baptism. Thus Paul would not regard them as "the firstfruits of Achaia."[4] But this rather pedantic distinction between "believing" and "turning to the Lord" as two stages in conversion is unconvincing.

Goudge suggested that Paul disregarded the few converts made at Athens since he "did not regard the passing visit to Athens as an integral part of his work."[5] In a similar vein is the suggestion that since the conversion of "the household of Stephanas" (1:16) was the first instance of the conversion of an entire family in the province, Paul saw in them, rather than in the scattered converts at Athens, the first promise of a great church in Achaia. Thus Edwards remarks, "To the Apostle's mind the pledge of a future Church came not in Athens, but in Corinth, and with the conversion of a whole family."[6] Such an ingenious explanation is possible. But it does not account for the strange fact that in 1 Corinthians 1:16 Paul's baptizing this family occurred to him only as a kind of afterthought. As Paul thought back on those whom he had personally baptized at Corinth, why should he have failed to think at once of this prominent family, if they were indeed "the firstfruits" of his work at *Corinth?* That Paul personally baptized this family contradicted his usual practice (1 Co 1:17). He usually left this task to his assistants. Goudge observes, "In each case, the persons baptized by S. Paul were of special importance."[7] That makes it difficult to understand why Paul would not immediately have thought of them, if he had actually baptized them at Corinth.

Zahn and Lenski hold that the true answer is that as "the firstfruits of Achaia," Stephanas and his family were actually baptized by Paul in Athens.[8] This view harmonizes with Paul's habitual use of the term *Achaia,* and explains why they did not come to mind immediately when recalling his work at Corinth. Since Stephanas was with Paul at Ephesus when he wrote 1 Corinthians (16:17), he may himself have reminded Paul that of the different members of the Corinthian church whom Paul had baptized, the apostle must include him and his family. This family would then be included among the "others with them" mentioned in Acts 17:34, if "others" includes all converts made at Athens. Then they were baptized by Paul while he was "at Athens alone" (1 Th 3:1), before his sermon to "the Areopagus" (Ac 17:22). Then, apparently, some time after their conversion, Stephanas and his family shifted their residence to Corinth; they had resided there a good while already and had firmly established themselves in the Corinthian church when Paul wrote 1 Corinthians.

FAMILY SERVICE

A further distinction of this family was that "they have set themselves to minister unto the saints" (1 Co 16:15). Voluntarily and spontaneously they had set or appointed themselves to this service. As a self-imposed duty, they made it their regular business to render service to their fellow believers, because they recognized that it needed to be done for the good of the church. Since the subject of the verb is *they* and refers to the whole family, their "ministry" cannot be taken to mean an official ministry in the church. The forms that their "ministry unto the saints" took is not indicated. Paul's quite general expression would include any and all types of service. Kling suggests that it probably consisted "in services of love to individuals such as the poor, the sick, in hospitality towards brethren visiting from abroad, and in the undertaking of various responsibilities in behalf of the church."[9] That this family systematically engaged in such services implies that they were free, according to their own choice, to dispose of their time and means, thus indicating that they could not have been slaves. The family of Stephanas must have had financial means and probably social prominence. It is, however, a well-known fact that often families of restricted financial means distinguish themselves by the abundance of their loving services to others in need. In view of the parallel admonition in 1 Thessalonians 5:12-13, perhaps Stephanas himself held some official position in the Corinthian church.

An example of the services rendered by this family was the coming of Stephanas, accompanied by Fortunatus and Achaicus, to Paul at Ephesus as the official representatives of the Corinthian church (1 Co 16:17). Paul expressed his joy at their presence with him, assuring the Corinthians that they had refreshed his spirit (16:18). They had supplied his need of direct personal contact with his Corinthian converts. The information thus secured relieved his anxiety and gave him a better understanding of circumstances.

This delegation had brought Paul a letter from the Corinthian church (1 Co 7:1). Large portions of 1 Corinthians are given over to his answers to the questions they had presented to him (cf. 7:1; 8:1; 12:1; 16:1), although Paul took the occasion to deal also with certain matters that their letter had not touched on (cf. 1:10-11; 5:1). It seems a natural conclusion that this delegation returned to Corinth with Paul's reply to the letter which they had brought, our 1 Corinthians.

APPROPRIATE RECOGNITION

Paul highly appreciated the services of this worthy family. But he felt it necessary to enjoin the Corinthians to show the house of Stephanas the respect and deference due such workers. He began his appeal with his kindly words, "I beseech you, brethren," but interrupted himself to insert a parenthetical statement justifying the appeal before stating, "That ye also be in subjection unto such" (16:15-16). Since the family of Stephanas voluntarily "set" or stationed itself to serve the saints, let the church also "be in subjection" or station themselves under, "such" excellent Christians. Let them respect and give proper heed to their counsel and advice.

Paul recognized that the Corinthians "were wanting in respect for such practical Christian activity, their admiration being reserved for 'excellency of speech or of wisdom' (2:1; cf. 1:18-25)."[10] Apparently Stephanas had just grounds for complaint and may have poured out his heart to Paul in regard to the unappreciative attitude of the church. Meyer feels that Paul's "commendation of Stephanas must have been grounded in some antagonism unknown to us, which the man had to lament in his work for the church."[11]

With his added words, "And to every one that helpeth in the

work and laboreth" (16:16), Paul generalized the duty. It was a standing obligation of the church, not merely in the case of this one family. They were but representative of a class which all the Corinthians should be proud of and gladly defer to. "Those who serve, should be served."[12]

Paul gratefully acknowledged the services of this delegation from Corinth (16:18). Their coming had brought him joy and refreshing of spirit. But as a gracious afterthought, Paul added that they also were the means of refreshing "your" spirit. He was confident that when they returned with Paul's reply to their letter and reported their interview with him, the Corinthian assembly would also experience refreshment through them. This service justified his appeal that the Corinthians acknowledge and treat with due respect men that had such qualities. Respect and esteem are due to Christian workers in proportion to their service and usefulness. Let everyone learn that lesson in connection with the house of Stephanas.

24

TROPHIMUS

Acts 20:4; 21:29
2 Timothy 4:20

TROPHIMUS, a Gentile Christian, on three occasions is named as a companion of Paul; yet we never get a direct picture of him. Once his name appears as a member of a group of men with Paul, and twice reference is made to him as a member of Paul's company but not actually in his presence when referred to.

BEARER OF COLLECTION

Trophimus first appears in Acts 20:4 as one of seven men who were waiting for Paul at Troas. They had been selected by the churches to accompany Paul to Jerusalem as bearers of the collection for the poor saints in that city (Ro 15:25-28; 1 Co 16:3-4; 2 Co 8:18-21). The last two men named were "of Asia, Tychicus and Trophimus." Obviously the Asian churches had selected them to act as their deputies, since both men were natives of the province of Asia. In Acts 21:29, Luke identifies Trophimus more specifically as "the Ephesian," a native of that important city where Paul had labored on the third missionary journey for nearly three years (Ac 20:31).

Although he had not achieved recognition previously, the selection of Trophimus for this important mission indicates that he was a trusted and esteemed believer whose associations with Paul well qualified him for the assignment. He may have been one of Paul's converts at Ephesus. From Acts 21:28-29, we ascertain that the Ephesian Jews knew he was a Gentile convert who had embraced Christianity without having received circumcision. Possibly, prior to Paul's ministry at Ephesus, he attended the Jewish synagogue as a seeker after the truth; but more probably, he was converted directly from paganism.

OCCASION FOR ARREST

Of the seven men named in Acts 20:4, only Trophimus is named as being with Paul in Jerusalem. Surely, the whole group went all the way to Jerusalem with Paul, but Trophimus receives specific mention only because he became the innocent cause for Paul's arrest in Jerusalem.

Paul's successful ministry at Ephesus had stirred up a Gentile riot (Ac 19:23-41) as well as having elicited numerous plots against him by the Jews (Ac 20:19). When the Asian Jews, Paul's implacable enemies, discovered his presence in Jerusalem at the feast of Pentecost, their hatred caused them to be on the alert for a possible opportunity to attack Paul. When they observed Paul within the temple accompanied by four men whom they did not recognize (Ac 21:22-26), they rashly assumed that they had found the occasion they were looking for. Immediately they raised an outcry against Paul, charging that the well-known traitor to the Jewish people and the law had defiled the holy temple by illegally bringing Greeks into it (21:27-28). The resultant riot culminated in Paul's arrest and imprisonment (21:31-33).

Luke thus recorded the basis for the charge by the Asian Jews, "For they had before seen with him in the city Trophimus the Ephesian, whom they supposed that Paul had brought into the temple" (v. 29). Somewhere in the city, perhaps not too far from the temple area, they had seen Paul in the company of Trophimus, whom they quickly recognized as an uncircumcised companion of Paul. Their hatred gave wings to their imagination and multiplied the supposed offense which they had detected. Their exaggerated charge in their public outcry was that he had "brought Greeks into the temple." The charge "was an erroneous suspicion expressed as a certainty, to which zealotry so easily leads!"[1] To bring uncircumcised Gentiles into the temple proper was regarded as profaning the holy temple and was a capital offence. It was a serious charge, well calculated to create a riot against Paul. Gentiles could walk into the large Court of the Gentiles surrounding the temple, but could not enter into the temple proper. At the stone balustrade surrounding the temple, inscriptions in Greek or Latin warned that no Gentile might enter the enclosure; violation would be punished by death. Two of these warning notices have been recovered.* The right to inflict capital punishment upon an offender was a concession made by the Romans to the deep religious feelings of the Jews.

If the charge had been true, the Jews legally could have executed Trophimus immediately. Paul himself would not have received the punishment as a circumcised individual, but the charge skillfully directed the hatred against him as the one responsible for the desecration. The Jews therefore immediately attempted to kill him. Only the timely intervention of the Roman chiliarch (Ac 21:33) prevented his death.

The Jewish scholar, Klausner, asserts, "It is possible that Paul may actually have brought Trophimus into the Temple, since Paul would not have seen any harm in an act like this, after he had put aside the differences between Jew and Greek in all matters pertaining to religion."[2] But such a claim is totally inconsistent with the very reason for Paul's presence in the temple at the time. Bruce well remarks, "It is absurd to think that Paul, who on this very occasion was going out of his way to appease Jewish susceptibilities, should have thus wantonly flouted Jewish law and run his own head into danger."[3]

Upon investigation, the Jewish religious leaders recognized that the charge raised by the Asian Jews could not be substantiated. In pressing his charges against Paul before the Roman governor, Felix, the orator Tertullus simply claimed that Paul "assayed to profane the temple" (24:6). They lowered the charge to the claim that they had caught Paul in the attempt to do so. Even this reduced charge, transferring it to the realm of motive, fanned Jewish hatred against Paul.

How Trophimus must have felt when he learned that he had

---

* One of these, discovered in 1871, reads: "No man of another nation to enter within the fence and enclosure round the temple. And whoever is caught will have himself to blame that his death ensues." Barrett, *The New Testament Background: Selected Documents*, p. 50. For the Greek text, see Lake and Cadbury, *The Beginnings of Christianity*, vol. 4, p. 274, and Jack Finegan, *Light From the Ancient Past*, (1946), illustration 111 for a picture of the original. A second inscription was found near St. Stephen's Gate in 1935.

been the unconscious and unjustified cause for Paul's imprisonment was best left unrecorded.

INACTIVATED BY SICKNESS

For at least five years, nothing further is known concerning Trophimus. The last passing mention of him occurs in 2 Timothy 4:20, "But Trophimus I left at Miletus sick." In requesting Timothy to come to him at Rome, Paul explained that his request was due to the fact that he was almost alone (4:11). In 4:10, Paul informed Timothy concerning his companions who had been with him in Rome; while in 4:20 he added a further explanation concerning two companions who had not arrived in Rome with him. Sickness had made it impossible for Trophimus to continue his old association with Paul. His absence was not due to disloyalty. The verb *left*, more literally, "left behind," implies that the resultant separation was the desire of neither Paul nor Trophimus.

This statement concerning Trophimus is not reconcilable with the story in Acts. In Acts, Trophimus was not left behind at Miletus but continued with Paul all the way to Jerusalem (Ac 21:29). On his trip to Rome as a prisoner Paul did not pass through Miletus (Ac 27:7-8), hence could not have "left" Trophimus there. The movements recorded in 2 Timothy clearly belong to a time following the close of Acts. The intricate schemes suggested by Harrison and Duncan attempting to fit the reference into the story of Acts are unconvincing.† The traditional view that 2 Timothy was written during Paul's second imprisonment in Rome is still the most satisfactory.

The nature and purpose behind Paul's visit to Miletus, some thirty-three miles from Ephesus, cannot be determined. Neither do we know the cause of the prostrating sickness of Trophimus. It must have been a deep disappointment to him to be unable to continue with Paul, and Paul must have keenly regretted the necessity of leaving his sick companion behind. The nearness of Miletus to Ephesus would assure that Trophimus would not remain unattended in his sickness.

---

† P. N. Harrison, *The Problem of the Pastoral Epistles*, thought that Trophimus was left at Miletus when Paul was en route to Troas (cf. 2 Co 2:12). Duncan, *St. Paul's Ephesian Ministry*, suggested that it was while Paul was returning from Corinth to Asia (cf. 2 Co 1:8).

Many have called attention to the fact that Paul did not heal his devoted companion. This has been thought strange in view of the fact that Paul did possess the gift of healing (Ac 19:11-12; 28:8). But of course such "miracles of healing were not at the command of their performers."[4] The miracles were divinely given attestations of the authenticity of the gospel (Heb 2:4). Vine points out that when the apostles exercised the power to heal "they were acting simply as the Lord's servants and their power was controlled by their Master, and not by their personal affections or desires. The healing was accomplished by faith, but faith-healing was not practiced as an art."[5]

Although our glimpses of Trophimus are few, they do leave us with some impressions concerning this rather elusive companion of Paul. He never seemed to have acted independently. He probably did not have the aggressive personality which fitted him to be an independent worker. He seems to have had ordinary gifts and attainments but preferred to work under the leadership of others. Hall characterizes him as "a good team-man."[6] He doubtlessly was happiest when working under the direction of Paul, his beloved friend and guide. Such faithful and dependable team members may never make the headlines, but they are vital to the success of the whole endeavor.

25

TYCHICUS

Acts 20:4
Ephesians 6:21-22
Colossians 4:7-8
Titus 3:12
2 Timothy 4:12

EACH TIME TYCHICUS APPEARS in Scripture, he is traveling with or for Paul. Of Paul's various associates, we may best characterize Tychicus as the apostle's trusted and faithful courier. The five occurrences of his name connect him with four different periods in Paul's life.

TRAVELS WITH PAUL

Tychicus first appears in Scripture during the latter part of Paul's third missionary journey. In Acts 20:4 he was one of the delegates who traveled with Paul in taking the collection to Jerusalem. Luke's statement, "And of Asia, Tychicus and Trophimus," makes it clear that Tychicus and Trophimus had been selected to represent the Asian churches. "Of Asia" identifies him as a native of that Roman province, probably of Ephesus. Codex D explicitly asserted that Tychicus and Trophimus were "Ephesians." While this reading is clearly a deliberate emendation, Ramsay holds that it may well embody an accurate local tradition which made Tychicus, like Trophimus (Ac 21:29), a native of Ephesus.[1]

Just when Tychicus first became associated with Paul is not given. He obviously became a Christian during the time that Paul worked at Ephesus on the third missionary journey, but there is no

213

hint that he was Paul's personal convert. His selection as one of the bearers of the funds raised in the Asian churches gives witness to his character as an esteemed and trusted believer. He may have started working with Paul before his selection for this task. Some authors conjecture that Tychicus was one of the unnamed companions of Paul in 2 Corinthians 8:18-22, but this cannot be established. If Tychicus had not previously worked with Paul, certainly the close contacts between Paul and Tychicus on this journey to Jerusalem welded strong and enduring ties between them.

COURIER OF PAUL

The second and most explicit picture of Tychicus must be dated some four years later, during Paul's first Roman imprisonment. He was one of the group of faithful companions with Paul during a part of that imprisonment. Paul commissioned him to take his companion letters, Colossians and Ephesians, to the province of Asia. Paul's warmhearted commendation of Tychicus in these epistles brings the personality of Tychicus clearly before us.

"All my affairs shall Tychicus make known unto you, the beloved brother and faithful minister and fellow-servant in the Lord: whom I have sent unto you for this very purpose, that ye may know our state, and that he may comfort your hearts" (Col 4:7-8). The same commendation, with minor variations, appears also in Ephesians 6:21-22. The claim of Norris that the commendation "in Ephesians is quite artificial — constituting a part of its pseudepigraphical presentation"[2] is less plausible than the conservative view that Paul in writing a companion letter to the same province would naturally use the same words in commending the courier of both communications.

Paul's warm words concerning Tychicus in the Colossian epistle not only identified the courier but informed the Colossians of his assignment. "All my affairs shall Tychicus make known unto you" reminded the Colossians that while urgent doctrinal matters had been dealt with in writing, further personal matters would be conveyed to them orally by Tychicus. Tychicus and Onesimus, speaking out of personal knowledge, would "make known unto you all things that *are done* here" (Col 4:9). Since he was sending such a capable messenger as Tychicus, Paul felt it unnecessary to write about his personal affairs.

Although Paul had not personally visited the Colossian church (Col 2:1), the Colossian believers would be eager to learn about Paul's circumstances at Rome. Such information would be more satisfactorily provided orally than in writing.

Paul's closely knit, threefold description of Tychicus, "the beloved brother and faithful minister and fellow-servant in the Lord," reveals his high personal esteem of his messenger. The absence of any possessive pronoun *my* or *your* suggests that it was not simply his own subjective evaluation of Tychicus but an objective declaration. "The beloved brother" identified him as a member of that spiritual brotherhood to which believers belonged, while "beloved" pointed out the reaction of those who knew him personally. It warmly commended Tychicus as a lovable character.

The following two designations relate to his activities. He was a "faithful minister," one who engaged in active service on behalf of the gospel. In its technical sense the term *minister* (*diakonos*) means "deacon," but there is no indication that Paul was using it here in that special sense. As Paul's faithful assistant, Tychicus helped forward the work of the Lord by carrying out the ministries Paul assigned to him. His commission in relation to the Colossian church was an instance of his ministries. He did not merely work for Paul but rendered ministries beneficial to the whole church. He did not have the rank of an apostle, but he faithfully served in a subordinate position under the guidance of Paul.

With his third term, "fellow-servant," Paul placed Tychicus on a level with himself as his colleague in Christian service. The designation (which Paul used elsewhere only in Col 1:7, of Epaphras) is literally "fellow-slave" and indicates that Tychicus too had submitted his will completely to the Lord Jesus to do His bidding. This term is omitted in Ephesians 6:21, and efforts have been made to use the omission as evidence of the pseudonymous authorship of Ephesians. Bruce remarks, "The idea that the omission is due to a later writer's unwillingness to appear to bring Paul down to Tychicus' level is far-fetched."[3]

The scope of the added phrase "in the Lord" (Col 4:7) has been differently understood. Some would limit it to the last expression only, since the other two already have modifiers.[4] This would mean that Tychicus was called a "fellow-slave" only in a spiritual sense, because of his union with the Lord. Abbott holds that "in the Lord" modifies the last two terms, indicating that his ministry as a devoted slave was motivated by his spiritual union with Christ.[5] Others, like Carson, feel that "in the Lord" is best taken as qualifying all three expressions.[6] Then this means that Tychicus stood in all three designated relations because of his spiritual relationship to Christ. His life and work were spiritually motivated.

Having identified his messenger, Paul with a double statement amplified his purpose in sending Tychicus to Colosse, "whom I have sent unto you for this very purpose, that ye may know our state, and that he may comfort your hearts" (4:8). "That ye may know our state" restates the purpose already indicated in verse 7, to provide them with information concerning Paul and his colleagues at Rome. The reading in the King James Version, "that he might know your estate," is based on a variant text which means that Tychicus was sent to Colosse to gather information about the situation there. The context disproves this as the true reading. Paul had already received information concerning the situation at Colosse through Epaphras (1:8) and wrote in response to that information. Tychicus was not sent to investigate the accuracy of that information. Also Paul's words "for this very purpose" indicate that his statement of purpose is parallel to that in the previous verse. Having been informed about them, Paul was anxious that Tychicus should minister to them. Besides informing them about affairs at Rome, Tychicus was to serve the Colossian believers personally, "that he may comfort your hearts." The rendering "comfort" indicates that he would relieve them of their anxiety. But more probably the meaning is that he was to "encourage" them by his news, explanations, and exhortations. The Colossians needed not so much to be consoled as to be encouraged to stand firm against the heretical teaching which was bidding for their adherence.

The added words "together with Onesimus" (Col 4:9) point to a further phase of the task given to Tychicus. A comparison of Colossians 4:9 with Philemon 1, 8-22 makes it clear that Tychicus was also given the duty of safely returning the fugitive Onesimus to his master, Philemon. In presenting the slave to him, Tychicus would also deliver

Paul's letter to Philemon, wherein the apostle pleaded for the forgiveness and restoration of the converted slave.

From the epistle to the Ephesians, we see that Tychicus had a
still wider ministry to perform. He carried that important epistle also.
Whether the epistle was originally addressed to the church at Ephesus,
it is commonly recognized that Paul intended it for the various churches in proconsular Asia. Apparently he wanted Tychicus to read the
letter to the various churches.

The most priceless ministry that Tychicus performed for the
Christian church was his safe transmission of the three letters destined
for Asia, which Paul entrusted to him. His faithful performance of
this laborious service is evidence that "his was the strong limb, the
brave heart, and the tireless zeal."[7] In Paul's day, private letters had
to be taken to their destination by a personal messenger, and their
safe transmission was often uncertain. Tychicus rendered Paul and
the whole Christian church a great service in reliably performing this
important yet tedious task. Lees well remarks, "The long journeys of
Tychicus are quickly marked upon the map, but it needs imagination
to picture the weariness of the road and the perils of the way."[8] These
Tychicus gladly assumed because of his ungrudging zeal and unflinch-
ing earnestness in the service of his Lord. His spirit of devotion
transformed an obscure and laborious task into a ministry of abiding
spiritual value.

The critical suggestion that the epistle to the Ephesians was
"composed by Tychicus, but presenting the Gospel in the phraseology,
language and ideas used by Paul, with which Tychicus was thoroughly
familiar,"[9] is farfetched. It can appeal only to those whose critical
presuppositions cause them to reject the explicit scriptural statement
of the Pauline authorship of the epistle.

REPLACEMENT FOR TITUS

A further fleeting glimpse of Tychicus is contained in Titus 3:12,
where Paul told Titus, "When I shall send Artemas unto thee, or
Tychicus, give diligence to come unto me to Nicopolis." This passing
reference to Tychicus reveals that he was again with Paul when he
wrote his letter to Titus on the island of Crete. We have no sure information as to where Paul and Tychicus were at the time. Those

who deny the Pauline authorship of the epistle find no historical value in this reference to Tychicus. Other critics admit that the words are probably a genuine Pauline fragment embodied in the letter, but add that there is no way of knowing to what period in Paul's life it belongs. Those who accept the Pauline authorship of the epistle believe that it belongs to a time following the close of the book of Acts. Thus the reference gives us a glimpse of Tychicus again with Paul following Paul's release from his Roman imprisonment (Ac 28:30-31).[10]

This passage adds a further touch to our understanding of the stature of Tychicus. Titus had received a difficult assignment from Paul on the island of Crete. The very fact that Paul contemplated sending Tychicus to take his place indicated his confidence that Tychicus would be able to carry on the work there. Paul regarded him as more than a dull but faithful plodder to whom he could safely entrust the delivery of his letters; he also had great ability and would be able to further the cause of Christ on Crete.

Paul's words indicated that he had not yet decided which of the two men, Artemas or Tychicus, to send to replace Titus. Clearly Paul had in mind some other important assignment for Tychicus if he did not go to Crete.

MINISTRY IN EPHESUS

The last reference to Tychicus, chronologically, is 2 Timothy 4:12, "But Tychicus I sent to Ephesus." Paul was again a prisoner when he wrote 2 Timothy (1:12, 16-18; 2:9). The traditional view, accepting the Pauline authorship of the epistle, is that Paul wrote this during his second Roman imprisonment. It was his last known letter before his execution.

Tychicus had loyally remained with Paul while others were turning away from him (1:15; 4:10). But in 4:12 we read, Paul "sent" him to Ephesus. The aorist verb *sent* is open to two interpretations. If it is a historical aorist, then he had been dispatched to Ephesus before the writing of the letter. But if it refers to a past event, Paul would have mentioned him in verse 10 after Titus, without inserting an additional verb. More probable is the view that "sent" is an "epistolary aorist," a common Greek idiom wherein the writer placed himself at the time that the readers read his letter. Then the meaning is that Paul was sending Tychicus to Ephesus with the letter to Timothy. Paul's statement is sometimes taken to mean that Timothy had left Ephesus. Huther feels that if Timothy was at Ephesus, "Paul would have certainly written *pros se*" ["unto thee"].[11] But this does not stand up, since Paul did not contemplate Timothy's continued presence at Ephesus, as he asked him to leave for Rome as soon as possible.

Tychicus was certainly not sent to Ephesus simply to deliver the letter to Timothy. He apparently was supposed to replace Timothy at Ephesus. Thus Hendriksen remarks, "He is also the right man to serve for a while as director of affairs in the churches of Asia Minor, as a substitute for Timothy during the latter's absence, which would be of rather lengthy duration."[12] If so, it further proves Paul's high regard for the abilities of Tychicus.

Tychicus distinguished himself for his faithful performance of common laborious tasks. His unswerving faithfulness and tireless zeal earned for him the affection and confidence of Paul. He also proved himself qualified to carry out important spiritual ministries in the work of the Lord. Tychicus may well be thought of as a man whose faithful performance of lowly tasks opened up for him the way to higher and more demanding ministries in the service of the Christ whom he deeply loved and zealously served.

Part 3

All the Others, Named and Unnamed

To portray the remarkable variety of all those around Paul, two lists of individuals are given. The first list contains those mentioned by name in relation to Paul but who have not been discussed in Parts 1 or 2. The second list presents those individuals who appear, however briefly, in one capacity or another, yet are left unnamed.

In the Acts and the Pauline epistles, the names of at least one hundred twenty-five different people are recorded in connection with Paul. Some of these individuals had no known personal contact with Paul; yet in various ways they were related to his story. Whenever a reasonable probability stands that two or more individuals appear with the same name, I have distinguished between them.

The list of unnamed personalities is much briefer. They generally appear in connection with some specific activity but were left anonymous. Usually the problem of their identity creates great difficulty.

Obviously, these numerous men and women did not all know Paul in the same degree of intimacy. Some of them stood in close personal relation with Paul as his active associates in missionary service. Others appear as his loyal friends and supporters, while still others belong with that larger circle of believers who approved of the ministry of Paul. A few in the story were friendly to Paul, even though they were not personally committed to the Christ whom Paul preached. Some remained aloof to Paul or showed open hostility to him.

26

NAMED INDIVIDUALS

THIS ALPHABETICAL LIST of the remaining individuals named in connection with the life of Paul does not attempt to discuss in full the information concerning them. Each name is simply followed by a complete listing of the scriptural references and a brief statement of identification. Whenever the form of the name used in the American Standard Version differs from the King James Version, the American Standard Version comes first, and the King James follows in brackets. The names of those individuals discussed in Parts 1 and 2 are included only if there is a second person with the same name. An Index of all the people around Paul, from this entire book, follows the Bibliography.

ACHAICUS (1 Co 16:17-18): third named member of a three-man delegation from the Corinthian church sent to Paul at Ephesus

AGABUS (Ac 11:27-28; 21:10-11): New Testament prophet who predicted a coming famine and later the arrest of Paul in Jerusalem

AGRIPPA II (Ac 25:13 – 26:32): great-grandson of Herod the Great, before whom, during a festive arrangement by Festus, Paul the prisoner made his defense

ALEXANDER

1. (Ac 19:33-34): member of the Jewish community at Ephesus whose attempt to speak to the followers of Artemis (Diana) during their riot was unsuccessful

2. (1 Ti 1:20): convert to Christianity who became an apostate and whom Paul delivered unto Satan

3. (2 Ti 4:14-15): "the coppersmith"; strong opponent of Paul, against whom Paul warned Timothy; possibly the same as number 2

AMPLIATUS [Ampilas] (Ro 16:8): Christian in Rome whom Paul greeted as "my beloved in the Lord"

ANANIAS

1. See 125-130.

2. (Ac 23:1-5; 24:1): "the high priest"; Jewish high priest, who, following Paul's arrest in Jerusalem, accused him at a Sanhedrin meeting and led the delegation accusing Paul before Felix at Caesarea

APELLES (Ro 16:10): Christian in Rome whom Paul greeted as "the approved in Christ"

APPHIA (Phile 2): Christian woman at Colosse addressed in the epistle to Philemon, generally held to be Philemon's wife

ARCHIPPUS (Col 4:17; Phile 2): Christian worker in the church at Colosse, perhaps the son of Philemon, exhorted to fulfill his ministry

ARETAS (2 Co 11:32): Nabatean king whose deputy unsuccessfully sought to apprehend Paul at Damascus (cf. Ac 9:24)

ARISTOBULUS (Ro 16:10): individual in Rome to the Christian members of whose household Paul sent greetings; unknown if he himself was a Christian

ARTEMAS (Titus 3:12): one of two co-workers whom Paul had in mind as a possible replacement for Titus on Crete

ASYNCRITUS (Ro 16:14): first of five believers in Rome whom Paul grouped together as the recipients of his greetings

BAR-JESUS [Bar-jesus] (also ELYMAS) (Ac 13:6-11): Jewish sorcerer at Paphos whose attempt to oppose the gospel was punished with temporary blindness through the instrumentality of Paul

BARSABBAS [Barsabas]: See Judas, number 2

BERNICE (Ac 25:13, 23; 26:30): oldest sister of Agrippa II with whom she heard Paul's defense at Caesarea at the arrangement of Festus

CAESAR (Ac 25:8, 10-12, 21; 26:32; 27:24; 28:19; Phil 4:22): name taken by all the Roman emperors after Julius Caesar; also referred to as "the Augustus" (Greek), "the emperor," (Ac 25:21, 25)

1. CLAUDIUS (Ac 11:28; 18:2): Roman emperor A.D. 41-54, whose expulsion of the Jews from Rome indirectly led to the lifelong friendship between Paul and Aquila and Priscilla; the Caesar in Ac 17:7.

2. NERO (Ac 25:8, 10-12, 21, 25; 26:32; 27:24; 28:19; Phil 4:22) Roman emperor A.D. 54-68; not personally named in the New Testa-

ment; used the Christians as a scapegoat to divest himself of the suspicion of having ordered the burning of Rome, A.D. 64; 2 Ti 4:17, "I was delivered out of the mouth of the lion" possibly Paul's personal reference to Nero

CARPUS (2 Ti 4:13): Christian friend at Troas with whom Paul had left his cloak, books, and parchments which Paul asked Timothy to bring with him

CEPHAS (1 Co 1:12; 3:22; 9:5; 15:5; Gal 1:18; 2:9, 11, 14): Aramaic form of the name "Peter," given to Simon by Jesus (Jn 1:42); according to the critical text, used eight times by Paul (See PETER.)

CHLOE (1 Co 1:11): woman living either at Corinth or Ephesus from the members of whose household Paul learned of the Corinthian party factions; not certain that she was a Christian

CLAUDIA (2 Ti 4:21): Christian woman in Rome who was a friend to Paul during his second Roman imprisonment and joined others in sending greetings to Timothy

CLAUDIUS [Caesar]: See CAESAR, number 1.

CLAUDIUS LYSIAS: See LYSIAS.

CLEMENT (Phil 4:3): fellow worker with Paul at Philippi but apparently no longer there when Paul wrote to the Philippians

CRESCENS (2 Ti 4:10): companion of Paul during his second Roman imprisonment but who had departed to Galatia when Paul wrote 2 Timothy

CRISPUS (Ac 18:8; 1 Co 1:14): former synagogue ruler at Corinth, converted through Paul and baptized by him

DAMARIS (Ac 17:34): Athenian woman converted through Paul's preaching

DEMETRIUS (Ac 19:23-41): silversmith of Ephesus who led the other silversmiths in stirring up a tumult against Paul because the effectiveness of his preaching adversely affected their lucrative business

DIONYSIUS (Ac 17:34): "the Areopagite"; member of the Areopagus, the Athenian supreme court, converted through Paul's preaching

DRUSILLA (Ac 24:24-25): Jewess, wife of Felix, who with her husband heard Paul's penetrating preaching "of righteousness, and self-control, and the judgment to come"

ELYMAS: See BAR-JESUS.

EPAENETUS (Ro 16:5): Christian in Rome whom Paul warmly greeted as "the firstfruits of Asia"

EUBULUS (2 Ti 4:21): first named of four of Paul's friends who sent greetings to Timothy during Paul's second Roman imprisonment

EUNICE (2 Ti 1:5): devout mother of Timothy whom Paul commended for her unfeigned faith

EUTYCHUS (Ac 20:9-12): young man at Troas overcome by sleep during Paul's prolonged message, fell from a third-story window but was restored to life by Paul

FELIX (Ac 23:23 – 24:27; 25:14): Roman procurator of Judea, a freedman appointed by Claudius, before whom Paul was arraigned but whose procrastination and greedy hope for a bribe left Paul an uncondemned prisoner in Caesarea for two years

FESTUS, PORCIUS (Ac 24:27 – 26:32): Roman procurator who, succeeding Felix, at once took up Paul's case but whose compromising suggestion that the case be transferred to Jerusalem caused Paul to appeal to Caesar

FORTUNATUS (1 Co 16:17): the second named of a three-man delegation that came to Paul at Ephesus from the Corinthian church

GALLIO (Ac 18:12-17): Roman proconsul at Corinth before whom Paul was brought by the Jews but who, regarding their charges as intra-Jewish religious questions, refused to rule in the case and had the complaining Jews driven from his judgment seat

GAMALIEL (Ac 22:3): eminent Pharisee doctor of the law; named by Paul as his early teacher at Jerusalem; whose tolerant attitude toward Christianity (Ac 5:34-40) his pupil, as the persecutor of the church, did not share

HERMAS (Ro 16:14): named last in a group of five persons "and the brethren that are with them" to whom Paul sent greetings at Rome

HERMES (Ro 16:14): named third in a group of five believers in Rome to whom Paul sent greetings

HERMOGENES (2 Ti 1:15): second of two men named by Paul as among the disciples in proconsular Asia who "turned away" from him when he had expected their help during his second Roman imprisonment

HERODIAN (Ro 16:11): Christian at Rome, greeted by Paul, whom he called "my kinsman"

HYMENAEUS (1 Ti 1:20; 2 Ti 2:17-18): leading heretical teacher at Ephesus whose chief doctrinal error lay in maintaining that "the resurrection is past already"; whom, having made shipwreck of his faith, Paul turned over to Satan

JAMES (Ac 15:13-21; 21:18-25; 1 Co 15:7; Gal 1:19; 2:2-9, 12): "the Lord's brother"; eminent leader of the Jerusalem church; converted through Christ's postresurrection appearance to him; formulated the decision of the Jerusalem Conference; later proposed to Paul the plan, aimed at pacifying the radical element in the Jerusalem church, which unwittingly set the stage for Paul's arrest in Jerusalem

JASON

1. (Ac 17:5-9): Christian at Thessalonica; host of Paul and Silas; seized with certain others by the Jewish-led rabble, charged before the rulers with harboring seditious agitators, and released after giving security

2. (Ro 16:21): second of three men whom Paul called "my kinsmen" who sent their greetings to the Roman saints from Corinth; probably the same as number 1

JESUS (Col 4:11): "called Justus"; Jewish Christian co-worker with Paul at Rome during the first Roman imprisonment; joined in sending greetings to the Colossian church

JOHN

1. "Whose surname was Mark": See pp. 76-87.

2. (Gal 2:9): "disciple"; directly mentioned as having contact with Paul only during the private meeting which Paul and Barnabas had with James, Cephas, and John at the time of the Jerusalem Conference

JUDAS

1. (Ac 9:11): owner of the house on Straight Street in Damascus where Saul of Tarsus stayed during his three days of blindness

2. (Ac 15:22, 27, 32-33): "called Barsabbas" [Barsabas]; one of the two chief men of the Jerusalem church sent to Antioch following the Jerusalem Conference, who as prophets confirmed the Syrian believers

JULIA (Ro 16:15): Christian woman at Rome to whom Paul sent greetings; perhaps the wife of Philologus with whom her name is linked

JULIUS (Ac 27:1 — 28:16): the centurion of the Augustan band in whose care Paul was placed for the journey to Rome and who treated Paul with consideration and kindness; listened, though he did not follow Paul's advice on staying at Fair Havens, shows personal esteem for Paul

JUSTUS

1. See JESUS.

2. TITUS JUSTUS [Justus] (Ac 18:7): Gentile adherent of the synagogue at Corinth who opened his house, next to the synagogue, as a preaching center for Paul when the synagogue was closed to him

LINUS (2 Ti 4:21): believer at Rome; named third among four friends with Paul during the second Roman imprisonment, who sent greetings to Timothy

LOIS (2 Ti 1:5): maternal grandmother of Timothy; commended by Paul for her unfeigned faith

LUCIUS

1. (Ac 13:1-3): "of Cyrene"; named third among the five "prophets and teachers" who ministered in the church at Syrian Antioch; proposed identification with Luke the evangelist very improbable

2. (Ro 16:21): named first among three men whom Paul identified as "my kinsmen" who sent greetings to the Roman believers; probably not the same as number 1

LYSIAS (CLAUDIUS LYSIAS) (Ac 21:31-39; 22:23 — 23:30; 24:7 KJV, 22): "the chief captain"; the Roman chiliarch whose prompt action saved Paul from death at the hands of the mob in the temple; shielded Paul from a plot to assassinate him by sending him to Caesarea under military guard

MANAEN (Ac 13:1-3): named fourth among the five "prophets and teachers" in the church at Antioch; described as "the foster-brother of Herod [Antipas] the tetrarch"

MARY (Ro 16:6): diligent Christian worker to whom Paul sent his greetings at Rome

MNASON (Ac 21:16): "an early disciple"; native of Cyprus, with whom Paul and his party lodged in Jerusalem during the third missionary journey

NARCISSUS (Ro 16:11): Roman, to the Christian members of whose household Paul sent greetings; probably not himself a believer

Nereus (Ro 16:15): named third in a group of five Christians in Rome to whom Paul sent greetings "and all the saints that are with them"; possibly the son of Philologus and Julia

Niger: See Symeon, number 1.

Nymphas (Col 4:15): Christian in Laodicea, may be either a man or a woman; greeted by Paul with "the church that is in their house," or "her house" according to some manuscripts

Olympas (Ro 16:15): believer in Rome; named fifth in a group of five Christians, to whom Paul sent greetings; possibly the son of Philologus and Julia

Patrobas (Ro 16:14): Christian in Rome to whom Paul sent greetings; named fourth in a group of five men "and the brethren which are with them"

Paulus: See Sergius Paulus.

Persis (Ro 16:12): Christian woman in Rome greeted by Paul; characterized as "the beloved, who labored much in the Lord"

Peter (Ac 15:7-11; Gal 2:6-9): leading apostle of Christ, whom Paul went to visit three years after his conversion (Gal 1:18), with whom he conferred during the time of the Jerusalem Conference; later had to rebuke publicly at Antioch (Gal 2:11-21); also referred to as Cephas and Symeon

Philetus (2 Ti 2:17): heretical teacher, named with Hymenaeus; held that "the resurrection is past already" and thus overthrew the faith of some

Philip (Ac 21:8-10): "the evangelist"; noted early Christian worker; identified as "one of the seven" (Ac 6:5); at whose home Paul and his party stayed a few days while on the way to Jerusalem during the third missionary journey

Philologus (Ro 16:15): Christian in Rome greeted by Paul, named first in a group of five believers; apparently the father of a family which opened their home for a gathering of the saints

Phlegon (Rom 16:14): Christian in Rome greeted by Paul, named second in a group of five believers

Phygelus [Phygellus] (2 Ti 1:15): first of two men named by Paul as among the disciples in proconsular Asia who "turned away" from him when he had expected their help during his second Roman imprisonment

PORCIUS FESTUS: See FESTUS.

PUBLIUS (Ac 28:7-8): "chief man" on the island of Melita, modern Malta; hospitably entertained Paul's shipwrecked party for three days; whose father Paul healed

PUDENS (2 Ti 4:21): named second among a group of four friends with Paul during his second Roman imprisonment who sent greetings to Timothy

PYRRHUS (Ac 20:4): father of Sopater of Berea; otherwise unknown but apparently named as a well-known Christian

QUARTUS (Ro 16:23): Christian at Corinth; simply styled "the brother"; named last in a group of eight friends sending greetings to the saints at Rome

RUFUS (Ro 16:13): believer at Rome whom Paul greeted as "the chosen in the Lord," together with "his mother and mine"; possibly the same as the second son of Simon of Cyrene who was compelled to bear the cross for Jesus (Mk 15:21)

SCEVA (Ac 19:14): Jew at Ephesus identified as "a chief priest," whose seven sons were exorcists; two of whom, attempting to expel a demon "by Jesus whom Paul preacheth" were severely injured by the demoniac

SECUNDUS (Ac 20:4): one of the deputies from the Thessalonian church appointed to travel with Paul in taking the collection to Jerusalem

SERGIUS PAULUS (Ac 13:7-12): Roman proconsul at Paphos; "a man of understanding"; had come under the evil influence of a Jewish sorcerer but revealed his prudence in requesting to hear Barnabas and Saul; deeply impressed by what he heard and saw, "believed" — became a Christian

SOPATER (Ac 20:4): Christian of Berea, whose father's name was Pyrrhus; named first among the seven men awaiting Paul at Troas as the bearers of the collection to Jerusalem on the third missionary journey; perhaps the same as Sosipater (Ro 16:21)

SOSIPATER (Ro 16:21): Christian at Corinth; identified by Paul with two others as "my kinsmen"; sent greetings to the Roman believers; perhaps to be identified with Sopater

SOSTHENES

1. (Ac 18:17): ruler of the Corinthian synagogue who was beat-

en before the judgment seat of Gallio when the governor refused to act against Paul as the Jews desired

2. (1 Co 1:1): believer; identified as "our brother," whose name Paul joined with his own in the salutation of 1 Corinthians; possibly same as number 1, assuming that he later became a Christian

STACHYS (Ro 16:9): believer at Rome; identified as "my beloved"; to whom Paul sent his greetings

STEPHEN (Ac 6:8 – 8:2; 11:19; 22:20): first Christian martyr in Jerusalem, to whose death Saul of Tarsus consented and whose executors laid their garments at his feet, opening Saul's career as a persecutor

SYMEON [Simeon]

1. (Ac 13:1): "called Niger"; named second among the five "prophets and teachers" ministering in the church at Antioch of Syria

2. (Ac 15:14): reference to Simon Peter by James, using the Semitic form of the common Greek name "Simon"

TERTIUS (Ro 16:22): scribe to whom Paul dictated the epistle to the Romans; penned a greeting to the believers at Rome in his own name

TERTULLUS (Ac 24:1-9): professional "orator" whom the Jewish high priest employed to present their case against Paul before Felix

TITUS JUSTUS: See JUSTUS, number 2.

TRYPHAENA [Tryphena] (Ro 16:12): active Christian worker in Rome; greeted by Paul with Tryphosa; perhaps her twin sister

TRYPHOSA (Ro 16:12): second of two active Christian women in Rome greeted by Paul; perhaps twin sisters

TYRANNUS (Ac 19:9-10): either the founder or the owner of the "school" or lecture hall in Ephesus where Paul daily presented the gospel for two years

URBANUS [Urbane] (Ro 16:9): Christian in Rome; identified as "our fellow-worker in Christ," to whom Paul sent greetings

ZENAS (Titus 3:13): Christian traveler; identified as "the lawyer"; who with Apollos apparently brought the letter to Titus on Crete and whom Titus was asked to assist by supplying what was needed for their further journey.

27

UNNAMED INDIVIDUALS

IN THE ACTS and the Pauline epistles occasional references to unnamed individuals appear in the story of Paul. Some of their activities were recorded but not their names. These anonymous characters represent that vast host of inconspicuous individuals who formed part of the New Testament scene, yet whose names were not preserved in the inspired record. These individuals are listed in the canonical order of the scriptural passages where they appear.

JEWISH HIGH PRIEST (Ac 9:1; 22:5): The high priest, from whom Saul the persecutor asked and received documented authorization to the synagogues of Damascus to act against any Christians in their membership, apparently was Caiaphas; but the authorization given Saul was the action of the whole Sanhedrin (Ac 22:5; 26:10). This refers to Paul's pre-Christian days; yet he referred to this high priest in his testimony to the mob at Jerusalem upon his arrest (Ac 22:5).

CRIPPLE HEALED AT LYSTRA (Ac 14:8-10): When the congenital cripple at Lystra showed his desire to be made whole, Paul responded by commanding him to stand up, and he was instantly healed. Nothing further is told of him, but he probably became a Christian.

PRIEST OF JUPITER (Ac 14:13): The priest of Jupiter (Greek, Zeus) led the effort to worship Barnabas and Paul, whom he regarded as gods in human form because of the healing of the cripple. He apparently directed a college of priests at the temple and "may be conceived as ordering and guiding the whole scene."[1] He maintained a position of prominence and influence at Lystra.

SOOTHSAYING SLAVE GIRL (Ac 16:16-18): A demon-possessed

slave girl at Philippi repeated supernatural cries identifying the missionaries. This disturbed Paul, and he cast out the evil spirit empowering her soothsaying abilities. The exorcism, terminating her usefulness to her masters, they regarded as an attack upon their financial interests, and this led directly to the mistreatment and imprisonment of the missionaries at Philippi. Although commonly assumed, it is not recorded that the delivered girl became a Christian.

PHILIPPIAN JAILER (Ac 16:23-36): The Roman jailer at Philippi, upon receiving orders, threw Paul and Silas into the inner prison and fastened their feet in the stocks. Following the midnight earthquake, Paul prevented him from committing suicide; he then was converted and proved his change of heart by his treatment of the prisoners and his reception of baptism the same night with all his house. Paul strangely did not mention him in the letter to the Philippians. The suggestion that he really was Epaphroditus is an interesting but unprovable conjecture.

EPHESIAN TOWN-CLERK (Ac 19:35-41): The speech of this officer of the Ephesian assembly skillfully quieted the mob in the theater and effectively blunted the feeling of antagonism against the Christians. While no personal contacts with Paul are indicated, his characterization of the companions of Paul being held by the mob (v. 37) shows that he had personal knowledge of Paul and his ministry.

CENTURION IN JERUSALEM (Ac 22:25-26): The Roman centurion who — at the order of the chief captain — supervised preparations for the scourging of Paul, upon learning that Paul was a Roman citizen, immediately warned Lysias about the violation of Roman law involved in his order. Like all centurions in the New Testament, he showed himself a trustworthy officer who honestly fulfilled his duties.

PAUL'S NEPHEW (Ac 23:16-21): "Paul's sister's son," characterized as a "young man" (v. 18), overheard the plot of more than forty Jews in Jerusalem to assassinate Paul. He saved his uncle's life by reporting the plot to the chief captain. This constitutes the only appearance in the New Testament of any members of Paul's immediate family. Whether the sister lived in Jerusalem or if she or her son were Christians is unknown.

PILOT AND THE OWNER OF THE SHIP THAT WAS WRECKED (Ac 27:11): "The master" or chief pilot and "the owner of the ship" gave professional advice which Julius accepted over Paul's arguments in the discussion about remaining at Fair Havens for the winter.

FATHER OF PUBLIUS (Ac 28:8): While Paul was lodged in the home of Publius on Malta, Publius's father was striken by fever and dysentery. The apostle visited him, and after prayer, healed him by laying his hands on him. This prompted a healing session on Malta and furthered the cause of the Lord.

MOTHER OF RUFUS (Ro 16:13): Paul sent greetings to this Christian woman in Rome with her son Rufus and affectionately described her as "his mother and mine." Paul used *mother* in its natural significance in relation to Rufus but undoubtedly in a nonliteral sense in relation to Paul himself. (Paul made reference to his mother only in Gal 1:15.) Somewhere, the mother of Rufus had treated Paul with kindness, affection, and tenderness of a mother; Paul's comment only half concealed his ardent gratitude for the care she lavished on him. He had apparently lived in her home. If her son Rufus is the same as the Rufus mentioned in Mark 15:21, then she was the wife of Simon of Cyrene, the man who had to bear the cross for Jesus. This identification is very probable and is generally accepted because of the Roman origin of the gospel of Mark. From the name of his sons, Alexander and Rufus, we may assume that Simon was a Hellenistic Jew, a member of the large Jewish colony in Cyrene. Therefore, I do not agree with Miller that his wife was a Negro.[2] Whether the family lived in or near Jerusalem at the time of the crucifixion of Jesus is not known. Zahn holds that Simon was not a festival pilgrim from Cyrene when the Roman soldiers impressed him but was rather a Jew from Cyrene residing in Palestine.[3] If so, Godet's conjecture that Paul lived in her home while he studied in Jerusalem under Gamaliel has merit.[4] Others have conjectured that Paul enjoyed her motherly care during the time that he worked in the church at Antioch.[5]

SISTER OF NEREUS (Ro 16:15): This unnamed Christian lady was included in a group of five believers at Rome to whom Paul sent his greetings. Nothing is known of her beyond the fact that she was the sister of Nereus. Possibly they were the children of Philologus and Julia.

INCESTUOUS CORINTHIAN CHURCH MEMBER (1 Co 5:1-5, 13): One Corinthian church member actually lived in sin with his father's wife.

Paul passed judgment upon him and demanded that he be excommunicated by the lax Corinthian church. Paul may not have known the man personally, but he received accurate information about his identity and conduct. If 2 Corinthians 2:5-11 refers to the same situation, Paul urged his forgiveness and restoration, because the administered discipline had wrought its intended result.

REPENTANT OFFENDER AT CORINTH (2 Co 2:5-11; 7:12): Who was the offender at Corinth whom the church had disciplined and whose forgiveness and restoration Paul requested? Paul's studied ambiguity in referring to this individual has occasioned much discussion and diversity of understanding. Until modern times, it was the almost universal view that this referred to the incestuous offender in 1 Corinthians 5:1-5, 13. The guilty member had been excommunicated by the church as Paul had demanded; the disciplinary action had induced repentance in the offender, and thus Paul's desired result had been achieved in regard to the church as well as the guilty individual. Consequently Paul now asked the church to forgive and restore him.[6] But in the last few years, this identification of the offender has been brought under sharp question, and an entirely different reconstruction of the scene has been advanced. The reference could relate to an occurrence at Corinth on a hypothetical visit by Paul during the interval between our canonical Corinthian letters. Possibly a certain individual, apparently the ringleader of the opposition to Paul's authority at Corinth, publicly insulted Paul; deeply offended, he returned to Ephesus and wrote a "severe letter" demanding that the offender be disciplined. Since the church had complied with Paul's demand, he now asked them to forgive and restore the offender. This reading of the situation makes it necessary to postulate a whole series of events between 1 and 2 Corinthians. (Some, like Strachan, theorize that part of this "severe letter" is preserved in 2 Co 10:1 − 13:10.[7]) This new reading is largely motivated by the feeling that if it relates to the incestuous offender, Paul dealt too leniently with the gross sin of incest.[8]

BROTHER SENT WITH TITUS (2 Co 8:18-19; 12:18): Paul sent someone, simply called "the brother," to Corinth with Titus in connection with the completion of the offering in the Corinthian church. His presence with Titus was intended as a precaution against any slanderous charges that Paul and his associates were misappropriating the funds being collected for the poor saints at Jerusalem (vv. 20-21). Paul identified him as "the brother whose praise in the gospel is spread through all the churches" and who had been appointed by the Macedonian churches to travel with Paul in taking the collection to its destination. The double description marked him as an aggressive Christian worker, one who held the confidence of the churches as to his personal integrity. Some have taken Paul's expression "the brother" to mean that he was the physical brother of Titus, with the further conclusion that the brother was Luke.⁹ But verses 22-23 show that Paul used the term in the sense of a Christian brother; besides, to have sent Titus with his own brother would have undermined the very purpose for which he needed a companion. The identity of this Christian worker has been the subject of much speculation. Chrysostom and Theodoret suggested that he was Barnabas; while Origen and Jerome thought that he was Luke. Modern writers in addition have suggested the names of Silas, Mark, Erastus, Trophimus, Aristarchus, Secundus, and Sopater of Berea.¹⁰ The best guess seems to be Luke, but the identification must remain conjectural.

SECOND BROTHER SENT WITH TITUS (2 Co 8:22): Paul sent a second companion for Titus, called "our brother." Here again "our brother" cannot mean Paul's brother but denotes a fellow Christian, for, as Plummer remarks, "If he had a brother, he could not have made use of him as a check on himself."¹¹ Paul identified this second companion for Titus as an individual whom he had often proved to be a reliable and zealous co-worker and who had great interest in the Corinthians. He therefore was a man in whom the Corinthians could have confidence. Apparently he was not personally known at Corinth. As in the case of the other companion to Titus, his identity remains shrouded in anonymity, although various guesses as to his identity have been offered.

GOVERNOR OF DAMASCUS (2 Co 11:32): The governor under Aretas, literally, "the ethnarch of Aretas the king," unsuccessfully sought to apprehend Saul in Damascus. Luke's account in Acts 9:23-25 makes it clear that the governor acted in cooperation with or at the instigation of the Jews at Damascus. Certainly the governor knew enough about Saul as an aggressive young preacher in Damascus to feel that his arrest would help to preserve peace in the city under his rule.

PAUL'S TRUE YOKEFELLOW (Phil 4:3): To a certain individual, Paul appealed in writing, "I beseech thee also, true yokefellow, help these women." Whom Paul meant by that epithet has been a perpetual puzzle to the interpreters, and conjectures have been numerous and ingenious. Scholars are divided as to whether the one thus addressed was with Paul when he wrote or, like the two women just addressed, was at Philippi. Lightfoot favors the former opinion and writes that Paul spoke directly to Epaphroditus, the bearer of the letter.[12] But such a direct address to the bearer of the letter in the body of the letter would be very unusual. The suggestion of Jones that Paul was making his comment to Timothy "who was actually writing the letter and was to visit Philippi shortly" is even more farfetched.[13] It would have been out of Paul's style to make a parenthetical remark to someone in his presence while dictating the letter. More naturally, Paul was probably addressing someone who, like Euodia and Syntyche, lived at Philippi. According to this, Silas has been nominated for the honor of being the "true yokefellow," but we have no evidence that he had returned to labor at Philippi. That Paul meant Luke seems more plausible. Smith supports this view with the comment, "There is no one whom Paul could more fittingly have designated as his 'true yoke-fellow.'"[14] But it rests on the unverified assumption that Luke had returned to Philippi during the latter part of Paul's first Roman imprisonment.

A suggestion as old as Chrysostom is that Paul was addressing a member of the Philippian church with the actual name of Syzygus (or Syzygus). This seems to give the most natural meaning to the passage. It is receiving the support of a growing number of modern scholars.[15] It harmonizes with the fact that Paul used proper names both before and after and gave no hint that a figurative term was being introduced in their midst. Paul nowhere else applied the words "true yokefellow" as a descriptive designation to any of his co-workers, not even the most intimate. Those who say that it is a proper name, explain that Paul with a smile was making a play upon the meaning of the name of the individual addressed. Then the adjective *true* was eminently proper as indicating that Paul regarded Syzygus as a true or genuine yokefellow, who would demonstrate the propriety of his beautiful name and pull together with Paul in helping these two women to work together again in effective service.

Admittedly, Syzygus is not known elsewhere as a proper name, but obviously not all proper names then in use have been preserved for us. Michael suggests that this rather unusual name "may have been a name assumed at baptism."[16] Its very rarity would make it easy for Paul thus to appeal to this man without any further identification. This view adds a new name to the list of Paul's co-workers of whom nothing more is told.

❄   ❄   ❄

That Paul did have other friends and co-workers of whom we do not even catch a passing glimpse seems evident from his reference to "the rest of my fellow-workers, whose names are in the book of life" (Phil 4:3). The remark seems to be his instinctive acknowledgment that there were other co-workers worthy of mention whom he had not named. While he had not recorded their names, they were written in "the book of life." Our list of Paul's unnamed friends and co-workers might be considerably extended if we knew the details concerning those who made up the various groups around Paul mentioned from time to time. Surely there were warm and lasting heart ties between Paul and "his disciples" at Damascus who aided his escape from that city (Ac 9:25), the Ephesian elders who fell on Paul's neck with their affectionate kiss and sorrowed that they would see him no more (Ac 20:37-38), and the beloved members of the different churches that Paul founded. Certainly these and others must be recognized as gladly taking their place among that undefined number of individuals who confessed that they belonged to "those around Paul."

NOTES

INTRODUCTION
1. D. A. Hayes, *Paul and His Epistles*, p. 65.
2. Reginald E. O. White, *Apostle Extraordinary*, p. 100.
3. Herbert S. Seekings, *The Men of the Pauline Circle*, p. 18.
4. Frederic W. H. Myers, *Saint Paul*, pp. 5-6.
5. William M. Taylor, *Paul the Missionary*, p. 553.
6. Hayes, p. 48.
7. Edgar J. Goodspeed, *An Introduction to the New Testament*, p. 4.
8. White, p. 105.
9. Seekings, p. 18.
10. G. Adolf Deissmann, *Paul. A Study in Social and Religious History*, p. 241.
11. Harrington C. Lees, *St. Paul's Friends*, p. 183.
12. F. W. Farrar, *The Life and Work of St. Paul*, p. 194.
13. E. Earle Ellis, "Paul and His Co-Workers," *New Testament Studies* (Jul 1971), pp. 452.

CHAPTER 1
1. Adam Clarke, *Clarke's Commentary* 5:839; David James Burrell, *Life and Letters of St. Paul*, pp. 264-265.
2. Charles W. Carter and Ralph Earle, *The Acts of the Apostles*, The Evangelical Commentary, p. 275.
3. Lees, *St. Paul's Friends*, p. 71.
4. James Hope Moulton and George Milligan, *The Vocabulary of the Greek Testament*, p. 378.
5. J. W. McGarvey, *New Commentary on Acts of Apostles*, 2:147.
6. Richard Belward Rackham, *The Acts of the Apostles*, Westminster Commentaries, p. 341.
7. John S. Howson, *The Companions of St. Paul*, pp. 66-67.
8. Herbert Lockyer, *All the Men of the Bible*, p. 51.
9. J. Rawson Lumby, "The Acts of the Apostles," in *Cambridge Greek Testament*, p. 327.
10. Albert Barnes, *Notes, Explanatory and Practical, on the Acts of the Apostles*, p. 258. Horatio B. Hackett, "A Commentary on the Acts of the Apostles," in *An American Commentary on the New Testament*, pp. 217-18.
11. Olaf Moe, *The Apostle Paul, His Life and His Work*, p. 323. Moe's italics.
12. Seekings, *The Men of the Pauline Circle*, p. 110.
13. E. M. Blaiklock, *The Acts of the Apostles*, Tyndale New Testament Commentaries.
14. R. C. H. Lenski, *The Interpretation of the Acts of the Apostles*, p. 768.
15. Marvin L. Fieldhouse, *The Book of the Acts*, The Missionary's Bible Commentary, p. 298.
16. Carter and Earle, p. 277.
17. Giuseppe Ricciotti, *The Acts of the Apostles*, p. 294.
18. Lenski, p. 774.
19. R. J. Knowling, "The Acts of the Apostles," in *The Expositor's Greek Testament*, 2:398.

20. Ellis, "Paul and His Co-Workers," *New Testament Studies* (Jul 1971), p. 439, note 6.
21. Farrar, *The Life and Work of St. Paul*, p. 362.
22. J. M. Norris, "Apollos," in *The Interpreter's Dictionary of the Bible*, 1:170.
23. Lees, pp. 71-72.
24. James Hastings, *The Greater Men and Women of the Bible, St. Luke — Titus*, p. 294.

CHAPTER 2
1. Arthur Cushman McGiffert, *A History of Christianity in the Apostolic Age*, p. 428.
2. Lees, *St. Paul's Friends*, p. 47.
3. Knowling, "The Acts of the Apostles," in *The Expositor's Greek Testament*, 2:383.
4. William Sanford LaSor, *Great Personalities of the New Testament*, p. 138.
5. Ibid., pp. 138-139.
6. W. M. Ramsay, *St. Paul the Traveller and the Roman Citizen*, p. 268.
7. Josephus *Antiquities* 8. 3. 5.
8. Ramsay, p. 268.
9. Lenski, *The Interpretation of the Acts of the Apostles*, p. 759.
10. E. H. Plumptre, "The Acts of the Apostles," in *Ellicott's Commentary on the Whole Bible*, 7:120.
11. Archibald M. Hunter, *Interpreting the New Testament*, p. 115.
12. Ramsay, p. 268.
13. Walter F. Adeney, *Women of the New Testament*, p. 242.
14. W. Sanday and A. C. Headlam, "The Epistle to the Romans," in *International Critical Commentary*, p. 420.
15. A. T. Robertson, *Types of Preachers in the New Testament*, pp. 54-55.
16. Ramsay, p. 268.
17. Lees, p. 49.
18. Suetonius *Claudius* 25.
19. Lenski, p. 741.
20. Blaiklock, *The Acts of the Apostles*, Tyndale New Testament Commentaries, p. 149.
21. See Blaiklock, *Out of the Earth. The Witness of Archaeology to the New Testament*, chap. 3.
22. Heinrich August Wilhelm Meyer, *Critical and Exegetical Handbook to the Acts of the Apostles*, p. 346.
23. Plumptre, p. 120.
24. Lees, p. 57. Lees' italics.
25. Herman Olshausen, *Biblical Commentary on the New Testament*, 3:360.
26. LaSor, p. 141.
27. Meyer, p. 349; Hackett, "A Commentary on the Acts of the Apostles," in *An American Commentary*, p. 211.
28. Kirsopp Lake and Henry J. Cadbury, *The Beginnings of Christianity*, 4:223.
29. Moe, *The Apostle Paul, His Life and His Work*, p. 313.
30. J. S. Howson and H. D. M. Spence, "The Acts of the Apostles," in *International Revision Commentary on the New Testament*, 5:271.
31. Lenski, p. 770.
32. Charles Hodge, *An Exposition of the First Epistle to the Corinthians*, p. 371.
33. Isabella Reid Buchanan, *The Women of the Bible*, p. 109.
34. Lees, p. 60.
35. Moses E. Lard, *Commentary on Paul's Letter to Romans*, p. 454.
36. Robertson, p. 67.
37. Guthrie, p. 404.
38. John Knox and Gerald R. Cragg, "The Epistle to the Romans," in *The Interpreter's Bible*, 9:654. For his discussion see pp. 365-368; 653-658.
39. M. J. Shroyer, "Aquila and Priscilla," in *The Interpreter's Dictionary of the Bible*, 1:176.

Chapter 3

1. Plumptre, "The Acts of the Apostles," in *Ellicott's Commentary on the Whole Bible*, 7:25.
2. A. C. Hervey, "Acts of the Apostles," in *The Pulpit Commentary*, 1:126.
3. J. Vernon Bartlet, "The Acts," in *The Century Bible*, p. 172.
4. Lenski, *The Interpretation of the Acts of the Apostles*, p. 189.
5. James Alex. Robertson, *The Hidden Romance of the New Testament*, pp. 46-47.
6. Plumptre, p. 25.
7. Floyd V. Filson, *Pioneers of the Primitive Church*, p. 84.
8. Paul S. Rees, *Men of Action in the Book of Acts*, p. 43. Rees' italics.
9. A. T. Robertson, *Types of Preachers in the New Testament*, p. 32.
10. Matthew Henry, *Commentary on the Whole Bible, New One Volume Edition*, p. 470.
11. Plumptre, p. 62.
12. Seekings, *The Men of the Pauline Circle*, p. 36.
13. Charles W. Carter and Ralph Earle, *The Acts of the Apostles*, The Evangelical Commentary, p. 58.
14. D. D. Whedon, *A Popular Commentary on the New Testament*, 3:144.
15. Filson, p. 99.
16. A. T. Robertson, p. 40.
17. Moulton and Milligan, *The Vocabulary of the Greek Testament*, p. 32.
18. Filson, p. 95.
19. Ramsay, *St. Paul the Traveller and the Roman Citizen*, pp. 51-52.
20. Joseph Henry Thayer, *A Greek-English Lexicon of the New Testament*, p. 138.
21. Ramsay, p. 66.
22. Bruce, *Commentary on the Book of the Acts*, The New International Commentary on the New Testament, p. 261.
23. Ramsay, pp. 84-85.
24. Ogg, p. 72.
25. Herbert F. Stevenson, *A Galaxy of Saints*, p. 118.
26. Filson, p. 87.
27. Moulton, *A Grammar of New Testament Greek*, vol. 1, *Prolegomena*, p. 130.
28. Lumby, *The Acts of the Apostles, Cambridge Bible for Schools*, p. 201.
29. Bruce, p. 318.
30. A. T. Robertson, p. 49.
31. William Owen Carver, *The Acts of the Apostles*, p. 162.
32. William Jacobson, "The Acts of the Apostles," in *The Speaker's Commentary, New Testament*, 2:459.
33. Meyer, *Critical and Exegetical Handbook to the Acts of the Apostles*, p. 298.
34. Walter F. Adeney, "Barnabas," in *Men of the New Testament. Matthew to Timothy*, p. 319.
35. John Calvin, *Commentary on the Epistles of Paul the Apostle to the Corinthians*. 2:299.
36. Tertullian *On Modesty* 20.

Chapter 4

1. Ramsay, *The Bearing of Recent Discovery on the Trustworthiness of the New Testament*, chap. 25.
2. W. M. Calder, *Classical Review*, Vol. 38, 1924. Quoted in Bruce, p. 6.
3. Bo Reicke, *The Gospel of Luke*, pp. 21-22. Ellis, "The Gospel of Luke," in *The Century Bible. New Edition*, pp. 52-53.
4. E. P. Blair, "Luke (Evangelist)," in *The Interpreter's Dictionary of the Bible*, 3:179.
5. Ellis, p. 54.
6. Bruce, *Commentary on the Epistle to the Colossians*, New International Commentary, p. 307f.
7. F. W. Grosheide, "Acts of the Apostles," in *The Encyclopedia of Christianity*, 1:47.
8. Farrar, *The Life and Work of St. Paul*, p. 272, note 3.
9. Rackham, *The Acts of the Apostles*, Westminster Commentaries, p. xxviii.

10. Ramsay, *St. Paul the Traveller and the Roman Citizen,* pp. 200-210.
11. Rackham, pp. xxx-xxxi.
12. Plummer, "A Critical and Exegetical Commentary on the Gospel According to St. Luke," in *International Critical Commentary,* p. xxi.
13. LaSor, p. 130.
14. Lockyer, *All the Men of the Bible,* p. 220.
15. Moe, *The Apostle Paul, His Life and Work,* pp. 259-260.
16. Ramsay, *St. Paul the Traveller,* pp. 59, 390; Lees, *St. Paul's Friends,* p. 89; A. Souter, "Luke," in *Dictionary of Christ and the Gospels,* 2:84.
17. William Kelly, *Notes on The Second Epistle of Paul the Apostle to the Corinthians,* p. 169.
18. Ramsay, *St. Paul the Traveller,* pp. 59, 390.
19. Carter and Earle, *The Acts of the Apostles,* The Evangelical Commentary, p. 394.
20. Lenski, *The Interpretation of the Acts of the Apostles,* p. 1061-66.
21. Ramsay, *Luke the Physician,* pp. 16-17; Rackham, p. 494; A. T. Robertson, *Luke the Historian in the Light of Research,* pp. 10, 28.
22. Ibid., p. 10.
23. F. J. Mueller, *They Knew Christ,* p. 3.
24. Lees, pp. 174-175.
25. Ibid.
26. Lake, "Luke," in *Dictionary of the Apostolic Church,* 1:718.
27. Cf. Ramsay, *St. Paul the Traveller,* pp. 1-10.
28. See I. Howard Marshall, *Luke: Historian and Theologian,* especially chaps. 6-9.
29. For the evidence, see A. T. Robertson; and J. A. Thompson, *Luke, the Historian.*
30. See Leander E. Keck and J. Louis Martyn, ed., *Studies in Luke-Acts;* Marshall; and W. Ward Gasque and Ralph P. Martin, ed., *Apostolic History and the Gospel,* part 1.
31. Blair, p. 180.

CHAPTER 5
1. J. H. Farmer, "Mark," in *The International Standard Bible Encyclopaedia,* 3:1986.
2. A. Plummer, "The Gospel According to St. Mark," in *Cambridge Greek Testament,* pp. ix-x.
3. Rackham, *The Acts of the Apostles,* Westminster Commentaries, p. 178.
4. Alfred Edersheim, *The Life and Times of Jesus the Messiah,* 2:485.
5. E. Bickersteth, "The Gospel According to St. Mark," in *The Pulpit Commentary,* 1:v.
6. Eusebius *Ecclesiastical History* 3:39.
7. James Morison, *A Practical Commentary on the Gospel According to St. Mark,* p. xix.
8. Henry Barclay Swete, *The Gospel According to St. Mark,* p. xv.
9. Ramsay, *St. Paul the Traveller,* p. 71.
10. Hackett, "A Commentary on the Acts of the Apostles," in *An American Commentary,* p. 151.
11. Carter and Earle, *The Acts of the Apostles,* The Evangelical Commentary, p. 178.
12. Swete, p. xvi.
13. Rackham, p. 199.
14. Farmer, 3:1987.
15. Seekings, *The Men of the Pauline Circle,* p. 46f.
16. LaSor, *Great Personalities of the New Testament,* pp. 125-126.
17. Lenski, *The Interpretation of the Acts of the Apostles,* p. 504.
18. Ramsay, *The Church in the Roman Empire Before A.D. 170,* p. 24.
19. Swete, p. xvii.
20. James D. Hunter, *John Mark; or, The Making of a Saint,* p. 67.
21. Lees, *St. Paul's Friends,* p. 119.
22. Lenski, *The Interpretation of St. Paul's Epistles to the Colossians, to the Thessalonians, to Timothy, to Titus and to Philemon,* p. 202.
23. Swete, pp. xx-xxi.
24. A. T. Robertson, *Making Good in the Ministry, A Sketch of John Mark,* p. 111.

25. Hiebert, pp. 122-126.
26. Charles Bigg. "A Critical and Exegetical Commentary on the Epistles of St. Peter and Jude," in *International Critical Commentary*, pp. 82-83.
27. On the Marcan authorship of the second gospel, see B. Harvie Branscomb, *The Gospel of Mark*, Moffatt New Testament Commentary, pp. xxxi-xxxviii; C. E. B. Cranfield, "The Gospel According to Saint Mark," in *Cambridge Greek Testament Commentary*, pp. 5-6; Plummer, pp. xv-xviii; Swete, pp. xiii-xxviii; Vincent Taylor, *The Gospel According to St. Mark*, pp. 26-31.
28. Robertson pp. 139-145.
29. Lees, p. 110.
30. A. F. Hort, *The Gospel According to St. Mark*, p. xviii.
31. Swete, p. xx.

CHAPTER 6
1. Edward Gordon Selwyn, *The First Epistle of St. Peter*, p. 11.
2. Plumptre, "The Acts of the Apostles," in *Ellicott's Commentary on the Whole Bible*, 7:99.
3. Selwyn, p. 11.
4. Bruce, "1 and 2 Thessalonians," in *The New Bible Commentary, Revised*, p. 1157.
5. Joseph Addison Alexander, *The Acts of the Apostles*, 2:88.
6. Carter and Earle, *The Acts of the Apostles*, The Evangelical Commentary, p. 238.
7. C. S. C. Williams, *A Commentary on the Acts of the Apostles*, Harper's New Testament Commentaries, p. 184.
8. McGarvey, *New Commentary on Acts of Apostles*, 2:69.
9. Bruce, *Commentary on the Book of the Acts*, The New International Commentary, p. 317.
10. Ramsay, *St. Paul the Traveller and the Roman Citizen*, p. 174-175.
11. Meyer, *Critical and Exegetical Handbook to the Acts of the Apostles*, p. 299.
12. David Smith, *The Life and Letters of Paul*, p. 118.
13. Plumptre, p. 102.
14. R. E. Nixon, "Silas" in *The New Bible Dictionary*, p. 1186.
15. Lees, *St. Paul's Friends*, p. 33.
16. Lenski, *The Interpretation of the Acts of the Apostles*, p. 630.
17. Seekings, *The Men of the Pauline Circle*, p. 79.
18. Jacobson, "The Acts of the Apostles," in *The Speaker's Commentary, New Testament*, 2:456.
19. B. Wrey Savile, "Silas," in *Fairbairn's Imperial Standard Bible Encyclopedia*, 6:174.
20. J. H. A. Hart, "The First Epistle General of Peter," in *The Expositor's Greek Testament*, 5:79.
21. G. J. Polkinghorne, "The First Letter of Peter," in *A New Testament Commentary*, p. 597.
22. Lenski, *The Interpretation of the Epistles of St. Peter, St. John and St. Jude*, p. 233.
23. Selwyn, p. 241.
24. Joh. Ed. Huther, "Critical and Exegetical Handbook to the General Epistles of Peter and Jude," in *Meyer's Commentary on the New Testament*, p. 243; Lenski, pp. 233-234.
25. J. N. D. Kelly, *A Commentary on the Epistles of Peter and of Jude*, Harper's New Testament Commentaries, p. 215.
26. Theodor Zahn, *Introduction to the New Testament*, 2:150.
27. Guthrie, *New Testament Introduction*, p. 780.
28. Lees, p. 30.

CHAPTER 7
1. Francis Bourdillon, *Lesser Lights*, Second Series, p. 286.
2. Ramsay, *St. Paul the Traveller and the Roman Citizen*, p. 179.
3. Plumptre, "The Acts of the Apostles," in *Ellicott's Commentary on the Whole Bible*, 7:102.

4. Lenski, *The Interpretation of St. Paul's Epistles to the Colossians, to the Thessalonians, to Timothy, to Titus and to Philemon*, p. 850.
5. McGarvey, *New Commentary on Acts of Apostles*, 2:79.
6. Henri Daniel Rops, *Daily Life in the Time of Jesus*, p. 122.
7. Alexander, *The Acts of the Apostles*, 2:102.
8. William Mordaunt Furneaux, *The Acts of the Apostles*, p. 254; Lenski, *The Interpretation of the Acts of the Apostles*, p. 634; R. Martin Pope, *The Epistles of Paul the Apostle to Timothy and Titus*, p. 101.
9. Zahn, *Introduction to the New Testament*, 1:203, 523; Lenski, p. 685.
10. Zahn, 1:265.
11. Ramsay, p. 276.
12. Lenski, p. 797.
13. Assuming the Roman origin of the Prison Epistles. See Hiebert, *An Introduction to the Pauline Epistles*, pp. 205-214. For the view that Colossians and Ephesians were written from Caesarea, but Philippians from Rome, see Reicke, "Caesarea, Rome, and the Captivity Epistles," in *Apostolic History and the Gospel*, pp. 277-286.
14. Seekings, *The Men of the Pauline Circle*, p. 60.
15. H. O. Kee, "Timothy," in *The Interpreter's Dictionary of the Bible*, 4:651.
16. Ernest Findlay Scott, *The Literature of the New Testament*, p. 194.
17. Guthrie, p. 620.
18. W. J. Conybeare and Howson, *The Life and Epistles of Saint Paul*, p. 811.
19. Henry Alford, *The New Testament for English Readers*, p. 1393.
20. Lees, *St. Paul's Friends*, p. 142.

CHAPTER 8
1. Lees, *St. Paul's Friends*, p. 87; Seekings, *The Men of the Pauline Circle*, p. 65. Asa Zadel Hall, *A Cloud of Witnesses*, p. 27.
2. Ramsay, *St. Paul the Traveller and the Roman Citizen*, pp. 59, 390; A. Souter, "Luke," in *A Dictionary of Christ and the Gospels*, 2:84.
3. Lees, p. 89.
4. J. B. Lightfoot, *Biblical Essays*, p. 281.
5. Bruce, *Commentary on the Book of Acts*, New International Commentary, pp. 244, 298-300; A. W. F. Blunt, "The Epistle of Paul to the Galatians," *The Clarendon Bible*, pp. 77-84; George S. Duncan, *The Epistle of Paul to the Galatians*, The Moffatt New Testament Commentary, pp. xxii-xxvi.
6. A. E. Humphreys, "The Epistles to Timothy and Titus," in *Cambridge Bible for Schools and Colleges*, pp. 68-69.
7. LaSor, *Great Personalities of the New Testament*, p. 152.
8. John Eadie, *Commentary on the Epistle of Paul to the Galatians*, p. 112.
9. Farrar, *The Life and Work of St. Paul*, pp. 232-237; Duncan, pp. 41-45.
10. Farrar, p. 235.
11. Moe, *The Apostle Paul, His Life and His Work*, p. 232.
12. Ernest Faulkner Brown, *The Pastoral Epistles*, Westminster Commentaries, p. xix.
13. Ramsay, p. 286.
14. Humphreys, p. 70; Ramsay, p. 285.
15. Hiebert, *An Introduction to the Pauline Epistles*, pp. 137-146, 148.
16. Kee, "Titus, Companion of Paul," in *The Interpreter's Dictionary of the Bible*, p. 656.
17. Ibid.
18. Bourdillon, *Lesser Lights*, Second Series, p. 299.

CHAPTER 9
1. G. Campbell Morgan, *The Acts of the Apostles*, p. 231.
2. McGarvey, *New Commentary on Acts of Apostles*, 1:175.
3. William Kelly, *An Exposition of the Acts of the Apostles*, p. 130.
4. Seekings, *The Men of the Pauline Circle*, p. 129.
5. Carver, *The Acts of the Apostles*, pp. 95-96.
6. Plumptre, "The Acts of the Apostles," in *Ellicott's Commentary on the Whole Bible*, 8:60.

CHAPTER 10
1. Rudolf Schnackenburg, "Apostles Before and During Paul's Time," in *Apostolic History and the Gospel*, pp. 293-294.
2. H. P. Liddon, *Explanatory Analysis of St. Paul's Epistle to the Romans*, p. 296.
3. John Miller, *Commentary on Paul's Epistle to Romans*, p. 378-79.
4. Zahn, *Introduction to the New Testament*, 1:417.
5. Ibid.
6. Denney, "St. Paul's Epistle to the Romans," in *The Expositor's Greek Testament*, 2:719.
7. Conybeare and Howson, *The Life and Epistles of Saint Paul*, p. 581, note 4.
8. Ramsay, *The Cities of St. Paul*, pp. 177-178.
9. Meyer, *Critical and Exegetical Hand-Book to the Epistle to the Romans*, p. 586, note 1.
10. Sanday and Headlam, "A Critical and Exegetical Commentary on the Epistle to the Romans," in *The International Critical Commentary*, p. 423.
11. Denney, 2:719.
12. Zahn, 1:418.
13. Barrett, *A Commentary on the Epistle to the Romans*, Harper's New Testament Commentaries, p. 283.
14. Sanday and Headlam, p. 423.
15. Robert Haldane, *Exposition of the Epistle to the Romans*, stamps this suggestion as "a conclusion without premises." p. 637.
16. Lenski, *The Interpretation of St. Paul's Epistle to the Romans*, p. 907.
17. Zahn, 1:418.
18. Liddon, p. 296.
19. James M. Stifler, *The Epistle to the Romans*, p. 265.
20. J. T. L. Maggs, *The Spiritual Experience of St. Paul*, p. 112.

CHAPTER 11
1. Ramsay, *St. Paul the Traveller and the Roman Citizen*, p. 280.
2. Plumptre, "The Acts of the Apostles," in *Ellicott's Commentary on the Whole Bible*, 7:134.
3. Ramsay; p. 316; Smith, *The Life and Letters of St. Paul*, p. 491; Bruce, *Commentary on the Book of the Acts*, New International Commentary, p. 501; Carter and Earle, "The Acts of the Apostles," The Evangelical Commentary, p. 394; Lenski, *The Interpretation of the Acts of the Apostles*, p. 1056.
4. Farrar, *The Life and Work of St. Paul*, p. 563.
5. Lightfoot, *Saint Paul's Epistle to the Philippians*, p. 35, note 2.
6. Lightfoot, *Saint Paul's Epistles to the Colossians and to Philemon*, p. 234.
7. Norris, "Aristarchus," in *The Interpreter's Dictionary of the Bible*, 1:219.

CHAPTER 12
1. Smith, *The Life and Letters of St. Paul*, p. 522; Ramsay, *St. Paul the Traveller and the Roman Citizen*, p. 358.
2. Lenski, *The Interpretation of St. Paul's Epistles to the Colossians, to the Thessalonians, to Timothy, to Titus and to Philemon*, p. 206.
3. Lees, *St. Paul's Friends*, p. 188.
4. W. F. Boyd, "Demas," in *Dictionary of the Apostolic Church*, 1:287.
5. J. N. D. Kelly, *A Commentary on the Pastoral Epistles*, Harper's New Testament Commentaries, p. 213.
6. Seekings, *The Men of the Pauline Circle*, p. 187-88.

CHAPTER 13
1. A. T. Robertson, *Some Minor Characters in the New Testament*, p. 91.
2. Eadie, *A Commentary on the Greek Text of the Epistle of Paul to the Colossians*, p. 287.
3. Ibid.
4. Alexander Maclaren, "The Epistles of St. Paul to the Colossians and to Philemon," in *An Exposition of the Bible*, 6:286b.
5. Lightfoot, *Saint Paul's Epistles to the Colossians and to Philemon*, p. 238.

6. Joseph Agar Beet, *A Commentary on St. Paul's Epistles to the Ephesians, Philippians, Colossians, and to Philemon*, p. 236.
7. Seekings, *The Men of the Pauline Circle*, p. 153.
8. H. C. G. Moule, "The Epistles of Paul the Apostle to the Colossians and to Philemon," in *Cambridge Bible for Schools and Colleges*, p. 141.
9. Richard Chenevix Trench, *Synonyms of the New Testament*, p. 378.

CHAPTER 14
1. Howson, *The Companions of St. Paul*, p. 169.
2. Moe, *The Apostle Paul, His Life and His Work*, p. 478.
3. Farrar, *The Life and Work of St. Paul*, p. 594.
4. John Trapp, *Trapp's Commentary on the New Testament*, p. 607-608.
5. Lightfoot, *Saint Paul's Epistle to the Philippians*, pp. 195-196; Alfred Barry, "The Epistles of Paul the Apostle to the Ephesians, Philippians, and Colossians," in *Ellicott's Commentary on the Whole Bible*, 8:78.
6. H. A. A. Kennedy, "The Epistle of Paul to the Philippians," in *The Expositor's Greek Testament*, 3:445.
7. Herbert F. Stevenson, *A Galaxy of Saints*, p. 126-27.
8. William F. Arndt and F. Wilbur Gingrich, *A Greek-English Lexicon of the New Testament and Other Early Christian Literature*, p. 99; Hendriksen, *Exposition of Philippians, New Testament Commentary*, pp. 139-140.
9. Arndt and Gingrich, p. 472.
10. H. G. G. Herklots, *The Epistle of St. Paul to the Philippians*, p. 82.
11. Lenski, *The Interpretation of St. Paul's Epistles to the Galatians, to the Ephesians, and to the Philippians*, (1937), pp. 696-697.
12. Hendriksen, p. 140. Hendriksen's italics.
13. Lightfoot, p. 125.
14. Seekings, *The Men of the Pauline Circle*, p. 162.
15. Beet, *A Commentary on St. Paul's Epistles to the Ephesians, Philippians, Colossians, and to Philemon*, p. 86.
16. Quoted in J. B. Gough Pidge, "Commentary on the Epistle to the Philippians," in *An American Commentary*, p. 39.
17. Hendriksen, p. 141. Hendriksen's italics.
18. Farrar, p. 594.
19. A. H. Stewart, "Bodily Healing Since Pentecost," *Our Hope*, (Aug. 1953), p. 102.
20. W. E. Vine, *Epistles to the Philippians and Colossians*, p. 74.
21. Howson, p. 175.
22. Reicke, *Apostolic History and the Gospel*, p. 284.

CHAPTER 15
1. A. T. Robertson, *Word Pictures in the New Testament*, 4:430.
2. Marvin R. Vincent, *Word Studies in the New Testament*, 3:182.
3. Haldane, *Exposition of the Epistle to the Romans*, p. 647.
4. Bruce, *The Epistle of Paul to the Romans*, Tyndale Bible Commentaries, p. 280.
5. McGarvey, *New Commentary on Acts of Apostles*, 2:159.
6. Liddon, *Explanatory Analysis of St. Paul's Epistle to the Romans*, p. 304.
7. George S. Duncan, *St. Paul's Ephesian Ministry*, pp. 79-80.

CHAPTER 16
1. J. Gibb, "Euodia" in *A Dictionary of the Bible*, 1:794.
2. Moule, *Philippian Studies*, p. 224.
3. T. Walker, *The Epistle to the Philippians*, The Indian Church Commentaries, p. 97.
4. Meyer, *Critical and Exegetical Handbook to the Epistles to the Philippians and Colossians*, p. 193. Meyer's italics.
5. A. T. Robertson, *Paul's Joy in Christ, Studies in Philippians*, p. 230.

Chapter 17

1. Farrar, *The Early Days of Christianity*, p. 569.
2. Goodspeed, "Gaius Titius Justus," in *Journal of Biblical Literature*, 69:382-83; Bruce, *Commentary on the Book of the Acts*, New International Commentary, p. 371.
3. Clarke, *Clarke's Commentary*, 6:165.
4. Albert N. Arnold and B. D. Ford, "Commentary on the Epistle to the Romans," in *An American Commentary*, p. 310.
5. Moule, "The Epistle of Paul the Apostle to the Romans," in *Cambridge Bible for Schools*, p. 255.
6. Sanday, "The Epistle of Paul the Apostle to the Romans," in *Ellicott's Commentary on the Whole Bible*, 7:27.
7. Ramsay, *St. Paul the Traveller and the Roman Citizen*, p. 280; Blunt, *The Acts of the Apostles*, The Clarendon Bible, p. 226.
8. See R. C. H. Lenski, *The Interpretation of the Acts of the Apostles*, p. 817.
9. Olshausen, *Biblical Commentary on the New Testament*, 3:378; Plumptre, "The Acts of the Apostles," in *Ellicott's Commentary on the Whole Bible*, 7:137.
10. Williams, *The Acts of the Apostles*, Harper's New Testament Commentaries, p. 229-30; Bruce, *The Acts of the Apostles*, pp. 370-71.

Chapter 18

1. Adeney, *Women of the New Testament*, p. 225.
2. Lake and Cadbury, *The Beginnings of Christianity*, 4:191.
3. Horace, *Odes* 1:8; 3:9.
4. Rackham, *The Acts of the Apostles*, Westminster Commentaries, p. 283.
5. Lightfoot, *Saint Paul's Epistle to the Philippians*, pp. 55-57.
6. Smith, *The Life and Letters of St. Paul*, p. 128.
7. Rackham, p. 282.
8. Moulton and Milligan, *The Vocabulary of the Greek Testament*, p. 547 .
9. Arnold T. Olson, *The Pacemakers. The Story of Six Conversions to Christianity from the Acts of the Apostles*, p. 45.
10. Taylor, *Paul the Missionary*, p. 227.
11. Meyer, *Critical and Exegetical Handbook to the Acts of the Apostles*, p. 312.
12. Carter and Earle, *The Acts of the Apostles*, The Evangelical Commentary, p. 235.
13. Margaret E. Sangster, *The Women of the Bible: A Portrait Gallery*, p. 339.
14. Rackham, p. 283.
15. Sangster, p. 340.
16. Farrar, *The Life and Work of St. Paul*, p. 276.

Chapter 19

1. John Knox, *Philemon Among the Letters of Paul*, p. 58; Herbert M. Carson, *The Epistles of Paul to the Colossians and Philemon*, Tyndale New Testament Commentaries, pp. 19-20; Hendriksen, *Exposition of Colossians and Philemon*, New Testament Commentary, pp. 23-26; C. F. D. Moule, "The Epistles of Paul the Apostle to the Colossians and to Philemon," in *Cambridge Greek Testament Commentary*, pp.14-18.
2. Smith, *The Life and Letters of St. Paul*, p. 545.
3. Vincent, "A Critical and Exegetical Commentary on the Epistles to the Philippians and to Philemon," in *International Critical Commentary*, p. 158.
4. Sallust *Catiline* 37:5.
5. Duncan, *St. Paul's Ephesian Ministry*, p 73
6. Meyer, *Critical and Exegetical Hand-Book to the Epistle to the Ephesians*, pp. 299-301; Martin Dibelius and Werner Georg Kümmel, *Paul*, p. 146.
7. Reicke, "Caesarea, Rome, and the Captivity Epistles," in *Apostolic History and the Gospel*, p. 281.
8. Duncan, p. 73.
9. Moule, p. 24.
10. G. H. P. Thompson, "The Letters of Paul to the Ephesians to the Colossians and to Philemon," in *The Cambridge Bible Commentary*, p. 115.

11. Archibald Kelly MacMurchy, *The Epistle of Paul to Philemon*, p. 4.
12. J. Morgan Gibbon, "Onesimus," in *Men of the New Testament, Matthew to Timothy*, p. 326.
13. Lightfoot, *Saint Paul's Epistles to the Colossians and to Philemon*, p. 312.
14. Francis W. Beare and G. Preston MacLeod, "The Epistle to the Colossians," in *The Interpreter's Bible*, 11:235.
15. John Knox and George A. Buttrick, "The Epistle to Philemon," in *The Interpreter's Bible*, 11:557-560.

CHAPTER 20
1. J. N. D. Kelly, *A Commentary on the Pastoral Epistles*, Harper's New Testament Commentaries, p. 170.
2. Stevenson, *A Galaxy of Saints*, p. 133.
3. Scott, *The Pastoral Epistles*, The Moffatt New Testament Commentary, p. 99.
4. Don De Welt, *Paul's Letters to Timothy and Titus*, Bible Study Textbook, p. 206.
5. Seekings, *The Men of the Pauline Circle*, p. 172.
6. Scott, p. 99.
7. Lenski, *The Interpretation of St. Paul's Epistles to the Colossians, to the Thessalonians, to Timothy, to Titus and to Philemon*, p. 784.
8. See Plummer, "The Pastoral Epistles," *An Exposition of the Bible*, 6:464-466; Plumptre, *The Spirits in Prison*, pp. 128, 266; Newport J. D. White, "The Pastoral Epistles," in *The Expositor's Greek Testament*, 4:159; J. H. Bernard, "The Pastoral Epistles," in *Cambridge Greek Testament*, p. 114; J. N. D. Kelly, pp. 169-171.
9. Plummer, 6:465-66.
10. See Lenski, pp. 784-787; Simpson, *The Pastoral Epistles*, p. 129; Guthrie, *The Pastoral Epistles*, Tyndale New Testament Commentaries, p. 136; Hendriksen, *Exposition of the Pastoral Epistles*, New Testament Commentary, pp. 238-240; De Welt, p. 207.
11. Guthrie, p. 136.
12. Hendriksen, p. 238f.
13. A. R. Fausset, *Biblical Cyclopaedia, Critical and Expository*, p. 529b.
14. Scott, p. 99.

CHAPTER 21
1. Burrell, *Life and Letters of St. Paul*, p. 299.
2. Scott, *The Epistles of Paul to the Colossians, to Philemon and to the Ephesians*, The Moffatt New Testament Commentary, p. 97-98.
3. Lightfoot, *Saint Paul's Epistles to the Colossians and to Philemon*, p. 303.
4. Addition by Hackett in J. J. Van Oosterzee, "The Epistle of Paul to Philemon," in *Lange's Commentary on the Holy Scriptures*, p. 12.
5. Scott, p. 98.
6. John Knox, *Philemon Among the Letters of Paul;* introduction to "The Epistle to Philemon," in *The Interpreter's Bible*, 11:555-60.
7. Everett F. Harrison, *Introduction to the New Testament*, pp. 308-309; Hendriksen, *Exposition of Colossians and Philemon*, New Testament Commentary, pp. 23-26; C. F. D. Moule, "The Epistles of Paul the Apostle to the Colossians and to Philemon," in *Cambridge Greek Testament Commentary*, pp. 14-18.
8. In Van Oosterzee, p. 22.
9. Knox, "The Epistle to Philemon," in *The Interpreter's Bible*, 11:557.
10. Frank Bertram Clogg, *An Introduction to the New Testament*, p. 91.
11. William Barclay, *The Letters to Timothy, Titus and Philemon*, The Daily Study Bible, p. 317-18.
12. A. H. Drysdale, *The Epistle of St. Paul to Philemon*, Devotional Commentaries, p. 23.
13. Hackett, p. 5.
14. S. Angus, *The Environment of Early Christianity*, p. 38.

15. Kelly, *The Epistles of Peter and of Jude,* Harper's New Testament Commentaries, p. 115.
16. Richard Longenecker, *The Ministry and Message of Paul,* p. 84.
17. William Neil, *Harper's Bible Commentary,* p. 504.

CHAPTER 22
1. Meyer, *Critical and Exegetical Hand-Book to the Epistle to the Romans,* p. 565.
2. Quoted in Vincent, *Word Studies in the New Testament,* 3:177.
3. Barrett, *The New Testament Background: Selected Documents,* pp. 28-29. See also Barclay, *The Letter to the Romans,* The Daily Study Bible, pp. 226-227.
4. Denney, "St. Paul's Epistle to the Romans," in *The Expositor's Greek Testament,* 2:717.
5. Howson, *The Companions of St. Paul,* p. 101.
6. Dodd, *The Epistle of Paul to the Romans,* in The Moffatt New Testament Commentary, p. 235.
7. Lenski, *The Interpretation of St. Paul's Epistle to the Romans,* p. 900.
8. William R. Newell, *Romans Verse by Verse,* p. 549.
9. Cecil J. Pickering, "Phoebe's commendation," *The Witness* (Feb. 1963), p. 44.
10. Denney, p. 718.
11. J. W. Shepard, *The Life and Letters of St. Paul,* p. 449.
12. Stifler, *The Epistle to the Romans,* p. 283.
13. Conybeare and Howson, *The Life and Epistles of Saint Paul,* p. 581, note 1; Vincent, 3:177; H. C. G. Moule, "The Epistle of Paul the Apostle to the Romans, " in *The Cambridge Bible for Schools and Colleges,* p. 246.
14. Bourdillon, *Lesser Lights,* p. 198.
15. Howson, p. 104.
16. S. F. Hunter, "Phoebe," in *The International Standard Bible Encyclopaedia,* 4:2386.
17. Conybeare, p. 542, note 6.
18. Lenski, p. 901.
19. Howard Rhys, *The Epistle to the Romans,* p. 198.
20. Lenski, p. 901.
21. Floyd E. Hamilton, *The Epistle to the Romans,* p. 231; E. H. Gifford, "The Epistle of St. Paul to the Romans," in *The Speaker's Commentary,* 3:231; Smith, *The Life and Letters of St. Paul,* p. 189.

CHAPTER 23
1. Lenski, *The Interpretation of St. Paul's First and Second Epistle to the Corinthians,* p. 794.
2. Moffatt, *The First Epistle of Paul to the Corinthians,* The Moffatt New Testament Commentary, p. 278; Joseph Waite, "The Second Epistle of Paul the Apostle to the Corinthians," in *The Speaker's Commentary,* 3:390.
3. Zahn, *Introduction to the New Testament,* 1:175.
4. Ramsay, *The Bearing of Recent Discovery on the Trustworthiness of The New Testament,* pp. 385-387 with 164-166.
5. H. L. Goudge, *The First Epistle to the Corinthians,* Westminster Commentaries, p. 170.
6. Thomas Charles Edwards, *A Commentary on the First Epistle to the Corinthians,* p. 471.
7 Goudge, p 7
8. Zahn, pp. 265-266; Lenski, pp. 47-48, 794.
9. Christian Friedrich Kling, "The First Epistle to the Corinthians," in Lange's *Commentary on the Holy Scriptures,* p. 359.
10. Goudge, p. 170.
11. Meyer, *Critical and Exegetical Hand-Book to the Epistles to the Corinthians,* p. 400.
12. Charles Hodge, *An Exposition of the First Epistle to the Corinthians,* p. 370.

CHAPTER 24
1. Meyer, *Critical and Exegetical Handbook to the Acts of the Apostles,* p. 410.

2. Joseph Klausner, *From Jesus to Paul*, p. 400.
3. Bruce, *Commentary on the Book of the Acts*, New International Commentary, p. 434, note 46.
4. Simpson, *The Pastoral Epistles*, p. 162.
5. W. E. Vine, *Exposition of the Epistles to Timothy*, p. 98.
6. Hall, *A Cloud of Witnesses*, p. 56.

CHAPTER 25

1. Ramsay, *The Church in the Roman Empire*, p. 154.
2. Norris, "Tychicus," in *The Interpreter's Dictionary of the Bible*, 4:720.
3. Bruce, *Commentary on the Epistle to the Colossians*, New International Commentary, p. 302, note 23.
4. Eadie, *A Commentary on the Greek Text of the Epistle of Paul to the Colossians*, p. 280.
5. T. K. Abbott, "A Critical and Exegetical Commentary on the Epistles to the Ephesians and to the Colossians," in *International Critical Commentary*, p. 298.
6. Herbert M. Carson, *The Epistles of Paul to the Colossians and Philemon*, Tyndale New Testament Commentaries, p. 98.
7. Seekings, *The Men of the Pauline Circle*, p. 139.
8. Lees, *St. Paul's Friends*, p. 218.
9. G. H. P. Thompson, "The Letters of Paul to the Ephesians, to the Colossians and to Philemon," in *The Cambridge Bible Commentary*, p. 19. See also Wilfred L. Knox, *St. Paul and the Church of the Gentiles*, p. 203; C. L. Mitton, *The Epistle to the Ephesians*, p. 268.
10. Hiebert, *An Introduction to the Pauline Epistles*, pp. 319-324.
11. Joh. Ed. Huther, "Critical and Exegetical Handbook to the Epistles of St. Paul to Timothy and Titus," in *Meyer's Critical and Exegetical Commentary on the New Testament*, p. 324.
12. Hendriksen, *Exposition of the Pastoral Epistles*, New Testament Commentary, p. 322.

CHAPTER 27

1. Ramsay, *The Church in the Roman Empire*, p. 53. Ramsay accepts the plural "the priests" in Codex D.
2. Miller, *Commentary on Paul's Epistle to Romans*, p. 379.
3. Zahn, *Introduction to the New Testament*, 2:505.
4. F. Godet, *Commentary on the Epistle to the Romans*, p. 493.
5. Bruce, *The Epistle of Paul to the Romans*, Tyndale New Testament Commentaries, p. 274.
6. See Lenski, *The Interpretation of St. Paul's First and Second Epistle to the Corinthians*, pp. 900-918; Hughes, *Paul's Second Epistle to the Corinthians*, The New International Commentary on the New Testament, pp. 59-72.
7. R. H. Strachan, *The Second Epistle of Paul to the Corinthians*, Moffatt New Testament Commentary, pp. xvi-xxii.
8. See Alfred Plummer, "A Critical and Exegetical Commentary on the Second Epistle of St Paul to the Corinthians," in *International Critical Commentary*, pp. xv-xix, 52-64; G. R. Beasley-Murray, "2 Corinthians," in *The Broadman Bible Commentary*, vol. 11, pp. 15-17.
9. Ramsey, *St. Paul the Traveller and the Roman Citizen*, p. 390; Souter, "Luke," in *Dictionary of Christ and the Gospels*, 2:84.
10. Hughes, *Paul's Second Epistle to the Corinthians*, New International Commentary, pp. 312-316; Plummer, "A Critical and Exegetical Commentary on the Second Epistle of St. Paul to the Corinthians," in *International Critical Commentary*, p. 248.
11. Plummer, p. 250, second note.
12. Lightfoot, *Saint Paul's Epistle to the Philippians*, p. 158.
13. Maurice Jones, *The Epistle to the Philippians*, Westminster Commentaries, p. 65.
14. Smith, *The Life and Letters of St. Paul*, p. 519, note.

15. Arndt and Gingrich, *A Greek-English Lexicon of the New Testament and Other Early Christian Literature*, p. 783.
16. J. Hugh Michael, *The Epistle of Paul to the Philippians*, Moffatt New Testament Commentary, p. 191.

BIBLIOGRAPHY

BIBLICAL TEXTS

GREEK

Aland, Kurt; Black, Matthew; Metzger, Bruce M.; Wikgren, Allen. *The Greek New Testament.* London: United Bible Soc., 1966.

Nestle, Erwin; and Aland, Kurt. *Novum Testamentum Graece.* 24th ed. Stuttgart: Privileg. Württ. Bibleanstalt.

Souter, Alexander. *Novum Testamentum Graece.* 1910. Reprint. Oxford: Clarendon, 1962.

Wescott, Brooke Foss; and Hort, Fenton John Anthony. *The New Testament in the Original Greek.* Reprint. New York: Macmillan, 1935.

ENGLISH VERSIONS

American Standard Version. New York: Nelson, 1901.

King James Version. Cambridge: University Press.

New American Standard Bible. Carol Stream, Ill.: Creation House, 1971.

Rotherham, Joseph Bryant. *The Emphasized New Testament.* Reprint. Grand Rapids: Kregel, 1959.

Weymouth, Richard Francis. *The New Testament in Modern Speech.* 1902. 5th rev. ed. Reprint. New York: Harper, n.d.

Williams, Charles B. *The New Testament: A Private Translation in the Language of the People.* Chicago: Moody, 1949.

GRAMMARS, LEXICONS, WORD STUDIES

Arndt, William F.; and Gingrich, F. Wilbur. *A Greek-English Lexicon of the New Testament and Other Early Christian Literature.* Chicago: U. Chicago, 1957.

Moulton, James Hope. *A Grammar of New Testament Greek.* Vol. 1, *Prolegomena.* Edinburgh: T. & T. Clark, 1908.

Moulton, James Hope; and Milligan, George. *The Vocabulary of the Greek Testament.* Reprint. London: Hodder & Stoughton, 1952.

252

Robertson, Archibald Thomas. *Word Pictures in the New Testament.* Vol. 4. New York: Harper, 1930.

Thayer, Joseph Henry. *A Greek-English Lexicon of the New Testament.* Reprint. New York: Amer. Book, 1899.

Trench, Richard Chenevix. *Synonyms of the New Testament.* Reprint. Grand Rapids: Eerdmans, 1947.

Vincent, Marvin R. *Word Studies in the New Testament.* Vol. 3, *The Epistles of Paul.* Reprint. Grand Rapids: Eerdmans, 1946.

NEW TESTAMENT INTRODUCTION

Clogg, Frank Bertram. *An Introduction to the New Testament.* London: U. London, 1949.

Goodspeed, Edgar J. *An Introduction to the New Testament.* Chicago: U. Chicago, 1937.

Guthrie, Donald. *New Testament Introduction.* Rev. ed. Downers Grove, Ill.: Inter-Varsity, 1971.

Harrison, Everett F. *Introduction to the New Testament.* Grand Rapids: Eerdmans, 1964.

Hiebert, D. Edmond. *An Introduction to the Non-Pauline Epistles.* Chicago: Moody, 1962.

_____ *An Introduction to the Pauline Epistles.* Chicago: Moody, 1954.

Hunter, Archibald M. *Interpreting the New Testament, 1900-1950.* Philadelphia: Westminster, 1951.

Knox, John. *Philemon Among the Letters of Paul.* Chicago: U. Chicago, 1935.

Kümmel, Werner Georg. *Introduction to the New Testament.* Trans. A. J. Mattill, Jr. Nashville: Abingdon, 1966.

Marxsen, W. *Introduction to the New Testament. An Approach to Its Problems.* Trans. G. Buswell. Philadelphia: Fortress, 1968.

Moffatt, James. *An Introduction to the Literature of the New Testament.* Reprint. Edinburgh: T. & T. Clarke, 1949.

Scott, Ernest Findlay. *The Literature of the New Testament.* Reprint. New York: Columbia U., 1948.

Zahn, Theodor. *Introduction to the New Testament.* Vols. 1 & 2. Edinburgh: T. & T. Clark, 1909.

BOOKS ON PAUL

Burrell, David James. *Life and Letters of St. Paul.* New York: American Tract Soc., 1925.

Conybeare, W. J.; and Howson, J. S. *The Life and Epistles of Saint Paul.* People's edition. Hartford, Conn.: Scranton, 1902.

Deissman, G. Adolf. *Paul. A Study in Social and Religious History.* Trans. William E. Wilson. Reprint. New York: Harper & Row, 1957.

Dibelius, Martin; *Paul.* Ed. and completed Werner Georg Kümmel. Trans. Frank Clarke. Reprint. Philadelphia: Westminster, 1966.

Duncan, George S. *St. Paul's Ephesian Ministry. A Reconstruction.* New York: Scribner, 1930.

Farrar, F. W. *The Life and Work of St. Paul.* New York: Dutton, 1889.

Hayes, D. A. *Paul and His Epistles.* New York: Methodist Book Concern, 1915.

Knox, Wilfred L. *St. Paul and the Church of the Gentiles.* Reprint. Cambridge: U. Press, 1961.

Longenecker, Richard. *The Ministry and Message of Paul.* Grand Rapids: Zondervan, 1971.

Moe, Olaf. *The Apostle Paul, His Life and His Work.* Trans. L. A. Vigness. Minneapolis: Augsburg, 1950.

Ogg, George. *The Chronology of the Life of Paul.* London: Epworth, 1968.

Ramsay, W. M. *St. Paul the Traveller and the Roman Citizen.* New York: Putnam, 1896.

Shepard, J. W. *The Life and Letters of St. Paul.* Grand Rapids: Eerdmans, 1950.

Smith, David. *The Life and Letters of St. Paul.* New York: Harper, n.d.

Taylor, William M. *Paul the Missionary.* 1881. Reprint. New York: Richard R. Smith, 1930.

White, Reginald E. O. *Apostle Extraordinary. A Modern Portrait of St. Paul.* Grand Rapids: Eerdmans, 1962.

BOOKS ON COMPANIONS OF PAUL

Adeney, Walter F. "Barnabas." In *Men of the New Testament.* See under Milligan, George.

———. *Women of the New Testament.* London: Service & Paton, 1899.

Bourdillon, Francis. *Lesser Lights: or Some of the Minor Characters of Scripture.* Second Series. London: SPCK, n.d.

Buchanan, Isabella Reid. *The Women of the Bible.* New York: Appleton, 1924.

Filson, Floyd V. *Pioneers of the Primitive Church.* New York: Abingdon, 1940.

Gibbon, J. Morgan. "Onesimus." In *Men of the New Testament.* See under Milligan, George.

Hall, Asa Zadel. *A Cloud of Witnesses*. Grand Rapids: Zondervan, 1961.

Hastings James. *The Greater Men and Women of the Bible. St. Luke — Titus*. New York: Scribner, 1916.

Howson, John S. *The Companions of St. Paul*. Boston: Amer. Tract Soc., 1872.

Hunter, James D. *John Mark; or, The Making of a Saint*. New York: Amer. Tract Soc., 1903.

LaSor, William Sanford. *Great Personalities of the New Testament*. Westwood, N.J.: Revell, 1961.

Lees, Harrington C. *St. Paul's Friends*. London: Religious Tract Soc., 1918.

Lockyer, Herbert. *All the Men of the Bible*. Grand Rapids: Zondervan, 1958.

Milligan, George; Adeney, Walter F.; et al. *Men of the New Testament. Matthew to Timothy*. Manchester: James Robinson, 1905.

Rees, Paul S. *Men of Action in the Book of Acts*. Westwood, N.J.: Revell, 1966.

Robertson, A. T. *Making Good in the Ministry, a Sketch of John Mark*. New York: Revell, 1918.

_____. *Some Minor Characters in the New Testament*. Garden City, New York: Doubleday, Doran, 1928.

_____. *Types of Preachers in the New Testament*. New York: George H. Doran, 1922.

Sangster, Margaret E. *The Women of the Bible: A Portrait Gallery*. New York: Christian Herald, 1911.

Seekings, Herbert S. *The Men of the Pauline Circle*. London: Charles H. Kelly, 1914.

Stevenson, Herbert F. *A Galaxy of Saints*. Westwood, N.J.: Revell, 1958.

BIBLE COMMENTARIES

Abbott, T. K. "A Critical and Exegetical Commentary on the Epistles to the Ephesians and to the Colossians." In *International Critical Commentary*. Edinburgh: T. & T. Clark, n.d.

Alexander, Joseph Addison. *The Acts of the Apostles*. 2 vols. New York: Scribner, 1858.

Alford, Henry. *The New Testament for English Readers*. Reprint. Chicago: Moody, n.d.

Arnold, Albert N.; and Ford, D. B. "Commentary on the Epistle to the Romans." In *An American Commentary*. Philadelphia: Amer. Bapt. Pub. Soc. 1889.

Barclay, William. *The Letter to the Romans.* The Daily Study Bible. Edinburgh: Saint Andrew, 1955.

————. *The Letters to Timothy, Titus, and Philemon.* The Daily Study Bible. Edinburgh: Saint Andrew, 1956.

Barnes, Albert. *Notes, Explanatory and Practical, on the Acts of the Apostles.* New York: Harper, 1860.

Barrett, C. K. "A Commentary on the Epistle to the Romans." In *Harper's New Testament Commentaries.* New York: Harper & Row, 1957.

————. *The Pastoral Epistles in the New English Bible.* Oxford: Clarendon, 1963.

Barry, Alfred. "The Epistles of Paul the Apostle to the Ephesians, Philippians, and Colossians." In *Ellicott's Commentary on the Whole Bible,* ed. Charles John Ellicott. Vol. 8. Reprint. Grand Rapids: Zondervan, 1954.

Bartlet, J. Vernon. "The Acts." In *The Century Bible.* London: Blackwood, Le Bas, n.d.

Beare, Francis W.; and MacLeod, G. Preston. "The Epistle to the Colossians." In *The Interpreter's Bible.* Vol. 11. New York: Abingdon, 1955.

Beasley-Murray, G. R. "2 Corinthians." In *The Broadman Bible Commentary,* ed. Clifford J. Allen. Vol. 11. Nashville: Broadman, 1971.

Beet, Joseph Agar. *A Commentary on St. Paul's Epistles to the Ephesians, Philippians, Colossians, and to Philemon.* London: Hodder & Stoughton, 1890.

Bernard, J. H. "The Pastoral Epistles." In *Cambridge Greek Testament.* Reprint. Cambridge: U. Press, 1922.

Bickersteth, E. "The Gospel According to St. Mark." In *The Pulpit Commentary.* Vol. 1. Reprint. Chicago: Wilcox & Follett, n.d.

Bigg, Charles. "A Critical Commentary on the Epistles of St. Peter and St. Jude." In *International Critical Commentary.* Edinburgh: T. & T. Clark, 1910.

Blaiklock, E. M. *The Acts of the Apostles.* Tyndale New Testament Commentaries. Grand Rapids: Eerdmans, 1959.

Blunt, A. W. F. *The Acts of the Apostles.* The Clarendon Bible. Oxford: Clarendon, 1922.

————. *The Epistle of Paul to the Galatians.* The Clarendon Bible. Oxford: Clarendon, 1925.

Branscomb, B. Harvie. "The Gospel of Mark." In *Moffatt New Testament Commentary.* London: Hodder & Stoughton, 1937.

Brown, Ernest Faulkner. *The Pastoral Epistles* Westminster Commentaries. London: Methuen, 1917.

Bruce, F. F. *The Acts of the Apostles: The Greek Text with Introduction and Commentary.* London: Tyndale, 1951.

_____. "Commentary on the Book of the Acts." In *New International Commentary on the New Testament.* Grand Rapids: Eerdmans, 1954.

_____. "Commentary on the Epistle to the Colossians." In *New International Commentary on the New Testament.* Grand Rapids: Eerdmans, 1957.

_____. *The Epistle of Paul to the Romans.* Tyndale New Testament Commentaries. Grand Rapids: Eerdmans, 1963.

_____. "1 and 2 Thessalonians." In *The New Bible Commentary, Revised.* Ed. D. Guthrie and J. A. Motyer. Downers Grove, Ill.: Inter-Varsity, 1970.

Calvin, John. *Commentary on the Epistles of Paul the Apostle to the Corinthians.* 2 vols. Trans. John Pringle. Reprint. Grand Rapids: Eerdmans, 1948.

Carson, Herbert M. *The Epistles of Paul to the Colossians and Philemon.* Tyndale New Testament Commentaries. Grand Rapids: Eerdmans, 1960.

Carter, Charles W; and Earle, Ralph. *The Acts of the Apostles.* The Evangelical Commentary. Grand Rapids: Zondervan, 1959.

Carver, William Owen. *The Acts of the Apostles.* Nashville: Broadman, 1916.

Clarke, Adam. *Clarke's Commentary.* Vols. 5 & 6. New York: Carlton & Lanahan, n.d.

Cranfield, C. E. B. "The Gospel According to Saint Mark." In *Cambridge Greek Testament Commentary.* Cambridge: U. Press, 1966.

Creed, John Martin. *The Gospel According to St. Luke.* Reprint. London: Macmillan, 1960.

Denney, James. "St. Paul's Epistle to the Romans." In *The Expositor's Greek Testament.* Vol. 2. Reprint. Grand Rapids: Eerdmans, n.d.

De Welt, Don. *Paul's Letters to Timothy and Titus.* Bible Study Textbook. Joplin, Mo.: College, 1961.

Dodd, C. H. "The Epistle of Paul to the Romans." In *Moffatt New Testament Commentary.* New York: Ray Long & Richard R. Smith, 1932.

Drysdale, A. H. "The Epistle of St. Paul to Philemon." In *Devotional Commentaries.* London: Religious Tract Soc., 1906.

Duncan, George S. "The Epistle of Paul to the Galatians." In *Moffatt New Testament Commentary.* Reprint. London: Hodder & Stoughton, 1948.

Eadie, John. *Commentary on the Epistle of Paul to the Galatians.* Reprint. Grand Rapids: Zondervan, n.d.

_____. *A Commentary on the Greek Text of the Epistle of Paul to the Colossians.* Edinburgh: T. & T. Clark, 1884.

Edwards, Thomas Charles. *A Commentary on the First Epistle to the Corinthians.* London: Hodder & Stoughton, 1897.

Ellis, E. Earle. "The Gospel of Luke." In *The Century Bible, New Edition.* London: Nelson, 1966.

Fieldhouse, Marvin L. *The Book of the Acts.* The Missionary's Bible Commentary. Nagano Ken, Japan: Oriental Bible Study Fellowship, n.d.

Furneaux, William Mordaunt. *The Acts of the Apostles. A Commentary for English Readers.* Oxford: Clarendon, 1912.

Geldenhuys, Norval. *Commentary on the Gospel of Luke.* London: Marshall, Morgan & Scott, 1950.

Gifford, E. H. "The Epistle of Paul the Apostle to the Romans." In *The Speaker's Commentary. New Testament.* Vol. 3. London: John Murray, 1881.

Godet, F. *Commentary on the Epistle to the Romans.* Trans. Rev. A. Cusin. Translation rev. and ed. Talbot W. Chambers. Reprint. Grand Rapids: Zondervan, 1956.

Goudge, H. L. *The First Epistle to the Corinthians.* Westminster Commentaries. London: Methuen, 1911.

Guthrie, Donald. *The Pastoral Epistles.* Tyndale New Testament Commentaries. Grand Rapids: Eerdmans, 1957.

Hackett, Horatio B. Additions to J. J. Van Oosterzee. See under Van Oosterzee.

_____. "A Commentary on the Acts of the Apostles." In *An American Commentary.* Ed. Alvah Hovey. Philadelphia: American Bap. Pub. Soc., 1882.

Haldane, Robert. *Exposition of the Epistle of the Romans.* Reprint. Grand Rapids: Zondervan, 1956.

Hamilton, Floyd E. *The Epistle to the Romans.* Grand Rapids: Baker, 1958.

Hart, J. H. A. "The First Epistle General of Peter." In *The Expositor's Greek Testament.* Vol. 5. Reprint. Grand Rapids: Eerdmans, n.d.

Hendriksen, William. *Exposition of Colossians and Philemon.* New Testament Commentary. Grand Rapids: Baker, 1964.

_____. *Exposition of Philippians.* New Testament Commentary. Grand Rapids: Baker, 1962.

————. *Exposition of the Pastoral Epistles*. New Testament Commentary. Grand Rapids: Baker, 1957.

Henry Matthew. *Commentary on the Whole Bible. New One Volume Edition*. Ed. Leslie F. Church. Grand Rapids: Zondervan, 1960.

Herklots, H. G. G. *The Epistle of St. Paul to the Philippians*. London: Lutterworth, 1946.

Hervey, A. C. "Acts of the Apostles." In *The Pulpit Commentary*. Vol. 1. Reprint. Chicago: Wilcox & Follett, n.d.

Hodge, Charles. *An Exposition of the First Epistle to the Corinthians*. Reprint. Grand Rapids: Eerdmans, 1950.

Hort, A. F. *The Gospel According to St. Mark*. Reprint. Cambridge: U. Press, 1928.

Howson, J. S.; and Spence, H. D. M. "The Acts of the Apostles." In *The International Revision Commentary on the New Testament*. Vol. 5. Ed. Philip Schaff. Philadelphia: American Sunday School Union, 1882.

Hughes, Philip Edgcumbe. "Paul's Second Epistle to the Corinthians." In *The New International Commentary on the New Testament*. Grand Rapids: Eerdmans, 1962.

Humphreys, A. E. "The Epistles to Timothy and Titus." In *The Cambridge Bible for Schools and Colleges*. Reprint. Cambridge: U. Press, 1925.

Huther, Joh. Ed. "Critical and Exegetical Handbook to the General Epistles of Peter and Jude." In *Meyer's Commentary on the New Testament*. Edinburgh: T. & T. Clark, 1881.

————. "Critical and Exegetical Handbook to the Epistles of St. Paul to Timothy and Titus." In *Meyer's Critical and Exegetical Commentary on the New Testament*. Edinburgh: T. & T. Clark, 1893.

Jacobson, William. "The Acts of the Apostles." In *The Speaker's Commentary*. New Testament. Vol. 2. London: John Murray, 1880.

Jones, Maurice. *The Epistle to the Philippians*. Westminster Commentaries. London: Methuen, 1918.

Kelly, J. N. D. "A Commentary on the Epistles of Peter and of Jude." In *Harper's New Testament Commentaries*. New York: Harper & Row, 1969.

————. "A Commentary on the Pastoral Epistles." In *Harper's New Testament Commentaries*. New York: Harper & Row, 1963.

Kelly, William. *An Exposition of the Acts of the Apostles*. Reprint. London: C. A. Hammond, 1952.

————. *Notes on the Second Epistle of Paul the Apostle to the Corinthians.* Reprint. London: G. Moorish, n.d.

Kennedy, H. A. A. "The Epistle of Paul to the Philippians." In *The Expositor's Greek Testament.* Vol. 3. Reprint. Grand Rapids: Eerdmans, n.d.

Kling, Christian Friedrich. "The First Epistle to the Corinthians." In *Lange's Commentary on the Holy Scriptures.* Reprint. Grand Rapids: Zondervan, n.d.

Knowling, R. J. "The Acts of the Apostles." In *The Expositor's Greek Testament.* Vol. 2. Reprint. Grand Rapids: Eerdmans, n.d.

Knox, John; and Buttrick, George A. "The Epistle to Philemon." In *The Interpreter's Bible.* Vol. 11. New York: Abingdon, 1955.

Knox, John; and Cragg, Gerald R. "The Epistle to the Romans." In *The Interpreter's Bible.* Vol. 9. New York: Abingdon, 1954.

Lard, Moses E. *Commentary on Paul's Letter to Romans.* Reprint. Dallas, Tex.: Eugene S. Smith, n.d.

Lenski, R. C. H. *The Interpretation of the Acts of the Apostles.* Columbus, O.: Lutheran Book Concern, 1934.

————. *The Interpretation of St. Paul's Epistles to the Colossians, to the Thessalonians, to Timothy, to Titus and to Philemon.* Columbus, bus, O.: Lutheran Book Concern, 1937.

————. *The Interpretation of St. Paul's Epistles to the Galatians, to the Ephesians, and to the Philippians.* Columbus, O.: Lutheran Book Concern, 1937

————. *The Interpretation of St. Paul's First and Second Epistle to the Corinthians.* Columbus, O.: Lutheran Book Concern, 1935.

————. *The Interpretation of St. Paul's Epistle to the Romans.* Columbus, O.: Lutheran Book Concern, 1936.

Liddon, H. P. *Explanatory Analysis of St. Paul's Epistle to the Romans.* London: Longmans, Green, 1893.

Lightfoot, J. B. *Saint Paul's Epistle to the Philippians.* London: Macmillan, 1898.

————. *Saint Paul's Epistles to the Colossians and to Philemon.* Reprint. London: Macmillan, 1900.

Lumby, J. Rawson. "The Acts of the Apostles." In *Cambridge Bible for Schools and Colleges.* Ed. J. J. S. Perowne. Reprint. Cambridge: U. Press, 1897.

————. "The Acts of the Apostles." In *Cambridge Greek Testament.* 1885. Reprint. Cambridge: U. Press, 1904.

Maclaren, Alexander. "The Epistles of St. Paul to the Colossians and Philemon." In *An Exposition of the Bible*. Vol. 6. Hartford, Conn.: Scranton, 1903.

MacMurchy, Archibald Kelly. *The Epistle of Paul to Philemon*. Edinburgh: Oliphant, Anderson & Ferrier, 1898.

McGarvey, J. W. *New Commentary on Acts of Apostles*. 2 vols. 1892. Reprint. Cincinnati: Standard, n.d.

Meyer, Heinrich August Wilhelm. *Critical and Exegetical Handbook to the Acts of the Apostles*. New York: Funk & Wagnalls, 1889.

————. *Critical and Exegetical Handbook to the Epistles to the Corinthians*. New York: Funk & Wagnalls, 1884.

————. *Critical and Exegetical Handbook to the Epistle to the Ephesians*. New York: Funk & Wagnalls, 1892.

————. *Critical and Exegetical Handbook to the Epistle to the Romans*. New York: Funk & Wagnalls, 1884.

————. *Critical and Exegetical Handbook to the Epistles to the Philippians and Colossians*. Edinburgh: T. & T. Clark, 1879.

Michael, J. Hugh. "The Epistle of Paul to the Philippians." In *Moffatt New Testament Commentary*. London: Hodder & Stoughton, 1927.

Miller, John. *Commentary on Paul's Epistle to Romans*. Princeton, N.J.: Evangelical Reform, 1887.

Mitton, C. L. *The Epistle to the Ephesians*. Oxford: U. Press, 1951.

Moffatt, James. "The First Epistle of Paul to the Corinthians." In *Moffatt New Testament Commentary*. New York: Harper, n.d.

Morgan, G. Campbell. *The Acts of the Apostles*. New York: Revell, 1924.

Morison, James. *A Practical Commentary on the Gospel According to St. Mark*. London: Hodder & Stoughton, 1896.

Moule, C. F. D. "The Epistles of Paul the Apostle to the Colossians and to Philemon." In *Cambridge Greek Testament Commentary*. Cambridge: U. Press, 1957.

Moule, H. C. G. "The Epistle of Paul the Apostle to the Romans." In *The Cambridge Bible for Schools and Colleges*. Cambridge: U. Press, 1881.

————. "The Epistles of Paul the Apostle to the Colossians and to Philemon." In *Cambridge Bible for Schools and Colleges*. Reprint. Cambridge: U. Press, 1932.

————. *Philippian Studies*. London: Hodder & Stoughton, 1897.

Neil, William. *Harper's Bible Commentary*. New York: Harper & Row, 1962.

Newell, William R. *Romans Verse by Verse*. Reprint. Chicago: Moody, 1948.

Olshausen, Herman. *Biblical Commentary on the New Testament.* Rev. A. C. Kendrick. Vol. 3. New York: Sheldon, 1859.

Pidge, J. B. Gough. "Commentary on the Epistle to the Philippians." In *An American Commentary.* Reprint. Philadelphia: American Bapt. Pub. Soc., n.d.

Plummer, Alfred. "A Critical and Exegetical Commentary on the Gospel According to S. Luke." In *International Critical Commentary.* Edinburgh: T. & T. Clark, 1901.

————. "A Critical and Exegetical Commentary on the Second Epistle of St. Paul to the Corinthians." In *International Critical Commentary.* Reprint. Edinburgh: T. & T. Clark, 1951.

————. "The Gospel According to St. Mark." In *Cambridge Greek Testament.* Reprint. Cambridge: U. Press, 1938.

————. "The Pastoral Epistles." In *An Exposition of the Bible.* Vol. 6. Hartford, Conn.: Scranton, 1903.

Plumptre, E. H. "The Acts of the Apostles." In *Ellicott's Commentary on the Whole Bible.* Vol. 7. Ed. Charles John Ellicott. Reprint. Grand Rapids: Zondervan, n.d.

Polkinghorne, G. J. "The First Letter of Peter." In *A New Testament Commentary.* Ed. G. C. D. Howley. Grand Rapids: Zondervan, 1969.

Pope, R. Martin. *The Epistles of Paul the Apostle to Timothy and Titus.* London: Charles H. Kelly, 1901.

Rackham, Richard Belward. *The Acts of the Apostles.* 9th ed. Reprint. Westminster Commentaries. London: Methuen, 1922.

Reicke, Bo. *The Gospel of Luke.* Trans. Ross Mackenzie. Richmond, Va.: Knox, 1964.

Rhys, Howard. *The Epistle to the Romans.* New York: Macmillan, 1961.

Ricciotti, Giuseppe. *The Acts of the Apostles.* Trans. Laurence E. Bryne. Milwaukee: Bruce, 1958.

Robertson, A. T. *Paul's Joy in Christ. Studies in Philippians.* New York: Revell, 1917.

Sanday, W. "The Epistle of Paul the Apostle to the Romans." In *Ellicott's Commentary on the Whole Bible.* Vol. 7. Reprint. Grand Rapids: Zondervan, n.d.

Sanday, W.; and Headlam, A. C. "The Epistle to the Romans." In *International Critical Commentary.* New York: Scribner, 1902.

Scott, E. F. "The Epistles of Paul to the Colossians, to Philemon, and to the Ephesians." In *Moffatt New Testament Commentary.* London: Hodder & Stoughton, 1930.

————. "The Pastoral Epistles." In *Moffatt New Testament Commentary*. Reprint. London: Hodder & Stoughton, 1948.

Selwyn, Edward Gordon. *The First Epistle of St. Peter*. London: Macmillan, 1949.

Shaw, R. D. *The Pauline Epistles, Introductory and Expository Studies*. Reprint. Edinburgh: T. & T. Clark, 1924.

Simpson, E. K. *The Pastoral Epistles*. Grand Rapids: Eerdmans, 1954.

Stifler, James M. *The Epistle to the Romans*. New York: Revell, 1897.

Strachan, R. H. "The Second Epistle of Paul to the Corinthians." In *Moffatt New Testament Commentary*. New York: Harper, 1935.

Swete, Henry Barclay. *The Gospel According to St. Mark*. Reprint. London: Macmillan, 1905.

Taylor, Vincent. *The Gospel According to St. Mark*. New York: St. Martin's, 1966.

Thompson, G. H. P. "The Letters of Paul to the Ephesians, to the Colossians, and to Philemon." In *The Cambridge Bible Commentary*. Cambridge: U. Press, 1967.

Trapp, John. *Trapp's Commentary on the New Testament*. Reprint. Evansville, Ind.: Sovereign Grace, 1958.

Van Oosterzee, J. J. With additions by Horatio B. Hackett. "The Epistle of Paul to Philemon." In *Lange's Commentary on the Holy Scriptures*. Reprint. Grand Rapids: Zondervan, n.d.

Vincent, Marvin R. "A Critical and Exegetical Commentary on the Epistles to the Philippians and to Philemon." In *International Critical Commentary*. Reprint. Edinburgh: T. & T. Clark, 1950.

Vine, W. E. *Epistles to the Philippians and Colossians*. London: Oliphant, 1955.

————. *Exposition of the Epistles to Timothy*. London: Pickering & Inglis, 1925.

Waite, Joseph. "The Second Epistle of Paul the Apostle to the Corinthians." In *The Speaker's Commentary. New Testament*. Vol. 3. London: John Murray, 1881.

Walker, T. *The Epistle to the Philippians*. The Indian Church Commentaries. Madras: SPCK, 1909.

Whedon, D. D. *A Popular Commentary on the New Testament*. Vols. 3 & 4. London: Hodder & Stoughton, 1882, 1876.

White, Newport J. D. "The Pastoral Epistles." In *The Expositor's Greek Testament*. Vol. 4. Reprint. Grand Rapids: Eerdmans, n.d.

Williams, C. S. C. "A Commentary on the Acts of the Apostles." In *Harper's New Testament Commentaries*. New York: Harper, 1957.

MISCELLANEOUS BOOKS

Angus, S. *The Environment of Early Christianity*. New York: Scribner, 1932.

Barrett, C. K. *The New Testament Background: Selected Documents*. New York: Harper & Row, 1961.

Blaiklock, E. M. *Out of the Earth. The Witness of Archaeology to the New Testament*. Grand Rapids: Eerdmans, 1957.

Bruce, F. F. "The Dawn of Christianity." In *The Spreading Flame*. Grand Rapids: Eerdmans, 1954.

Daniel-Rops, Henri. *Daily Life in the Time of Jesus*. New York: Hawthorn, 1962.

Edersheim, Alfred. *The Life and Times of Jesus the Messiah*. 2 vols. New York: Longmans, Green, 1901.

Farrar, F. W. *The Early Days of Christianity*. Author's edition. New York: Cassell, n.d.

Finegan, Jack. *Light From the Ancient Past*. Princeton: Princeton U. Press, 1946.

Gasque, W. Ward; and Martin, Ralph P., eds. *Apostolic History and the Gospel*. Grand Rapids: Eerdmans, 1970.

Harrison, P. N. *The Problem of the Pastoral Epistles*. Oxford: U. Press, 1921.

Jackson, F. J. Foakes; and Lake, Kirsopp, eds. *The Beginnings of Christianity*. Vol. 2. London: Macmillan, 1922.

Keck, Leander E.; and Martyn, J. Louis, eds. *Studies in Luke-Acts* Nashville: Abingdon, 1966.

Klausner, Joseph. *From Jesus to Paul*. Trans. William F. Stinespring. Reprint. Boston: Beacon, 1961.

LaHaye, Tim. *Transformed Temperaments*. Wheaton, Ill.: Tyndale, 1971.

Lake, Kirsopp, and Cadbury, Henry J. *The Beginnings of Christianity*. Vol. 4. 1932. Reprint. Grand Rapids: Baker, 1965.

Lightfoot, J. B. *Biblical Essays*. London: Macmillan, 1893.

Marshall, I. Howard. *Luke: Historian and Theologian*. Grand Rapids: Zondervan, 1971.

Mueller, F. J. *They Knew Christ*. Milwaukee: Bruce, 1946.

McGiffert, Arthur Cushman. *A History of Christianity in the Apostolic Age*. Rev. New York: Scribner, 1916.

Maggs, J. T. L. *The Spiritual Experience of St. Paul*. London: Charles H. Kelly, 1901.

Myers, Frederic W. H. *Saint Paul*. London: H. R. Allenson, n.d.

Olson, Arnold T. *The Pacemakers. The Story of Six Conversions to Chris-*

tianity from the Acts of the Apostles. Minneapolis: Evangelical Free Church of America, 1957.

Plumptre, E. H. *The Spirits in Prison, and Other Studies on the Life After Death.* London: Wm. Isbister, 1885.

Ramsay, W. M. *The Bearing of Recent Discovery on the Trustworthiness of the New Testament.* Reprint. Grand Rapids: Baker, 1953.

————. *The Church in the Roman Empire Before A.D. 170.* Reprint. Grand Rapids: Baker, 1954.

————. *The Cities of St. Paul.* Reprint. Grand Rapids: Baker, 1949.

————. *Luke the Physician and Other Studies in History of Religion.* Reprint. Grand Rapids: Baker, 1956.

Reicke, Bo. "Caesarea, Rome and the Captivity Epistles." In *Apostolic History and the Gospels.* Ed. W. Ward Gasque and Ralph P. Martin. Grand Rapids: Eerdmans, 1970.

Robertson, A. T. *Luke the Historian in the Light of Research.* New York: Scribners, 1934.

Robertson, James Alex. *The Hidden Romance of the New Testament.* London: James Clarke, n.d.

Schnackenburg, Rudolf. "Apostles Before and During Paul's Time." In *Apostolic History and the Gospels.* Ed. W. Ward Gasque and Ralph P. Martin. Grand Rapids: Eerdmans, 1970.

Thompson, J. A. *Luke, the Historian.* Melbourne: Australian Institute of Archaeology, 1954.

Dictionary and Magazine Articles

Blair, E. P. "Luke (Evangelist)." In *The Interpreter's Dictionary of the Bible.* Ed. George Arthur Buttrick. 3:179-180. New York: Abingdon, 1962.

Boyd, W. F. "Demas." In *Dictionary of the Apostolic Church.* Ed. James Hastings. 1:286-287. 1915. Reprint. Edinburgh: T. &. T. Clark, 1951.

Ellis, E. Earle, "Paul and His Co-Workers." *New Testament Studies.* 17 (Jul 1971): 437-452.

Farmer, J. H. "Mark." In *The International Standard Bible Encyclopaedia.* Ed. James Orr. 3:1986-1987. Grand Rapids: Eerdmans, 1939.

Faussel, A. R. "Onesiphorus." In *Biblical Cyclopaedia, Critical and Expository.* Hartford, Conn.: Scranton, 1902.

Gibb, J. "Euodia." In *A Dictionary of the Bible.* Ed. James Hastings. 1:794. New York: Scribner, 1908.

Goodspeed, E. J. "Gaius Titius Justus." *Journal of Biblical Literature,* 69 (1950): 382-383.

Grosheide, F. W. "Acts of the Apostles, The." In *The Encyclopedia of Christianity*. Ed. Edwin H. Palmer. 1:47-73. Wilmington, Del.: National Foundation for Christian Education, 1964.

Hunter, S. F. "Phoebe." In *The International Standard Bible Encyclopaedia*. Ed. James Orr. 4:2386. Grand Rapids: Eerdmans, 1939.

Kee, H. C. "Timothy." In *The Interpreter's Dictionary of the Bible*. Ed. George Arthur Buttrick. 4:650-51. New York: Abingdon, 1962.

————. "Titus, Companion of Paul." In *The Interpreter's Dictionary of the Bible*. Ed. George Arthur Buttrick. 4:656-57. New York: Abingdon, 1962.

Lake, K. "Luke." In *Dictionary of the Apostolic Church*. Ed. James Hastings. 1915. Reprint. 1:718-220 Edinburgh: T. & T. Clark, 1951.

Nixon, R. E. "Silas." *The New Bible Dictionary*. Ed. J. D. Douglas. Grand Rapids: Eerdmans, 1962.

Norris, J. M. "Apollos." In *The Interpreter's Dictionary of the Bible*. Ed. George Arthur Buttrick. 1:169. New York: Abingdon, 1962.

————. "Aristarchus." In *The Interpreter's Dictionary of the Bible*. Ed. George Arthur Buttrick. 1:219. New York: Abingdon, 1962.

————. "Tychicus." In *The Interpreter's Dictionary of the Bible*. Ed. George Arthur Buttrick. 4:720. New York: Abingdon, 1962.

Pickering, Cecil J. "Pheobe's Commendation." *The Witness* 93 (Feb. 1963): 43-44.

Savile, B. Wray. "Silas." In *Fairbairn's Imperial Bible Encyclopedia*. Ed. Patrick Fairbairn. Reprint. 6:174. Grand Rapids: Zondervan, 1957.

Shroyer, M. J. "Aquila and Priscilla." In *The Interpreter's Dictionary of the Bible*. Ed. George Arthur Buttrick. 1:176. New York: Abingdon, 1962.

Souter, A. "Luke." In *A Dictionary of Christ and the Gospels*. Ed. James Hastings. 2:83-84. Edinburgh: T. & T. Clark, 1909.

Stewart, A. H. "Bodily Healing Since Pentecost." *Our Hope*, 50 (Aug. 1953): 94-106.

INDEX OF PERSONALITIES

267

SELECTED SCRIPTURE INDEX

Included in this index are only those passages which received some specific interpretation. Many passages which were simply cited have not been included.